C m & G m fugues

4

MATERIALS
AND
STRUCTURE
OF
MUSIC

VOLUME TWO

MATERIALS AND STRUCTURE OF MUSIC

Second Edition

William Christ
Richard DeLone
Vernon Kliewer
Indiana University

Lewis Rowell
University of Hawaii

William Thomson
Case Western Reserve University

Prentice-Hall, Inc., Englewood Cliffs, New Jersey

Library of Congress Cataloging in Publication Data

CHRIST, WILLIAM.
    Materials and structure of music.

-- ---Workbook.
    1. Music--Theory. I. Title.
MT6.C49M43   781   70-152713
ISBN   0-13-560342-0 (v. 1)
ISBN   0-13560367-6 (v. 2)

© 1973, 1967 by PRENTICE-HALL, INC.
Englewood Cliffs, New Jersey

Printed in the United States of America

10   9   8   7   6   5   4   3   2   1

PRENTICE-HALL INTERNATIONAL, INC., London
PRENTICE-HALL OF AUSTRALIA, PTY. LTD., Sydney
PRENTICE-HALL OF CANADA, LTD., Toronto
PRENTICE-HALL OF INDIA PRIVATE LIMITED, New Delhi
PRENTICE-HALL OF JAPAN, INC., Tokyo

To

NELDA, JOANNE, DIANE, ANNETTE, and BETTY

who were so patient

CONTENTS

PREFACE, xi

Chapter 1

TONAL STRUCTURE AND FORM, 1

Tonal Form of a Baroque Prelude. Key Relationships in a Recitative. Tonality Design Involving Distant-related Keys. Tonality Scheme of an Extended Movement.

Chapter 2

RONDO FORM, 32

Chapter 3

DIATONIC SEVENTH CHORDS (NONDOMINANT), 48

Treatment of the Dissonance. Uses of Diatonic Seventh Chords. The Supertonic Seventh Chord. Uses of the Supertonic Seventh Chord.

Chapter 4

DIATONIC SEVENTHS (CONCLUDED): NINTH CHORDS, 69

Leading Tone Seventh Chord. Uses of the Leading Tone Seventh Chord. The Tonic Seventh Chord. Some Uses of the Tonic Seventh Chord. Subdominant Seventh Chord. Uses of Subdominant Seventh Chord. The Submediant Seventh Chord. Uses of the Submediant Seventh Chord. The Mediant Seventh Chord. Uses of the Mediant Seventh Chord. Ninth Chords. The Dominant Ninth Chord (V_9). Inversions of V_9. Nondominant Ninth Chords.

Chapter 5

EMBELLISHING DIMINISHED CHORDS, 102

Embellishing Diminished Triads. Embellishing $°_7$ Chords. Irregular Resolutions of $°_7$ Chords. The $°_7$ Chord as an Agent of Tonal Instability. The $°_7$ Chord as Modulatory Pivot. The $ᵠ_7$ Chord.

Chapter 6

CANTUS FIRMUS TECHNIQUE: THE CHORALE PRELUDE, 126

The Imitative (or "Fugal") Chorale Prelude. The Embellished Chorale.

Chapter 7

NEAPOLITAN AND AUGMENTED SIXTH CHORDS, 141

The Neapolitan Chord. Uses of the Neapolitan "Sixth." The Root Position Neapolitan Chord. Other Forms and Uses of the Neapolitan. The Neapolitan Key Relationship. Augmented Sixth Chords. Resolutions of Augmented Sixth Chords. "Inverted" Augmented Sixth Chords. The Gr^{+6}_5 and Enharmonic Uses. Augmented Sixth Chord as Related to Tonic. Augmented Sixth Chords in Other Relationships.

Chapter 8

VARIATION FORMS, 172

Cantus Firmus Variation Types. Independent Variations.

Chapter 9

THEMATIC DEVELOPMENT IN TWO-VOICE COUNTERPOINT, 207

General Characteristics. Beginning Section of the Invention. Developmental Sections. Closing Section. Contrapuntal Association.

Chapter 10

FUGUE, 231

Exposition. Developmental Sections. Sectional Linkage. Tonality Relations in the Fugue.

Chapter 11

FURTHER DETAILS OF FUGUE, 254

*Fugal Exposition.   Tonal and Real Answers.   Order of Voice Entries.   Tonality
Contrasts of Entries.   The Countersubject; Invertible Counterpoint at Twelfth.*

Chapter 12

SONATA-ALLEGRO FORM, 277

*The Classical Sonata-Allegro.   Exposition.   Development.   Recapitulation.
Coda.   The Tonal Design.   Preparation for and Beginning of the Recapitulation.
Other Factors Influencing the Perception of Form.   The Flexibility of the
Pattern.   The Function of the Introduction.   Sonata-Allegro Form in
Twentieth-Century Compositions.*

Chapter 13

ENRICHED TONAL RESOURCES, 310

*Extended Tertian Chords; Eleventh and Thirteenth Chords.   Augmented Eleventh
Chords (+11).   The Dominant Thirteenth Chord.   Nondominant Thirteenth
Chords.   Variable Tonal Relations and Harmonic Ambiguity.   Deceptive Harmonic
Action.   Harmonic Sequences.   Expanded Key Relations.   Key and Chord
Relationships by Seconds and Thirds.   Chords Containing Tritones and
Contrapuntal Factors.   Modality.   Tonal Regions.*

Chapter 14

MELODY IN TWENTIETH-CENTURY MUSIC, 366

*Rhythmic Structure.   Pitch Organization.   Atonal and Serial Melody.
Other Organizational Factors.*

Chapter 15

HARMONY IN TWENTIETH-CENTURY MUSIC, 385

*Tertian Chords.   Nontertian Chords.   Stacked Chords.   Other Chord Types.
Harmonic Succession.   Serialized Harmony.   Melodic and Harmonic Interaction.*

Chapter 16

TONALITY AND ATONALITY IN TWENTIETH-CENTURY MUSIC, 416

Tonal Relations. Bitonality and Polytonality. Atonality. Pandiatonicism. Tonality Schemes.

Chapter 17

FORMAL PROCESSES IN TWENTIETH-CENTURY MUSIC, 429

Formal Punctuation. Other Factors Which Delineate Phrases and Create Continuity. The Variation Process. Organization and Structure of Three Contemporary Compositions.

GLOSSARY, 463

INDEX OF MUSICAL EXCERPTS, 467

INDEX, 472

PREFACE

In these two volumes we have attempted to accomplish two main tasks: (1) To set out in effective pedagogical order a framework of understanding for the materials and structure of music; and (2) to transmit this understanding by means of the actual music produced in the Western world.

To achieve the first goal, Volume I begins with a study of melody. The complexities of the traditional four-part "harmony" work have been deferred until step-by-step knowledge of basic pitch organization in two- and three-voice combinations has been introduced. In this way the learning sequence is realistically geared to student comprehension, and a true ordering from simple to complex is realized.

The format of introducing pitch organization through study of counterpoint in these early chapters (9-12) is more akin to the traditions of sixteenth-century contrapuntal teaching than to any other, for the *interval* is the basis of pitch determination. We believe that the teaching of counterpoint *as a compositional discipline* is more properly within the domain of the composition class than the theory class; in the theory class the work aims more toward comprehension of music than toward demonstrable skill in writing, for the written work is only a means to the more basic and significant goal of understanding. The object of this early introduction to rudimentary counterpoint is not to provide a rigidly disciplined course in contrapuntal skill, but rather to enrich the student's understanding of music.

In these two volumes the different structural elements of music, such as tonality, melody, harmony, texture, and form, are presented as interrelated phenomena without unwarranted emphasis upon the formulation and application of contrived principles. Through this approach, and through his own involvement with *all* of the materials of music, the student develops a wider perspective and a deeper understanding of its organization.

To meet the second goal, an abundance of musical examples accompanies the text of Volumes I and II. There is an emphasis, of course, on the music of the so-called "period of common practice" which is included with the full realization of the significance of this repertoire both to the performing and listening musician.

Materials and Structure of Music I and *II* are designed for a basic music theory curriculum. It is assumed that the materials of the two volumes and accompanying workbooks will be used as the basis for the entire course of study, with the supplementation of melodies for music-reading practice and at least some of the scores for works that are discussed in the texts. Each chapter concludes with suggested *Exercises* designed for the application of information exposed in the text. These *Exercises* are minimal and are intended only as outlines of supplementary work that should be done. Both Workbooks I and II are planned to furnish sufficient materials for a comprehensive course of study, and for maximum efficiency it is highly recommended that they be utilized.

The teacher should by all means plan his use of the texts and workbooks to meet the needs of his own class and his own academic situation. The separate volumes are planned around the thirty-week academic year of a four-semester course, the "freshman and sophomore *theory* classes." The concepts and procedures presented here have been applied successfully in music programs of diverse institutions throughout the United States and Canada. It should be noted that both volumes have been tested and adopted for use in comprehensive musicianship courses, i.e., courses interrelating theory, music history, and literature.

Some of the chapters might well be dealt with in less than a week of class time, while others conceivably should be granted more time for discussion and assimilation. The experienced teacher should encounter no difficulty in establishing a workable time sequence that will fit the texts and workbooks to the needs of his own classes. *

It is intended that Volume I be the basis of a beginning theory program with the primary prerequisites being demonstrable performance skill on an instrument and knowledge of the rudiments of music. Chapter 1 of Volume I is a review of fundamental matters which the music major must know.

Volume II is a logical continuation of Volume I. While Volume I is devoted mainly to the materials of music, Volume II deals more with the organization of these materials. The subjects covered in Volume II represent some departures from the conventional second-year theory text. In addition to the treatment of musical forms, melodic, harmonic, and rhythmic concepts and materials are introduced which exceed the bounds of the "traditional." Their inclusion is essential because the student of music will not be equipped to understand the music of this century if his study is terminated with the materials that were typical of Bach, Mozart, Beethoven, or even Wagner.

These "new" materials are introduced when possible as the extension of matters fundamental to *all* music. For instance, chords are built of intervals: therefore, chords can be constructed of *fourths,* or *seconds* as logically as from thirds, even though the past four hundred years of musical practice might lead one to assume that tertian chords are normative for all music.

There is a shift of basic approach during the final four chapters, a shift necessitated by the fact that the music involved represents a diversity of musical types for which no universal pattern of common practice has been developed. These final chapters are devoted to a systematic and comparative examination of significant musical resources and individual techniques both "old" and "new," with an

---

*A teacher's manual for Volume I is available through the publisher and one for Volume II is anticipated.

explanation of the musical logic of each. Though no all-embracing rationale of analysis is offered to elucidate all contemporary music, techniques of analysis and points of view are explained.

We acknowledge the influence, both implicit and explicit, of Hindemith, Schenker, and other twentieth-century writers on our collective efforts.

Finally, we wish to thank all of those who were directly helpful in the preparation of the manuscript and the compilation of musical examples.

THE AUTHORS

There is a certain marvellous order which belongs to the nature of harmony in general; in this order every instrument, to the best of its ability, participates under the direction of that faculty of sense-perception on which they, as well as everything else in music, finally depend.

Aristoxenus
The Harmonics, Book II

MATERIALS
AND
STRUCTURE
OF
MUSIC

1

TONAL STRUCTURE
AND FORM

The discussions of modulation and tonal shift in *Materials and Structure of Music I* concentrated on the processes through which one tonic supersedes another. We shall now consider the set of relationships formed between different tonalities within a work and their function in delineating musical form.

In this sense we can speak of *tonal form*, which corresponds to sectional divisions within a composition according to the tonality scheme.[1] Tonality changes fulfill a structural need for variety. In short works tonality changes often punctuate and delineate small form units; in extended movements tonality changes delineate *large* sections within the total design as well.

In this chapter we shall examine the tonal form of four different movements. We shall be concerned primarily with sectionalization that results from the contrasts of different tonalities. Other form-producing elements will be discussed only as they relate to the tonal form.

Tonal Form of a Baroque Prelude

By tradition, *prelude* refers to many diverse types of compositions that are either independent or introductory movements. The prelude that is discussed below is the opening movement of a *suite*. In this work the *prelude* is a multi-section movement containing many returns of an initial musical idea. As a whole, the prelude consists of continuous rhythmic unfolding, which Ex. 1-1 makes clear.

---

[1] All musical dimensions are form creating, and each may be examined as a set of relationships that delineate form.

Ex. 1-1. Bach: English Suite in F, Prelude.

I V7

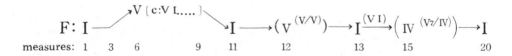

Rhythmic invariance[2] tends to make us ignore phrases and restatements of the principal melodic material. Consequently, changes of key are introduced to highlight a restatement, as can be heard by performing Ex. 1-1.

Considering only the section in Ex. 1-1, the tonal center is *F*; however, other tonal emphases also appear. For example, the dominant, *C*, is a tonal goal in measure 6. In retrospect, the tonal play beginning in measure 3 initiates a motion away from *F* to *C*. Measures 12–15 are tonally unstable because several potential tonics appear in a small span of time. *F* is reasserted in measure 15, and dominates through measure 20. The tonal structure shapes this section, first by an immediate motion to the dominant tonal region, and second by the rapid succession of secondary dominants.

The next section of this movement introduces new melodic material in association with a rearticulated pedal, as well as chord outlining. Contrary to our expectations, the section (Ex. 1-2a) begins in *F*, rather than in a new key. There is a subsequent modulation to *C* (shown in Ex. 1-2b).

---

[2] Also referred to as *Fortspinnung*. Rhythmic invariance designates continuous rhythmic activity.

Ex. 1-2. Ibid.

Section 3 of this movement is a modified restatement of the initial material in the dominant key. Similarly to the first, this section opens and closes in the same key; contrary to the first, motion away from *C* is not a strong shaping aspect.

Ex. 1-3. Ibid.

The fourth section brings back material that was heard in the second. As before, this section begins in the key of the preceding section (*C*), but subsequent activity leads to *d* minor. Furthermore, still another tonal region (*g* minor) connects *C* to *d*. Thus the tonal design of this section is

V (c:) ⟋(ii (g:))⟋ vi [d:]

measures: 34   36   38

Ex. 1-4. Ibid.

Since we have heard the contrasting material of Ex. 1-4 in a particular formal role, we expect it to precede a restatement of the opening material at a different tonal level, which in this case is *d* (Ex. 1-5).

Ex. 1-5. Ibid.

Ex. 1-5 continued.

Subsequent sections of this movement reveal similar structural procedures. In short, the formal design unfolds through alternate statements of the initial musical idea and a contrasting idea. In addition, the initial statement generally begins and ends in the same key, whereas the contrasting idea always begins in the preceding key and then establishes a new key for the next statement. Although space does not permit a quotation of the entire work, the movement should be heard to confirm the role of tonality in establishing its sectional form.

The tonal form and the consequent key relationships for the entire movement are shown below. Reduced to principal key centers, the tonality scheme of this movement is *F C d a F*. The tonal form, then, consists entirely of motion between near-related keys.

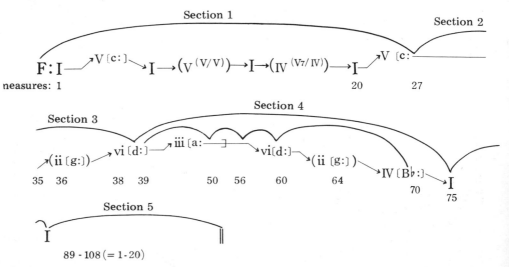

Thus, even though the movement is characterized by rhythmic invariance, tonality changes clearly divide its parts. Of particular significance in this composition is the juxtaposition of stable sections and modulatory sections. The latter provide contrast and connect the different stable tonal areas.

Key Relationships in a Recitative

A *recitative,* by its very nature, is through composed. In operas, recitatives are generally set to a prose text that narrates the action of the plot. Since the narration often contains abrupt idea changes, the music accompanying the recitative also changes character frequently. For example, to give added rhythmic emphasis to a line of text, a more strictly measured type of accompanimental pattern often is used.

The tonality scheme of most recitatives is characterized by constantly changing tonics. At times there is only an allusion to a tonic, or at most, a departure is made from a tonal center as soon as it has been established. The general effect is that of successive tonal regions, thereby heightening the "arrival impact" of the tonality of the aria or chorus that follows.

The recitative by Mozart discussed below begins and ends in g minor, which is reaffirmed in several sections of the recitative. Ex. 1-6 shows the opening eleven measures. As can be seen, g begins to give way to the subdominant region, c minor, in measure 4.

Ex. 1-6. Mozart: *Idomeneo,* Act I, Scene I, "Quando avran fine . . ."

Ex. 1-6 continued.

In the first section *c* minor is an important structural goal; however, the digression to *E-flat* in measure 12 (shown in Ex. 1-7) displaces it. The accompanimental material of this second section is sequentially restated four measures later. Since it is an exact sequence at the second above, *F* is heard as a new tonic. The return of the chordal accompaniment in measure 21 continues to confirm *F*.

Ex. 1-7. Ibid.

Ex. 1-7 continued.

A new accompanimental pattern appears with the return of *g* minor in measure 27. Once again, a new reference point, the relative major of *g* minor (*B-flat* major), is quickly introduced (Ex. 1-8).

Ex. 1-8. Ibid.

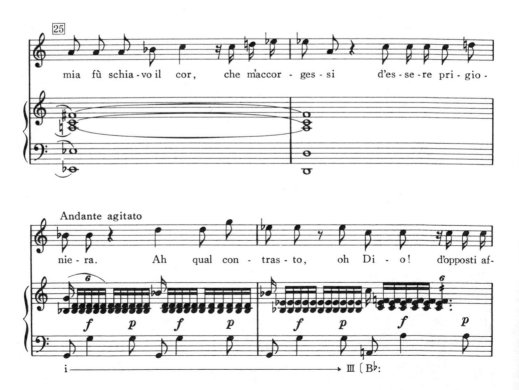

Motion increases considerably in the next section of the recitative, where there are four potential keys in the space of five measures: *E-flat, A-flat, F,* and *B-flat*. The section as a whole is in *E-flat*, as is confirmed by the last measure of Ex. 1-9.

Ex. 1-9. Ibid.

Ex. 1-9 continued.

Even more frequent changes appear in the next section. Here sequential unfolding in the first three measures of Ex. 1-10 exposes a succession of secondary dominants each of which implies a motion to a tonal region that is not completed.

Ex. 1-10. Ibid.

The appearance of *G* major re-emphasizes the principal tonic. The implication of *b* minor in Ex. 1-10 now becomes clear; it connects the constantly changing references to *G*. As in the first section, there is a decisive motion to the subdominant region. Consequently, the tonal design of these two sections is similar, except that the opening is *g* minor to the subdominant whereas here it is *G* major to the subdominant. The movement closes in *g* minor, which is the key of the aria that follows.

Ex. 1-11. Ibid.

ARIA

In comparison with our earlier Bach example, our Mozart recitative is quite unstable. Nevertheless, *G* is a stabilizing factor because of its predominant role. The other keys that appear represent variety-producing digressions. Moreover, the frequent changes of tonic create a tension that is not resolved until the following aria. The diagram below illustrates the tonality design that is created by the succession of different keys; it also shows the relationships of the subsidiary tonal centers to *G*. As can be seen, the key scheme of the recitative is dominated by tonics that relate to the principal key by a major third below, a minor third above, and a perfect fifth below.

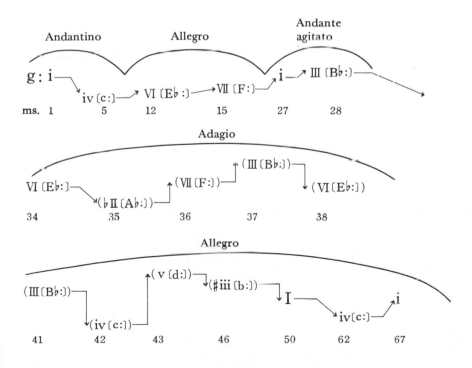

Tonality Design Involving Distant-related Keys

The tonal schemes of the two preceding works consist primarily of near-related keys. In other instances a design may contain distant key relations as well. If distantly related keys are incorporated, the resultant contrasts will usually be greater than when near-related keys are used.

Both near- and distant-related keys are used in the Schumann Trio discussed next. The principal tonic is *D-flat,* and *A-flat* occupies an important subsidiary position. In the first thirteen measures of the movement a partial restatement of the opening thematic material is set in the dominant region, clearly dividing this section into two parts. Thus a simple type of opposition is brought into play; the melodic material unifies the movement because it appears in four varied restatements, whereas change of key provides variety.

Ex. 1-12. Schumann: Trio, Op. 80, II.

Ex. 1-12 continued.

In the second section, Ex. 1-13, the distant relation of *A* major (enharmonically *B-double flat*) is introduced. In retrospect, this establishes a strong tonal contrast because it represents a departure from the juxtaposition of near-related keys in the opening section. As can be seen, the *A* tonic is a minor second above *A*♭ a major third lower than the initial tonic (an enharmonic ♭VI).

Ex. 1-13. Ibid.

Immediately following the confirmation of *A* in this section, tonal regions are introduced that are closely related to it: *c-sharp* minor, *b* minor, and *f-sharp* major-minor. In addition, *c-sharp* and *f-sharp* also are close relations of *D-flat* (enharmonically *C-sharp*). Thus the existing tonal contrast clearly results from juxtaposing *A-flat* and *A*.

Ex. 1-14. Ibid.

((c#:

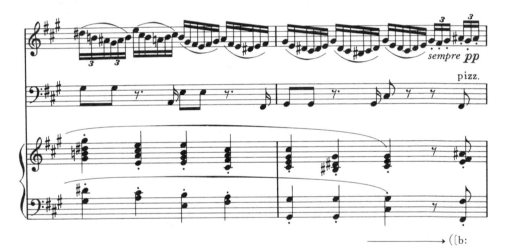

((b:

The return to *A-flat* in the third section of the movement coincides with a restatement of the opening melodic material. Similar to the first section, a change to its dominant key, *E-flat*, takes place. The restatement, however (a portion of which is shown in Ex. 1-15), is an abbreviated variation of the original.

Ex. 1-15. Ibid.

(a)

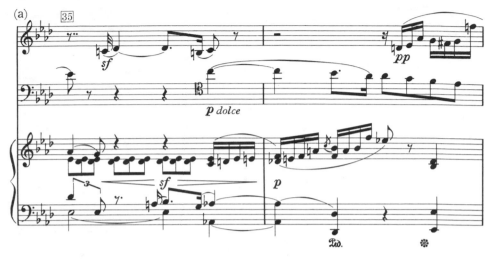

(b)

The subsequent reappearance of material from the second section begins in *B* major, which is the enharmonic subtonic area of *D-flat* major. Like the section in *A* major, the new tonic is followed by its own near-related keys, *e-flat* minor and *d-flat* (*c-sharp*) minor.

Ex. 1-16. Ibid., harmonic reduction, measures 44–62.

The fifth section continues as a varied statement of the second and sets the scene for the return of *D-flat* major. As the harmonic reduction in Ex. 1-17 shows, this portion begins in *E-flat* and changes to *A-flat*, which is the dominant of the original key.

Ex. 1-17. Ibid., harmonic reduction, measures 64–73.

With the return to *D-flat* major the tonal cycle is partially closed. Since this reappearance coincides with a restatement of the opening section (with a different accompaniment), the design also includes a restatement of the original change to *A-flat*. The latter subsequently functions as a dominant for the final return to *D-flat* major (shown in Ex. 1-18).

Ex. 1-18. Ibid.

The tonal form of this movement reveals complexities that are not present in the Bach or Mozart examples. First, the principal tonality of the movement marks off the outer form limits. Second, distant-related keys outline the large sectional form of the movement, while near-related keys create variety within sections. As before, a diagram makes this clear.

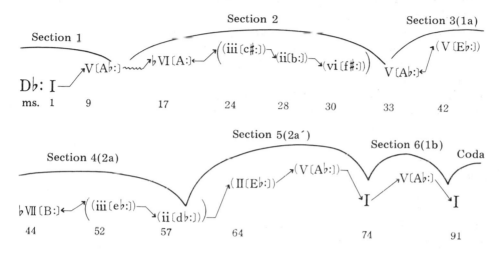

Each of the tonal centers is symbolized in relation to *D-flat* major. Broadly speaking, this means that successive areas of *D-flat* are given formal prominence. Considered in this manner, the contrast created by Sections 2 and 4 is readily apparent because these sections contain digressions far afield from *D-flat*. In addition, these two sections contribute tonal variety since they introduce minor keys. The overall key scheme, however, is represented by major keys that are framed by *D-flat*.

Tonality Scheme of an Extended Movement

The key designs of the preceding works illustrate the use of near- and distant-related tonics in delineating large formal sections and parts of sections. Naturally, the large formal units in an extended movement may have durations that are equal to any one of the complete movements discussed above. It follows, then, that large formal divisions may have a tonal form of their own. This can be seen in miniature in the second section of the Schumann movement, in which several keys appear in close succession. In the discussion that follows we shall see this same principle at work in a form of greater dimensions.

Viewed as a whole, the tonality scheme of the first movement of Kodaly's symphony is C⌒A⌒C ⌒C⌒C♭ C. Here the letters denote principal tonal centers; the wavy lines indicate tonal digressions during which a tonic may be present only briefly. The scheme shows that each of the three divisions begins in *C*, that the first and third sections are subdivided by tonalities subordinate to *C*, and that the movement closes in *C*.

To facilitate our discussion we shall refer to each division of the movement as Section 1, 2, or 3. Each of these divisions fulfills a particular role in the creation of the movement's design. Briefly, Section 1 presents or exposes the material that is basic to the movement, Section 2 is a recasting and reworking of the basic material, and Section 3 is a varied restatement of Section 1.

In the ensuing discussion we shall determine the role of other tonal centers that fill in the motion to and from the various sections of *C* tonality. Because of the length of the movement, the excerpts given do not always show a complete phrase or section. Therefore, the movement should be heard and seen in score before proceeding, keeping in mind the overall tonality scheme (shown above).

Section 1 divides into two parts, 1a and 1b, because of the change to the tonality of *A*. These divisions are recognized in retrospect because both of these parts also contain tonal regions. For example, part 1a consists of the following:

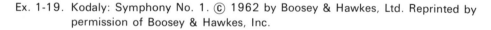

$$C \quad \left[\frac{C}{A^\flat} \quad A \quad f^\sharp \quad E \quad C^\sharp \text{\small wwww} \right]$$

1-46   46   53   56   63   73

C is a springboard for the appearance of the various tonal regions. More important, each of these brief reference points is associated with varied fragments of the melodic material, forecasting some of the activity that will take place in Section 2.

Ex. 1-19 shows the opening of the movement and the first tonality change. This change contrasts sharply with the simple opening of the movement because both *C* and *A-flat* occur simultaneously, succinctly delineating the beginning of a smaller formal unit within Section 1a.

Ex. 1-19. Kodaly: Symphony No. 1. © 1962 by Boosey & Hawkes, Ltd. Reprinted by permission of Boosey & Hawkes, Inc.

Each of the tonal regions shown in the previous diagram is significant because it illuminates the process of fragmentation. But more important, the successive tonics create an expectancy for the appearance of a tonal center that will control the texture for a longer period of time. In this movement tonal stability, following an unstable section, coincides with the appearance of an ostinato pattern (a change of texture) and new melodic material, thereby establishing the beginning of Section 1b.

Ex. 1-20. Ibid.

The brief successive use of distant-related tonics then becomes clear—with the exception of the bitonal statement shown in Ex. 1-19, each of the tonal regions is closely related to *A*. In this sense there is a motion from I–VI that is prepared by the successive tonal regions.

Section 1b differs from 1a in two respects: the tonality of *A* closes as well as opens the section, and only two tonal regions appear, namely *c-sharp* (measure 130) and *C* (measure 147). As in Section 1a, these digressions are fragmented statements of material presented earlier with the brief reference to *C* recalling the basic tonality. The restatement of the tonality, *A*, is associated with new thematic material. Thus Section 1b is tonally symmetrical, but thematically asymmetrical. Ex. 1-21 shows the beginning of the last part of Section 1b.

Ex. 1-21. Ibid.

The reappearance of the primary tonality in measure 192 signals the beginning of Section 2. Here the return to *C* is unmistakable because other organizational factors (such as the unison opening) also recur. Since thematic material from both 1a and 1b is recast in new settings, the formal role of Section 2 becomes evident—it highlights old melodic material in new ways. Consequently, Section 2 consists of numerous tonal regions.

Tonality:	C	G-flat	E-flat	B	A-flat	F	[C-flat]	F	B-flat	(D-flat)	G.P.
Measure:	192	212	220	224	232	240	244	250	264	272	

Ex. 1-22 illustrates some of the tonality changes that take place in Section 2. A thorough study reveals that not all of the tonics indicated in the preceding scheme are as distinctly established as others, and they might better be characterized as *tonal allusions.* In contrast to Section 1, the relationships are predominantly distant.

Ex. 1-22. Ibid.

Section 2 closes with a *Grand Pause*. Immediately thereafter a *C* pedal is heard marking the second return of the basic tonic and the beginning of the third section. As in Section 1a there is digression from *C*; however, each of these digressions now is interrupted by a reference to *C*, as can be seen in Ex. 1-23.

Ex. 1-23. Ibid.

A similar procedure continues until the appearance of Section 3b, which is the formal equivalent of Section 1b. However, instead of *A*, *C-flat* is the subordinate tonal center, and it is in turn replaced by another occurrence of *C* twenty measures later.

Ex. 1-24. Ibid.

Ex. 1-24 continued.

(b)

Immediately following the passage illustrated in Ex. 1-24b, several allusions to other, more transitory, tonics are heard. These brief references make use of melodic material already heard, leading the listener to expect a return to the tonality of *C*, and the subsequent close of the movement.

As the preceding discussion discloses, the basic tonality demarcates the large formal divisions of the movement. The subsidiary reference points in Sections 1 and 2 create formal subdivisions. The inclusion of brief tonic allusions and tonal regions delineates smaller formal units. Furthermore, except for the basic divisions into broad sections, the entire work is characterized by the use of distant-related tonics. While each section and each part of sections is delineated by different tonal centers, the total result is an example of expanded tonality.

If we designate relationships as in earlier diagrams, the complete tonal form of this movement is as follows:

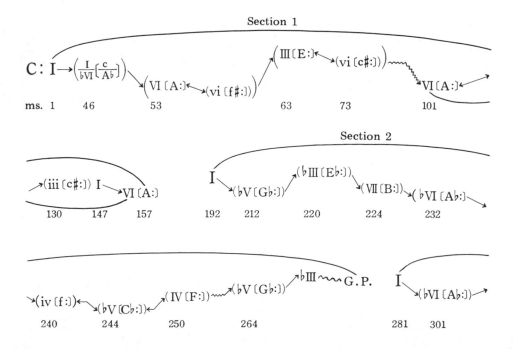

Section 3

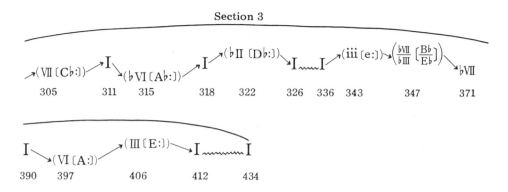

Each of the four compositions discussed in this chapter reveals various formal roles performed by tonality. Each contains a basic reference point to which all other tonalities and tonal regions can be related. Some of these relationships are described as *near*, others as *distant*. Ultimately, the specific set of tonality relationships is one of the factors that distinguishes one composition from another.

A continuing study of tonality schemes will reveal many important aspects of musical organization and structure. In general, the predominant use of near-related keys provides greater stability than frequent use of distant-related keys, or frequent changes of tonic. Furthermore, rapid tonality changes are often associated with transitional portions of a composition, as well as with passages that contain fragmented statements of earlier material. Many forms of music studied in subsequent chapters reveal the tonality schemes outlined in this chapter.

Exercises

For more detailed assignments see *Materials and Structure of Music II, Workbook*, Chapter 1.

1. Describe how changes of tonality are accomplished in the Prelude discussed at the beginning of this chapter.
2. Make a tonality scheme analysis of works such as the following:
   a. Beethoven, *Sonata*, Op. 2, No. 3
   b. Brahms, *Intermezzo*, Op. 116, No. 2
   c. Hindemith, *Mathis der Mahler*, I
   d. Recitatives from operas by Mozart and Rossini, and the recitatives from Bach's *St. Matthew Passion*
   e. Copland, *Symphony No. 3*
   f. Bartok, *Second String Quartet*
   g. Barber, *Piano Sonata*
   h. Carter, *Woodwind Quintet*
   i. Berg, *Seven Early Songs*
   j. Stravinsky, *Mass*
3. Write a recitative on a pre-existing text or an original text. Use the recitative discussed in this chapter as your model.
4. Sketch the basic framework of a composition comparable in length to the last movement of Beethoven's Fourth Symphony. Indicate the key relationships in your sketch, and show how the key changes could be brought about.
5. Analyze Ex. 1-12, Ex. 1-13, Ex. 1-14, and Ex. 1-15 to show basic harmony. Then, select at least one of these reductions as the harmonic model for a short piano and flute composition.

2

RONDO FORM

Forms in music result from the presentation of musical patterns in recognizable schemes of reiteration, variation, and contrast. Every aspect of music (melody, harmony, tonality, range, timbre, loudness, meter, rhythm, tempo, etc.) contributes to the establishment of musical form. When the listener recognizes patterns of like and unlike elements and discerns their order of arrangement, he is conscious of the organizational scheme—the form.

An extension of the basic idea of statement, contrast, restatement is seen in the medieval *rondeau* of Ex. 2-1. Form is achieved in this piece through two contrasting thematic ideas presented in a particular pattern of repetition and alternation accompanying lines of the text. The form can be represented as A B a A a b A B, with the capital letters indicating the music attending the refrain—the repeated text (underlined). Unity is achieved here by repetition of both text and themes.

Ex. 2-1. Trouveres: *En ma dame* (Rondeau).

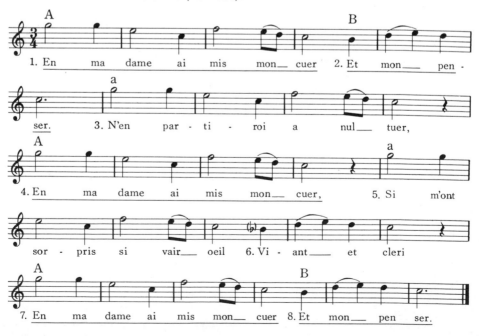

Although the main organizational feature of the old vocal rondeau was the recurrence of a refrain, an instrumental rondeau was developed during the seventeenth century that had certain similarities to this earlier vocal form. It consisted of a theme whose many repetitions alternated with numerous subordinate themes, which were frequently couched in different keys—the dominant, the relative minor, etc. This form is exemplified in a Gavotte by Bach, the main theme of which is illustrated in Ex. 2-2.

Ex. 2-2. Bach: Sonata in E Major for Solo Violin, Gavotte en Rondeau.

This Rondeau theme alternates with contrasting materials according to the following pattern:

Theme:	A	B	A	C	A		
Meas.:	(1-8)	(9-16)	(17-24)	(25-40)	(41-48)		
Tonality:	E	c♯	E	E-B	E		
		D	A	E			A
		(49-64)	(65-72)	(73-92)			(93-100)
		f♯	E	c♯	B g♯		E

The seventeenth-century *rondeau* was the direct ancestor of the modern *rondo* form, which generally differs from its predecessor in having fewer but longer sections. The form is achieved by the alternation of a main theme (the *rondo theme*) with contrasting sections. It is usually found as a movement in works of multiple movements, frequently as the last movement of symphonies, sonatas, concertos, and other instrumental works. Haydn was one of the first composers to make frequent use of the rondo principle in this modern manifestation.

The rondo theme usually is a simple, straightforward melody, a period or song form whose importance is emphasized by its appearance at the beginning of the movement. It is further stressed by its reappearances, frequently in unaltered form, following excursions into contrasting materials.

The following patterns represent common rondo schemes, a few of which will be discussed presently.

1. A B A B A   2. A B A C A   3. A B A C A B A
4. A B A C A D A   5. A B A B C B A D C B A C B A

The term *rondo* not only designates a form type, as defined above, but it also connotes a character type. Rondo movements are usually characterized by uncomplicated dance-like themes in an animated tempo. They thus become jaunty vehicles for the expression of whimsy, gaiety, flippancy, and humor. No rondo would better justify this statement than that whose main theme appears in Ex. 2-3.

Ex. 2-3. Haydn: Symphony No. 88, IV.

The movement partially illustrated in Ex. 2-4 is a simple rondo composed from limited materials. The characteristic effect is achieved through the use of rondo theme A, a variation a, and a contrasting theme b.

Ex. 2-4. Mozart: Sonatina in C Major, III.

Ex. 2-5. Mozart: Ibid.

Ex. 2-6. Mozart: Ibid.

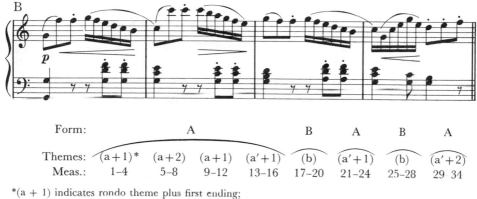

Form:	A				B	A	B	A
Themes:	(a+1)*	(a+2)	(a+1)	(a'+1)	(b)	(a'+1)	(b)	(a'+2)
Meas.:	1–4	5–8	9–12	13–16	17–20	21–24	25–28	29 34

*(a + 1) indicates rondo theme plus first ending;
(a' + 2), variation plus second ending, etc.

This five-part design illustrates certain important organizational features:

1. After its initial appearance the rondo theme is immediately repeated with slight variation.
2. The primacy of the main theme is further established by its recurrences and proportionate duration. Twenty-four of the total thirty-four measures are devoted to (a) and (a'), while (b) encompasses only eight measures.
3. The modification of the rondo theme adds a touch of variety, which relieves the monotony of literal repetition.
4. The subsidiary theme (four-measure phrase) differs markedly from the rondo theme because of its increased pitch-rhythm movement, the interruption of the Alberti accompaniment, and the rate of change of the harmonic rhythm.

With modest means, the twin masters of unity and variety have been served.

To develop further the topic of rondo form, consider a more extended example by the same composer:

Ex. 2-7. Mozart: Viennese Sonatinas, the A rondo theme.

Ex. 2-7 continued.

Ex. 2-8. Ibid., B theme.

Ex. 2-9. Ibid., C theme.

Ex. 2-10. Ibid., Coda.

The aforementioned thematic materials are arranged according to this scheme:

Section:	A	B	A	C	A	Coda
Tonality:	C	c	C	F	C	C
Meas.:	(1–32)	(33–64)	(65–96)	(97–128)	(129–160)	(161–189)

In addition to the points previously made concerning rondo forms, the following additional features are exemplified by the Viennese Sonatinas:

1. The five-part form (plus coda) consists of an A section alternating with two contrasting sections, B and C.
2. The rondo theme consists of a contrasting double period. Note that the first period is parallel in that, except for the cadences, the phrases are identical.
3. Sections B and C are cast in the contrasting keys of c minor and F major, respectively.
4. Sections B and C contrast with each other and with the rondo theme, in accompaniment, thematic character, and key.
5. The various theme groups (double periods) are juxtaposed with no intervening transitory or modulatory material.
6. A coda has been added to close the movement. It is made of materials which are similar to, or derivative of, previous themes.

The themes in Ex. 2-11 are from a rondo that is more complex in structure. The thematic materials are ordered in the pattern, A B A C A' B' A" Coda (based on A).

Ex. 2-11. Piston: Sonata for Violin and Piano, III. © 1940 by Associated Music Publishers, Inc., New York. Reprinted by permission.

These thematic materials are presented according to the following design:

Section:	A	(trans.)	B	(trans.)	A	C
						(canonic)
Meas.:	(1–41)	(42–47)	(48–78)	(79–99)	(100–125)	(126–150)
Dynamics:	*f*		*pp*		*f*	*p*	*p*

Section:	(trans.)	A		(trans)	B′	(trans.)
		(and elements of C)				
Meas.:	(151–163)	(164–185)		(186–191)	(192–220)	(221–236)
Dynamics:		*f*			*p pp*	*f*

Section:	A″	Coda
Meas.:	(237–254)	(255–290)
Dynamics:	*f*	*p ff*

The following important features should be noted: (1) The "canonic" character of the C section contributes an added element of variety through a change of texture as well as change of theme; (2) the dynamic levels of the various sections also provide variety; (3) theme A is accented and heavy, theme B is a combination of two patterns—a smooth, sustained line combined with a staccato, "nervous" bass—and theme C is angular and, in contrast to B, relatively ambiguous in tonality; (4) the overall dimensions have been increased by the inclusion of sections B′, A″ and Coda, as well as through the use of transitional materials. (In the works of many composers, themes and transition elements blend together so smoothly that it is sometimes impossible to determine precisely where one leaves off and the other begins.) Note the symmetrical design achieved in this seven-section pattern: A B A C A B A (Coda).

In the movement represented in Ex. 2-12, the technique of variation assumes importance; the rondo theme is constantly varied, never returning in its original form. Thus the basic repetitive character of the rondo (the unifying element) is maintained. The form here combines rondo characteristics with theme and variations. Only the main theme and the design of this movement are shown.

Ex. 2-12. Haydn: Sonata No. 9, III.

Form: A B A′ C A″ A‴

Another important factor in the study of rondo is that of *instrumentation* and its relation to form. Giuseppe Torelli, in his Solo Concerto for Violin and Orchestra, confines the repeated thematic materials (A sections) to *tutti* passages, whereas the contrasting sections are performed by the solo violin and continuo.

Ex. 2-13. Torelli: Solo Concerto for Violin and Orchestra.

Sections:	(Tutti) A	(Solo) B	(Tutti) A'	(Solo) C	(Tutti) A	Coda
Tonality:	(cgcg)	(g-c)	($E^b c$)	(fgc)	(cgcg)	(c)
Meas.:	(1–16)	(17–25)	(26–33)	(34–46)	(47–60)	(61–66)

A different technique is employed in the third movement of the Beethoven Violin Concerto in D major (A B A C A B A-Coda), whose rondo theme appears in Ex. 2-14. In the rondo sections of this movement the theme is stated first by the solo violin and then by the orchestra; in the episodic sections the solo instrument predominates, with the orchestra generally functioning as accompaniment.

Ex. 2-14. Beethoven: Violin Concerto in D Major, III.

Beethoven, seldom content to conform to a stereotyped pattern, constantly sought to inject new elements of variety into his works. He enlarged the formal dimensions, exploited new key relationships, and treated thematic materials with greater freedom than did his predecessors. In the fourth movement of his Piano Sonata in B-flat Major, Op. 22, he alters the seven-section rondo pattern in that the sixth section consists of a return of both the first and second contrasting materials transposed to the tonic key.

Sections:	A	B	A	C	A	(CB')	A	Coda
Tonality:	B-flat	F	B-flat	b-flat	B-flat	B-flat	B-flat	B-flat

In the third movement of his Symphony No. 7, Op. 92, Beethoven enlarges the form through repetition and arrives at the following arrangement:

	Scherzo*	Trio	Scherzo	Trio	Scherzo
Sections:	A B A	C(c1-c2)	A B A	C(c1-c2)	A B A
Tonality:	FA-FF	D	FA-FF	D	FA-FF

Note that the C sections (binary forms) are used to balance the ternary grouping of A B A, and also observe the key relations (chromatic third relations) F–A and F–D. The thematic materials are seen in Ex. 2-15:

---

*The *scherzo* was introduced by Beethoven to take the place of *minuet*. While it, too, is in triple meter, its character is generally more vigorous and bustling than that of the *minuet*.

Ex. 2-15. Beethoven: Symphony No. 7, Op. 92, III.

The previous survey demonstrates that, although a composition may generally conform to a basic rondo pattern, the composer, by necessity or by choice, frequently modifies the basic scheme as he creates music. One should recognize this fact and approach the study of each new work with the full realization that the stereotyped forms are mere frames of reference, since in practice they are subject to various modifications. Furthermore, there are compositions whose forms are subject to multiple interpretations, while others conform to no particular stereotyped design.

Although the rondo form is still used frequently, no significant deviations have been made since Beethoven's time. New tonal schemes and enriched harmonic vocabularies have been employed along with thematic materials of greater melodic complexity; yet, the formal patterns of more recent composers have generally borrowed from the past. This does not indicate a lack of ingenuity or imagination; rather, it suggests that certain formal schemes are, and continue to be, successful in a fundamental sense.

Composers such as Schubert, Mendelssohn, Chopin, and Brahms, to name but a few, employed the rondo form in numerous works, two of which are illustrated in Ex. 2-16 and Ex. 2-17:

Ex. 2-16. Schubert: Sonata for Piano in D Major, Op. 53, Finale.

Form: A B A' (var. A) C A'' (var. A) Coda

Ex. 2-17. Chopin: Mazurka in B-flat Major, Op. 7, No. 1.

Form: A   BA   CA

To exemplify more recent practices, several works by contemporary composers have been chosen. The themes and attendant form patterns should be used as points of departure for the study of the complete scores and recorded performances.

Ex. 2-18. Barber: Sonata for Piano, Op. 26, II. Reprinted by permission of the copyright owner, G. Schirmer, Inc.

Form: A B A C A Coda

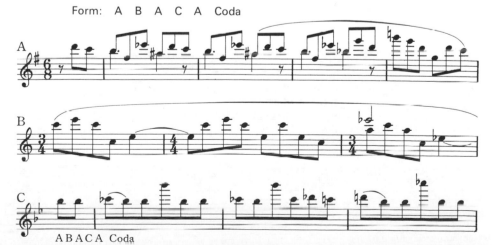

ABACA Coda

Ex. 2-19. Bartók: Music for Strings, Percussion and Celesta, IV. Copyright 1937 by Universal Edition; Renewed 1964. Copyright and Renewal assigned to Boosey & Hawkes, Inc., for U.S.A. and to Universal Edition for all other countries of the world. Reprinted by permission.

Ex. 2-20 illustrates a work of particular interest because sections B, D, and the Coda are made up of fragments of A treated developmentally. Section C contains new materials which are not derivatives of the rondo theme. The result is a highly unified movement that suggests a tri-part form yet possesses many characteristics of the rondo.

Ex. 2-20. Hindemith: Third Sonata for Piano, II. © 1936 by B. Schott's Soehne, Mainz. Renewed 1963. Reprinted by permission.

Form: A (trans.) B   (trans.)   A (trans.)   C (trans.)
                   (b1 b2 b3)
       A (trans.)   D (trans.)   A Coda

The two works of Ex. 2-21 and Ex. 2-22 illustrate more clearly delineated schemes.

Ex. 2-21. Milhaud: Suite Française, V. © Copyright MCMXLV, MCMXLVI, MCML by Leeds Music Corporation, New York, N. Y. Used by permission. All rights reserved.

Form: A B A C A B A

Ex. 2-22. Prokofiev: Violin Concerto No. 2, Op. 63, III. By permission of the
International Music Company, New York.

Form: A B   (trans.) A (trans.) C   A B   (trans.) A Coda
         (b1 b2)   (C & dev.) (b1 b2)

From a more thorough study of recent music it will become apparent that traditional practices have been modified considerably to fit the needs of twentieth-century composers. For example, literal repetition frequently is avoided, and tonality, once an obvious determinant of formal organization, has become tenuous or irrelevant as a determinant of form in the works of many composers. For an earlier composer such as Mozart, one of the primary unifying features of form was the return to the tonic key, an element of variety effected by departure from the tonic. Obviously, if the initial tonality is obscure or ambiguous, its strength as a unifying element is diminished. Although clearly established tonalities are found in many contemporary works, abrupt key changes are common and thus the need for extensive transitory (modulatory) materials is obviated.

Exercises

For more detailed assignments see *Materials and Structure of Music II, Workbook,* Chapter 2.

1. For further analysis of forms, see the following list. Outline the form, indicating themes, sections, keys, and measure numbers. Make a summary of the prominent features not apparent from the outline.
   Haydn: *Piano Sonata in C major,* III.
   Mozart: *Sonata in E-flat major for Violin and Piano,* K. 380, Rondo.
   Beethoven: *Quartet in A minor,* Op. 132, II.
   Mendelssohn: *Midsummer Night's Dream,* Scherzo (the C section is developmental in character).

Brahms: *Symphony No. 1,* III.
Mahler: *Symphony No. 4,* II.
Piston: *String Quartet No. 1,* III.
Sessions: *Symphony No. 2,* IV.
Barber: *Capricorn Concerto,* III.

2. Compose two characteristic rondo themes of two to three phrases in length, using at least one form of each of the following: V_7/V, V_7/iv, V_7/VI, V_7/ii.

3. Select one of the themes and make a setting for string quartet.

4. Compose a contrasting section to follow the rondo theme (Ex. 2-3) and experiment with changes of texture, thematic character, and key.

5. Arrange the materials of Exercises 3 and 4 to create a rondo form as follows: A B A B A (Coda). For the sake of variety, use different dynamic levels and ranges for the repeated sections. Append a short coda made of materials derived from the rondo theme.

6. Copy score and parts for class performance.

3

DIATONIC SEVENTH CHORDS (NONDOMINANT)

Diatonic seventh chords are tertian structures which appear frequently throughout music. These chords have as their roots or primes any of the degrees of the major or minor scales, the constituent intervals being a third, a fifth, and a seventh.

Ex. 3-1. Mozart: Piano Sonata, K. 332, I.

Ex. 3-2. Bacharach: *What the World Needs Now Is Love.*

The classification *nondominant diatonic seventh chords* includes those chords whose members are exclusively diatonic. It excludes the dominant seventh and secondary dominant seventh chords.

The seventh chords assume many guides and many musical roles. The following chart shows the types which occur most frequently in the eighteenth and nineteenth centuries; they are arranged according to chord quality, which is indicated by a series of symbols: Mm, MM, mm, etc. (The first letter represents the triad type, the second, the size of the interval of the seventh.)[1] The term *diminished-minor* and *diminished-diminished* are not commonly used, being replaced by *half-diminished* ($^{\circ}7$) and *diminished* ($^{\circ}7$), respectively

QUALITY	MAJOR MODE	MINOR MODE
Major-Major (MM)	I^7, IV^7	III^7, VI^7
Major-Minor (Mm)	V^7	V^7
Minor-Minor (mm)	ii^7, iii^7, vi^7	i^7, iv^7, (v^7)
Half-Diminished ($^{\circ}7$)	$vii^{\circ 7}$	$ii^{\circ 7}$
(Diminished-Minor)		
Diminished ($^{\circ}7$)		vii°_7 (harmonic and
(Diminished-Diminished)		melodic minor
		scales)

Although the chords illustrated in the chart above are in root position, all of these sonorities appear in 1st, 2nd, and 3rd inversions as well. Inversions are indicated as follows: first inversion—$^6_5$; second inversion—$^4_3$; and third inversion—$^4_2$.

Notational representation of the various common forms is shown in Ex. 3-3a. A few additional types are found in the minor mode, and these appear in Ex. 3-3b, following the initial chord of each measure.

Ex. 3-3a. Diatonic seventh chords.

D Major

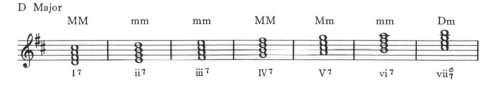

---

[1]Other types of seventh chords occur, often in a minor mode, as a result of chromatic inflection, for example, *minor-major* and *augmented-major*. (See measures 1 and 3 of Ex. 3-3b.)

Ex. 3-3b. Ibid.

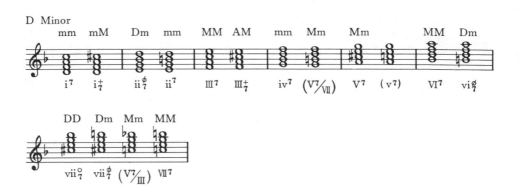

Treatment of the Dissonance

The seventh forms an unstable chordal element and thus merits some special attention. It often results from a purely melodic function; when it does it can be described, for example, as a passing tone, leaning tone, or suspension.

Ex. 3-4a. Palestrina: Motet, *Dies Sanctificatus.*

Ex. 3-4b. Ibid.

Note that in Ex. 3-4a the seventh appears in measures 2 and 5 as a passing tone, in the penultimate measure of Ex. 3-4b as a 7-6 suspension.

When no such explanation is possible, as in Ex. 3-5, it becomes apparent that the seventh is a bona fide chord member.

Ex. 3-5. Schubert: *Der Greise Kopf.*

It is often impossible to determine whether a chord is a seventh chord, or whether it is simply a triad with an attendant non-chord tone. Thus, the first two measures of Ex. 3-6 may be described as a basic harmonic movement from vi through I$_4^6$ to iii, being embellished by the escape tones *c-sharp* and *b.* An equally logical description would be the harmonic analysis indicated with the example.

Ex. 3-6. Puccini: *La Boheme,* Act I, "Si, mi chiamano Mimi."

We will consider such sonorities to be *seventh chords when the duration of the seventh is equal to that of the attendant chord.* Remember, however, that many chords are subject to multiple interpretations.

Composers of different periods and styles have used various means of approaching the seventh of the chord. In much music (particularly that of contrapuntal texture) the seventh is prepared, as a suspension, in that it appears as a member of the previous chord; it is either tied over as in Ex. 3-7, or rearticulated as in Ex. 3-8. The effect of the dissonance is minimized when the tie occurs.

Ex. 3-7. Handel: Suite No. 12 for Harpsichord, Gigue.

G: ii⁶₅   I⁶₅   vii⁰⁶₅   vi⁶₅   V⁷

Ex. 3-8. Mozart: Symphony in G Minor, No. 40, (K. 550), I.

ii⁰⁴₂

In other arrangements the seventh functions as part of a momentary seventh chord, being approached and left by step. When it follows its triadic form, the seventh chord prolongs the triad from which it is derived.

Ex. 3-9. Beethoven: Symphony No. 4 in B-flat Major, Op. 60, II.

E♭: I   (I⁷)   IV⁶₄

Ex. 3-10 has features in common with Ex. 3-9 in that the seventh of each of the seventh chords is part of a descending step-progression. In Ex. 3-10, however, the nondominant seventh chords are not preceded by their triadic counterparts. Here each member of the three-tone arpeggiation acts as a passing tone, thus linking the parallel members of the preceding and succeeding patterns. In this sense the whole chord is a *passing chord*.

Ex. 3-10. Beethoven: Piano Sonata, Op. 14, No. 1, III.

When the seventh of a chord is approached by leap, the dissonance is emphasized. Two subdominant seventh chords appear in Ex. 3-11; the seventh of each is initiated in this manner.

Ex. 3-11. Monteverdi: *Ariana*, "Lasciatomi morire!"

Composers have been consistent in their resolution of the chord's seventh, at least until the beginning of the twentieth century: *the seventh customarily resolves down by step* (Ex. 3-12a), and if such is not the case, it is most frequently held over, continuing as a member of the next chord (Ex. 3-12b).

Ex. 3-12. Resolution of chord sevenths.

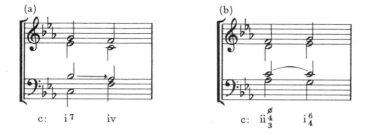

Seventh chords are used in progressions similar to those of their triadic counterparts. The usual resolution of such chords (except the subdominant and leading tone seventh chords) is to a chord with a root a perfect fifth below (or perfect fourth above) the root of the seventh chord.

Ex. 3-13. Usual resolutions.

Usual resolutions

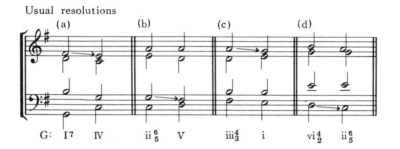

In other resolutions (a few of which appear in Ex. 3-14) the seventh is often held over. Four different root relations are represented by the progressions: (a)—step up; (b)—step down; (c)—third up; and (d)—third down.

Ex. 3-14. Other resolutions.

Other resolutions

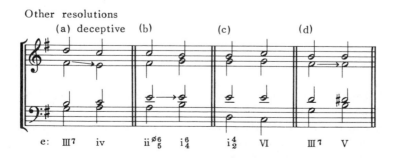

The subdominant (IV_7; iv_7) and leading tone ($vii_{ø7}$; vii_{o7}) seventh chords usually progress to dominant and tonic, respectively (see Ex. 3-15a). They too, however, may resolve to other than their more predictable successors (Ex. 3-15b).

Ex. 3-15. Resolutions of subdominant and leading tone seventh chords.

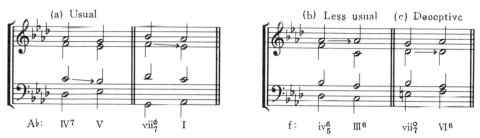

The following chart of common tonally related progressions (appearing in Volume I) will be helpful in planning progressions of diatonic seventh chords. Note how the chord resolutions cited in Examples 3-12 through 3-15 relate to this general scheme.

TONIC			PRE-DOMINANT (subdominant)	DOMINANT	TONIC
I, i	vi, VI		IV, iv	V, V_7	I, i
	iii, III, III⁺		ii, ii°	vii$_6^o$	(vi, VI)
				(iii$_6$, iii	
				III)	

The harmonic cycle may begin at any point.
Any step in the cycle may be omitted.
Any step or steps may be retraced before direction is resumed.

As a general rule, secondary seventh chords appear in complete form. Exceptions may be found in progressions of four-part textures in which the chord of resolution is another seventh chord (sequential passages, for example), and in such cases the fifth (or more rarely, the third) may be omitted and the root doubled. Because of its pronounced resolution tendency, the seventh of the chord is not doubled frequently.

Ex. 3-16. Sequence.

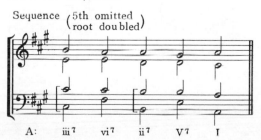

Uses of Diatonic Seventh Chords

Let us now turn our attention to a few of the *roles* diatonic seventh chords play in music. As previously stated, they may appear singly or in series as do the triads from which they derive. In addition, they often appear at important structural points, such as the beginning of a phrase, or at the point of climax as exemplified in measure 4 of Ex. 3-17.

Ex. 3-17. Mendelssohn: *Elijah,* ''Behold God the Lord'' (last 6 measures).

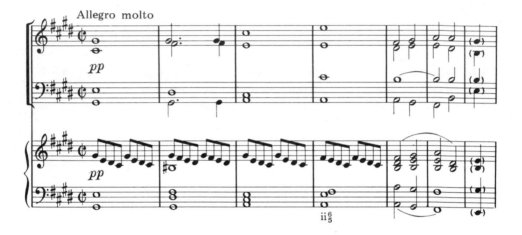

Seventh chords frequently function in connection with a cadence, both in the approach and in the cadence proper. The final cadence pattern in Ex. 3-18 consists of a series of triads appearing in conjunction with an *e-flat* pedal. Two of the resulting sonorities are seventh chords.

Ex. 3-18. Hindemith: *Mathis der Maler* (last 6 measures). © 1934 by B. Schott's Soehne, Mainz. Renewed 1963. Reprinted by permission.

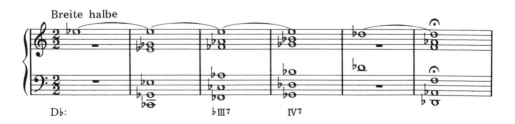

In contrast to the Hindemith work which ends on a *D-flat* triad, the excerpt of Ex. 3-19 ends on a MM7th chord.

Ex. 3-19.   Ravel: *Jeux d' Eau.* © 1941 by Editions Max Eschig, Paris.
Reprinted by permission.

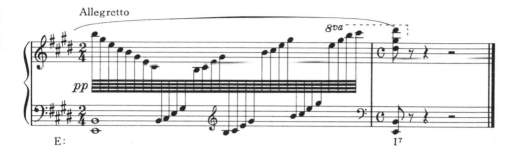

Chains of seventh chords provide the harmonic basis for sequential materials
in the same way as triads. Ex. 3-20, containing five nondominant diatonic seventh
chords, appears in a fugal passage at the juncture of two main thematic groups
and thus serves to dramatize the appearance of a new theme.

Ex. 3-20.   Brahms: Requiem, Section VI.

Seventh chords frequently serve as pivots in modulatory passages. In Ex. 3-21,
a mm$_2^4$ chord functions in this capacity, performing the dual role of iv$_2^4$ in *G* and
ii$_2^4$ in *B-flat*.

Ex. 3-21. Beethoven: String Quartet, Op. 18, No. 6, IV.

The Supertonic Seventh Chord

The supertonic seventh chord appears in two diatonic forms: ii_7 in major, and ii_7° in minor. The ii_7 contains one unstable interval, the seventh between root and seventh; the ii_7° contains two, the seventh and diminished fifth.

The common resolution of both ii_7 and ii_7° is to V. This progression is characterized by downward step resolution of the chord seventh, which moves in parallel thirds or sixths with another voice. In the resolution to V_7, the fifth of one chord or the other may be omitted and the root doubled, while the third of the first chord is held over to become the seventh of the second chord.

Ex. 3-22. Root position, resolutions to dominant.

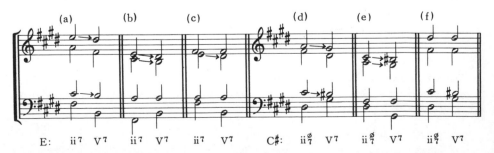

The inverted forms of the supertonic seventh are also often used to precede the dominant; resolutions of the various forms are summarized in Ex. 3-23.

Ex. 3-23. Inversion, resolutions to dominant.

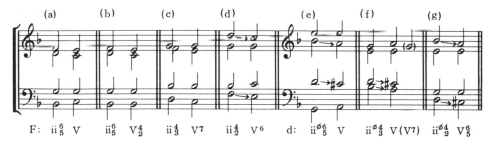

Progression (b) of Ex. 3-23 shows a resolution in which the third of ii$^6_5$ is retained, becoming the seventh of the subsequent V$^4_2$. Both ii$^4_3$ and ii$^4_2$ stand in fairly fixed relationship with the dominant chord in that they must resolve to V$_7$ and V$_6$, respectively, if the seventh is to resolve down by step.

Other resolutions are possible, a few of which appear in Ex. 3-24.

Ex. 3-24. Other resolutions.

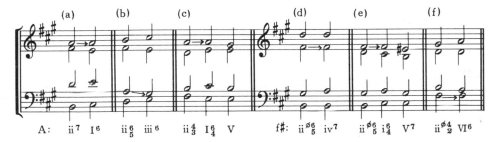

In such progressions the seventh chord may be held over rather than resolved downward. In Ex. 3-24, progressions (c) and (e) are variations of the regular resolution to V through the interpolation of the tonic $^6_4$ chord.

In the resolution to V, and to I, the supertonic $^6_5$ bears a marked resemblance to the subdominant.

Ex. 3-25. Comparison of ii$^6_5$ and IV.

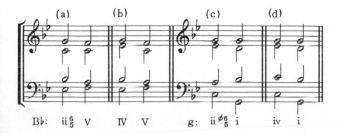

The "subdominant" character of the supertonic $\frac{6}{5}$ chord in (a) and (c) of Ex. 3-25 is intensified by the bass movement: ascent by step to V in the former, descent by a perfect fourth to i in the latter. Because of these characteristic features, and because of the role it plays in such patterns (cadential or otherwise), the supertonic $\frac{6}{5}$ chord has been regarded by some theorists as a subdominant chord with added sixth. In this form, a perfect fifth is formed between the bass tone and the seventh of the chord. Since two perfect fifths are present in the mm $\frac{6}{5}$ there is the possibility of two different root interpretations. In the $^{\circ}\frac{6}{5}$ only one *perfect* fifth is present (between the bass and chord seventh), thus making the bass pitch the probable root.

Ex. 3-26. ii$\frac{6}{5}$ and ii$^{\circ}\frac{6}{5}$.

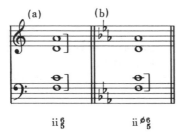

The chord seventh may be approached in various ways as exemplified in Ex. 3-27: in (a) the seventh is prepared and treated as a 7-6 suspension; in (b) it enters as a passing tone; and in (c) it assumes full significance as a chord member without melodic decorative implications.

Ex. 3-27. Approach to the seventh.

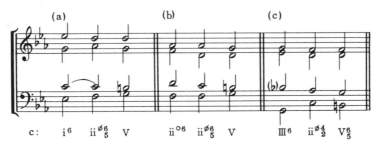

As subsequent examples will reveal, the supertonic chord appears in many contexts, most often preceded by tonic or submediant and resolving to the dominant, a progression that permits conventional resolution of the unstable interval or intervals. The ensuing musical materials illustrate varied uses of this sonority.

Uses of the Supertonic Seventh Chord

Since the root of the supertonic seventh chord forms a fifth relation with the root of the dominant chord, it frequently precedes the dominant in cadences. Both

Ex. 3-28 and Ex. 3-29 illustrate the root position supertonic seventh chord preceded by tonic. In each the unstable chord members are treated in a conventional manner.

Ex. 3-28. Verdi: Requiem, *Ingemisco*.

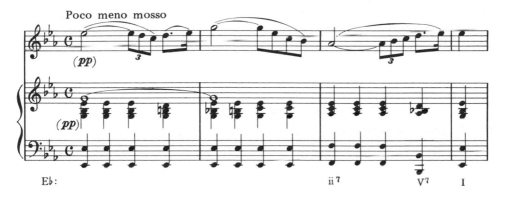

Ex. 3-29. Debussy: *Clair de Lune*.

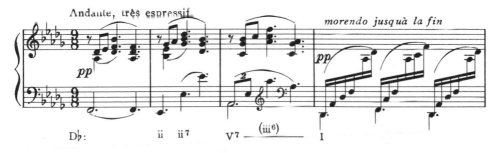

The first inversion is used in a similar fashion with a bass line that moves 4-5-1, as in Ex. 3-30. Here the ii_5^0 is preceded by the submediant chord.

Ex. 3-30. Schubert: Symphony No. 5 in B-flat Major, I.

A variation of the cadence pattern under discussion appears in Ex. 3-31. Here the ii_2^4 precedes the dominant, but instead of moving directly to V_5^6, it progresses to a mutated form (ii_2^{m4}), which then proceeds to the dominant.

Ex. 3-31. Mozart: Piano Sonata, K. 309, III.

The motion to the dominant may be indirect in still another way, the supertonic seventh resolving to tonic $\frac{6}{4}$, which in turn is followed by the dominant.

Ex. 3-32. Verdi: Requiem, *Libera Me*.

The ii°$_7$ chord in Ex. 3-33 is structurally important because it appears at the close of the climax of the passage, where it is sustained for two measures prior to the cadence pattern i$^6_4$-V-i. First and second inversions of the supertonic seventh also are used in approaching the progression (I$^6_4$-V).

Ex. 3-33. Beethoven: Symphony No. 9 in D Minor, Op. 125, III.

The supertonic seventh chord is frequently the penultimate chord in the progressive cadence on V, and in Ex. 3-34 a ii$_3^4$ serves this purpose. Note that, as is so often the case, the seventh forms a 4-3 suspension above the dominant.

Ex. 3-34. Beethoven: Symphony No. 3 in E-flat Major, Op. 55, I.

Ex. 3-35 illustrates a ii$_5^6$ followed by its mutated form, V$_5^6$/V. This secondary dominant links ii$_5^6$ to V, the cadence chord. Simultaneously, the motion of the bass line from *f* to *g* is strengthened by the *f-sharp* inflection.

Ex. 3-35. Mozart: *Marriage of Figaro,* Act III, Sextette.

Ex. 3-36 illustrates a typical use of a ii$^4_2$ in which it is preceded by tonic. As can be seen, the root of I is held over to form the seventh of ii$^4_2$, which then resolves to the third of V$^6_5$.

Ex. 3-36. Mozart: Motet, *Ave Verum Corpus*.

Interior progressions of the supertonic chord to the tonic chord are fairly usual, while cadences of this type are not. However, when they do serve a cadential function, the progression is most often in minor, with ii$^{ø6}_5$ moving to i, as in Ex. 3-37.

Ex. 3-37. Tschaikovsky: *Legende*

In interior progressions the ii$^4_2$ (or ii$^{ø4}_2$) often serves to embellish (to prolong) tonic in much the same way as does IV$^6_4$ (or iv$^6_4$).

Ex. 3-38. Schubert: *Gute Nacht*.

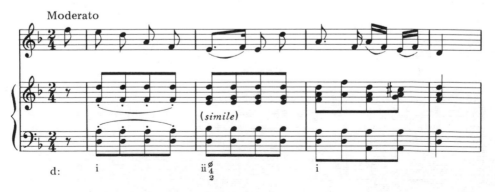

In Ex. 3-39 ii_7 and ii_5^6 are preceded and followed by tonic in a passage characterized by the similar movement of the lines.

Ex. 3-39. Puccini: *La Bohème,* Act I, "Si, mi chiamano Mimi."

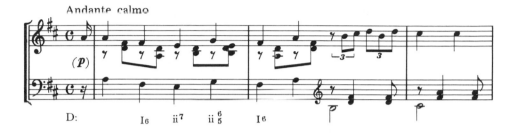

The supertonic seventh chord figures prominently in the approach to the authentic cadence of Ex. 3-40. Herein the cadential i_4^6 is prolonged by the interpolation of a $ii°_5^6$.

Ex. 3-40. Leoncavallo: *Pagliacci,* Act I, "Recitar."

In measure 1 of Ex. 3-41 the supertonic seventh chord links successive appearances of the tonic chord, while a "deceptive" relationship is formed in measures
2–3 where ii_7 resolves to iii.

Ex. 3-41. Fauré: *Poeme d'un Jour*.

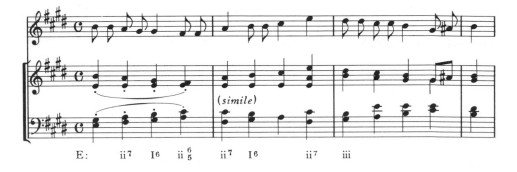

E: ii⁷   I⁶   ii ⁶₅   ii⁷   I⁶   ii⁷   iii

Root relation of a second is exemplified again in Ex. 3-42, in which ii⁶₅ resolves to V⁴₃/IV. This represents a variation of the supertonic seventh to tonic progression. Here the chord of resolution is a chromatically altered I that functions as a secondary dominant. The extensive prolongation of this chord creates the effect of a tonal region in *A-flat*.

Ex. 3-42. Mozart: *The Magic Flute*, Overture.

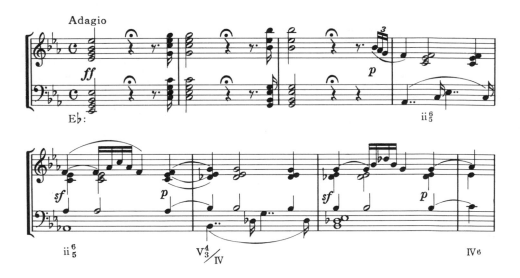

One other progression involving the supertonic seventh chord appears with enough frequency to justify its inclusion, i.e., the progression to submediant. Beginning at measure 5 of Ex. 3-43 the relative minor key receives durational and dynamic stress where for two measures the ii₇ assumes the temporary role of "iv₇" in support of *a* minor. In the last two measures the original tonality of *C* is reaffirmed by the authentic cadence.

Ex. 3-43. Chopin: Mazurka, Op. 17, No. 2.

The last example to be considered contains the ii°$_7$ as an integral chord in a deceptive passage that shifts from an initial minor key to its relative major. In this instance the ii°$^4_3$ serves as the pivot chord of the third-related modulation.

Ex. 3-44. Schubert: Quartet No. 14 in D Minor, *Death and the Maiden.*

Exercises

For more detailed assignments see *Materials and Structure of Music II, Workbook,* Chapter 3.

1. Spell various types of seventh chords (nondominant) from the bass up, and identify them as to chord type and function in various major and minor keys.
2. Considering *d* as the root, third, fifth, and seventh, respectively, of different non-dominant seventh chords, spell various types (mm^7, MM$^6_5$, $^{o4}_3$, $^o_7$, etc.) and indicate the function of each in the major and/or minor keys in which they might appear as diatonic chords.
3. Indicate the chord quality and function of each of the *seventh* chords appearing in Ex. 3-17, Ex. 3-18, Ex. 3-20 and Ex. 3-43.
4. Sing (from the bass up) various types of nondominant seventh chords (root position and inverted).
5. Make two different four-part settings of each of the following:
   a. ii$^o_7$—V   b. ii$^6_5$—I$^6_4$—V   c. ii$^{o4}_2$—V^7 d. ii$^4_2$—V$^6_5$ e. ii$^{o6}_5$—i$_6$—V
   f. ii$^{o4}_2$—V^7/iv—iv   g. ii$^{o6}_5$—VI—i$^6_4$—V
6. Construct a two-phrase period per the following specifications:
   a. Employ at least 4 of the following in typical progressions:
      ii$^6_5$, ii$^4_3$, ii$_7$, V$^4_3$/vi, V$^4_2$/IV
   b. Write in open score for string quartet.
7. Analyze several of the following, indicating keys, chords, and nonchord tones:
   a. Beethoven: *Piano Sonata,* Op. 2, No. 3, I (5-8)
   b. Brahms: *Symphony No. III,* Op. 90, III (1-8)
   c. Chopin: *Mazurka,* Op. 30, No. 1 (5-8)
              Nocturne, Op. 37, No. 1 (33-40)
              Nocturne, Op. 48, No. 1 (25-32)
   d. Franck: *Symphonic Variations,* Allegro non troppo
   e. Mozart: *Piano Sonata in D major,* K. 311, III (23-26)
   f. Schubert: *Symphony No. V,* III (1-18)
   g. Sibelius: *Symphony No. II,* Op. 43, III (Trio) (1-4)
8. Find other examples containing supertonic seventh chords, particularly in the music for your own instrument.

4

DIATONIC SEVENTHS (CONCLUDED): NINTH CHORDS

Leading Tone Seventh Chord

The leading tone seventh chord is a half-diminished seventh chord (vii°$_7$) in major, and a diminished seventh chord (vii°$_7$) in minor. Both sonorities share common features as well as differences. The vii°$_7$ contains two dissonant intervals, a diminished fifth and a minor seventh, whereas the vii°$_7$ contains two diminished fifths. While the former in root position contains both major and minor thirds, the latter contains only minor thirds.

Ex. 4-1. vii°$_7$ and vii°$_7$.

Within an established tonality both chords have strong resolution tendencies. They usually resolve to tonic, the diminished fifths contracting to thirds, the augmented intervals expanding to sixths, and the sevenths contracting to perfect fifths. To proceed by the resolution tendencies of the intervals contained in the vii°$_7$ will lead to a tonic with doubled third, as shown in (d), (e), and (f) of Ex. 4-2.

Ex. 4-2. Resolutions of vii°$_7$ and vii°$_7$.

Ex. 4-3. Parallel motion, upper voices.

g: vii°⁷   i   vii°⁷   i

No unique resolution problems arise in the inversions of these chords,[1] as shown in Ex. 4-4. The most significant feature of both chord forms is the usual resolution of the chord *prime* (leading tone) to the tonic pitch.

Ex. 4-4. Resolutions of inversions of $°_7$ and $°_7$.

The prevalence of the harmonic relationship vii°₇—I (vii°₇—i) has led some theorists to consider the leading tone seventh chord as a "dominant ninth chord" with the root omitted. Ex. 4-5 would tend to support this theory in that the vii°₇ is followed immediately by the dominant.

---

[1] Inversions of diminished seventh chords are recognizable only in context after a given chord has resolved.

Ex. 4-5. Chopin: Nocturne, Op. 37.

Both forms of the leading tone seventh chord (vii$_7^\circ$ and vii$_7^\circ$) are important members of the family of diatonic tertian structures, principally because of the role they play in relation to tonic. Although both customarily resolve to tonic, other possible resolutions are to iii (III), vi (VI), V/IV (V/iv), or V/vi (V/VI).

Ex. 4-6. Other resolutions of $^\circ{}_7$ and $^\circ{}_7$.

Uses of the Leading Tone Seventh Chord

The vii°$_7$ plays an important role in the passages from which the following two examples are taken. Here the leading tone seventh chord appears in three different forms (vii°$_7$, vii°$^6_5$, vii°$^4_3$), functioning at cadence points in excerpts 4-7 and 4-8 and as a neighbor embellishment of tonic in excerpt 4-8, with the vii°$_6$ resolving to vi$_6$ in the parallel descent to the cadence on V.

Ex. 4-7. Beethoven: Piano Sonata, Op. 10, No. 1, I.

Ex. 4-8. Ibid.

A vii$^4_3$ appears at the head of the second phrase in Ex. 4-9.

Ex. 4-9. Schubert: Symphony No. 5 in B-flat Major, III.

In the first movement of the same work the leading tone seventh chord passes between two tonic chords, serving an embellishing function in a passage in which imitation is an important feature.

Ex. 4-10. Schubert: Symphony No. 5 in B-flat Major, I.

In Ex. 4-11 the vii$_7^{\circ}$ and the three previous chords occur above a tonic pedal.

Ex. 4-11. Mendelssohn: *Elijah,* "Be Not Afraid."

Harmonic impetus is increased by the introduction of unstable harmonic elements. In Ex. 4-12 a vii$_3^4$ is introduced at the high point of the line, following a progressive cadence on V_6. Thus the climax is stressed and the motion to tonic strengthened because of the expected resolution.

Ex. 4-12. Mozart: Piano Sonata, K. 533, III.

Embellishment of the dominant is the function of the $vii^{\circ\frac{4}{2}}$ appearing in measures 1–6 of Ex. 4-13. This dominant elaboration dramatizes the reappearance of the movement's main theme in measure 9. The cadential $vii^{\circ\frac{6}{5}}$ (measure 19), resulting from the resolution of the 7-6 suspension in the melody, is a very "active" cadence chord.

Ex. 4-13. Mozart: Piano Sonata, K. 457, III.

Although the leading tone seventh chord customarily resolves to tonic, it may resolve to other triads or seventh chords as well. This is often true in passages containing consecutive seventh chords.

Ex. 4-14. Bizet: *Carmen,* Act II, "Faites-Lui Mes Aveux."

Ex. 4-15 is a phrase that follows a cadence on the dominant. The vii$^{\varnothing \frac{6}{5}}$ progresses to tonic which, by virtue of a passing minor seventh, functions as V$^6_5$/IV.

Ex. 4-15. Mendelssohn: Andante con Variazioni, Op. 82.

Still another type of secondary dominant, V/vi, appears as the chord of resolution of the vii$^{\varnothing \frac{6}{5}}$ in Ex. 4-16.

Ex. 4-16. Bartók: *Little Pieces for Children,* Vol. I, No. 7. Reprinted by permission of the copyright owner, Edwin F. Kalmus.

The Tonic Seventh Chord

Ex. 4-17. Stravinsky: *Petrouchka,* Third part. Copyright by Edition Russe de Musique. All rights assigned to Boosey & Hawkes, Inc. Revised Edition Copyright 1947 by Boosey & Hawkes, Inc. Reprinted by permission.

The passage of Ex. 4-17 appears as a cornet solo in a work for orchestra. It outlines the seventh chord which is the topic for this section. As study of the example reveals, the constituent intervals above its root (G) are: major third, perfect fifth, and major seventh.

In the minor mode i_7 is a mm_7 chord, which is identical in construction to the ii_7 (major mode) previously discussed. The i_7 usually employs the unaltered seventh degree (subtonic) of the minor scale rather than the leading tone.

Ex. 4-18. i_7 chord.

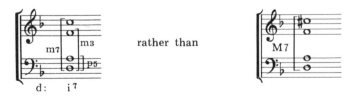

rather than

The tonic seventh chord generally moves to the subdominant, thus permitting the usual downward resolution of the chord's seventh. When the tonic seventh is a MM_7 chord (thus containing the leading tone), this resolution is contrary to the usual ascent of this scale member. In the progression to the subdominant the inversions generally follow the resolution patterns described for inversions of other seventh chords. That is, the bass of the first inversion generally moves up by step; that of third inversion, down by step; and that of second inversion, up or down by step.

Ex. 4-19. Usual resolution of I_7 and i_7 and inversions.

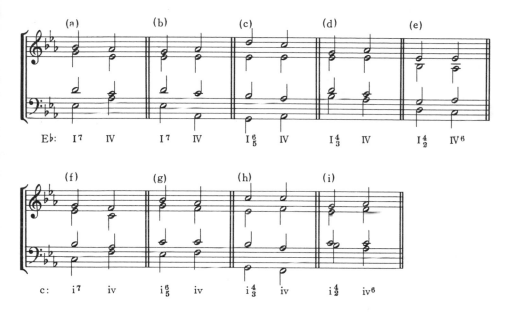

Other common resolutions are to the supertonic triad and its mutation as V_7/V, or to the submediant.

Ex. 4-20. Other resolutions of I_7 and i_7 and inversions.

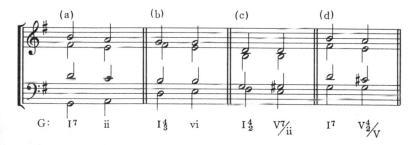

Some Uses of the Tonic Seventh Chord

In one typical occurrence the tonic seventh chord appears early in a phrase as an elaboration of the basic progression I-IV, as illustrated in Ex. 4-21. Here the chord's seventh results from the passing motion between 8 and 6, the root and third of the chords in measures 1 and 3.

Ex. 4-21. Puccini: *La Bohème,* Act II, ''Quando me'n vo.''

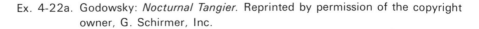

In other passages the MM_7 chord may serve as a cadence chord. Parts (a) and (b) of Ex. 4-22 illustrate this sonority as the terminal chord of two works for piano.

Ex. 4-22a. Godowsky: *Nocturnal Tangier.* Reprinted by permission of the copyright owner, G. Schirmer, Inc.

Ex. 4-22b. Krenek: "The Moon Rises." Reprinted by permission of the copyright owner, G. Schirmer, Inc.

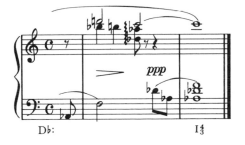

Db: I_3^4

In Ex. 4-23 the seventh of I^7 appears as a suspension, having been prepared as the third of the preceding V^7. The I^7 resolves to vi^6, following which the I^7 again appears.

Ex. 4-23. Mendelssohn: *Elijah,* "Behold God the Lord."

Subdominant Seventh Chord

The two unaltered forms of the subdominant chord are MM_7 in major and mm_7 in minor.

Ex. 4-24a. Copland: *Appalachian Spring*. Copyright 1945 by Aaron Copland.
Reprinted by permission of Aaron Copland, Copyright Owner, and
Boosey & Hawkes, Inc., Sole Licensees.

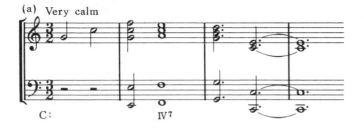

Ex. 4-24b. iv$_7$.

As we know, seventh chords generally resolve to a chord whose root is a perfect
fifth below that of the seventh chord. This is not the case with the subdominant
seventh chord, which more often resolves directly to V or indirectly through I$_4^6$
or ii$_7$.

Ex. 4-25. IV$_7$—V and iv$_7$—V.

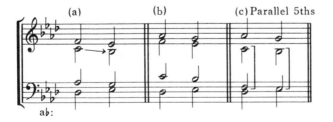

As shown in Ex. 4-25, the inverted forms are frequently treated so that the bass
moves by step. Less commonly, the subdominant seventh chord progresses to such
other chords as tonic, supertonic, and various secondary dominants; however, the
progressions to tonic and supertonic are most usual. A few possible resolutions are
seen in Ex. 4-26.

Ex. 4-26. Resolutions of IV₇, iv₇, and their inversions.

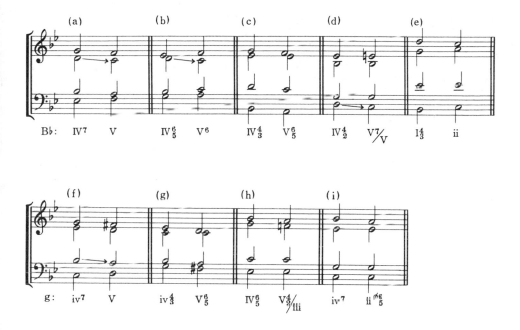

Uses of Subdominant Seventh Chords

The subdominant seventh chord sometimes performs an important function near the end of a phrase, either before a cadence or as a member of the cadence proper. In Ex. 4-27 a IV₇ appears following vi and functions as the penultimate chord in the progressive cadence on V.

Ex. 4-27. Bartók: Concerto for Piano, No. 3, II. Copyright 1947 by Boosey & Hawkes, Ltd. Reprinted by permission of Boosey & Hawkes, Inc.

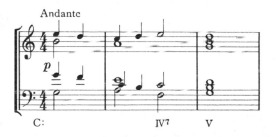

A plagal cadence closes Ex. 4-28. Here IV₇ resolves to I, which is embellished by a 6-5 suspension.

Ex. 4-28. Chopin: Nocturne, Op. 62, No. 2.

The subdominant seventh chord in Ex. 4-29 functions as a cadence chord, a mid-point in the movement to the transient-terminal cadence on V in the subsequent phrase.

Ex. 4-29. Mendelssohn: *Elijah*, "Yet Doth the Lord See It Not."

However, non-cadential uses of the subdominant seventh chord are more common, and often prepare the dominant.

Ex. 4-30. Chopin: Nocturne, Op. 48, No. 1.

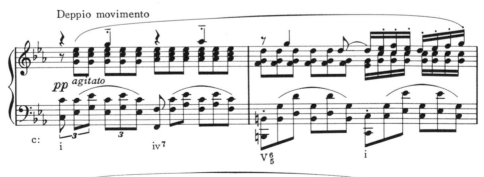

Two subdominant seventh chords appear in Ex. 4-31, the first resolving to V_5^6, and the second to ii^6. In the latter a 7-6 pattern forms the seventh of the IV^6, which resolves into the ii^6 chord. The similarity of these two chords seems to be an unfolding of the same harmonic unit.

Ex. 4-31. Handel: *Messiah*, "Surely He Hath Borne Our Griefs."

In a different setting, the subdominant seventh resolves to a minor dominant, which then progresses deceptively to VI. This passage is characterized by parallelism and, until the cadential V, by its adherence to the natural minor scale.

Ex. 4-32. Puccini: *Tosca*, Act II, "Vissi d'arte."

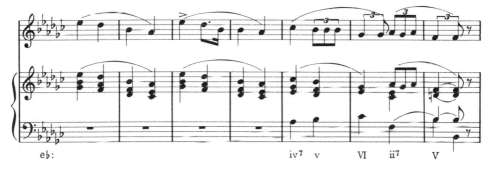

The IV_3^4 frequently functions as a tonic embellishment as does its triad counterpart. This is especially true in passages featuring a tonic pedal. Ex. 4-33 illustrates such a use near the close of a work.

Ex. 4-33. Chopin: Nocturne, Op. 37, No. 2.

The progression from IV^7 to V^6_5/V may be accomplished very smoothly as Ex. 4-34 demonstrates. In such a progression the secondary dominant serves as a chromatic interpolation heightening arrival of the dominant.

Ex. 4-34. Chopin: Waltz, Op. 69, No. 1.

$A\flat$: IV^7 V^6_5/V V^4_3/iii I^6_4 V^7 I

The Submediant Seventh Chord

The submediant seventh chord is generally found in one of two forms: as a mm_7 chord in major or as a MM_7 chord in minor. Its usual resolution is to the supertonic triad or supertonic seventh chord. Other resolutions are to subdominant, dominant, dominant of dominant, and occasionally directly to tonic. Ex. 4-35 illustrates a few such resolutions, in root position and inverted.

Ex. 4-35. Resolutions of vi_7 and VI_7 and inversions.

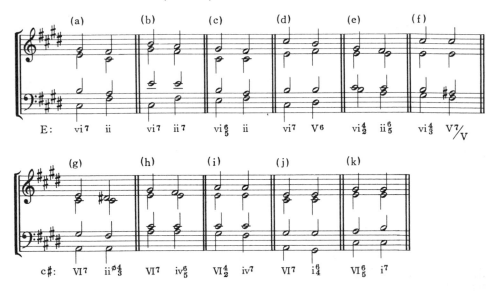

Uses of the Submediant Seventh Chord

In Ex. 4-37, vi_7 precedes ii_7 in the approach to a terminal cadence.

Ex. 4-37. Chopin: Ballade in F, Op. 37, Andantino.

Frequently the submediant seventh chord is followed by its mutation, the V_7/ii. This change accelerates the motion toward the supertonic, which in turn prepares the cadence.

Ex. 4-38. Offenbach: *Les Contes d'Hoffman,* "Elle a fui, La tourterelle."

The Mediant Seventh Chord

The mediant seventh chord usually appears as a min[7] in major, or as a MM[7] in minor. It regularly resolves to the submediant, whose root is a fifth below.

Ex. 4-39. Resolutions of ii[7], iii[7] and inversions.

Uses of the Mediant Seventh Chord

In Ex. 4-40 the mediant seventh chord appears twice. First it results from a passing bass tone which follows the submediant triad, creating the third inversion (iii$_2^4$). Its second appearance is in the form of a sequential continuation of a stream of secondary sevenths; here it is in root position (iii$_7$). Note that every secondary seventh chord appears in this passage.

Ex. 4-40. Debussy: *The Blessed Damozel.*

Every diatonic seventh chord is also used in the course of the first four measures of the next example, and in each instance the seventh resolves regularly. An interesting use is made of a sequential pattern in which the melodic fragments alternate between the accompaniment and the vocal line.

Ex. 4-41. Grieg: *An der Bahre einer Jungen Frau.*

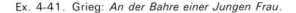

The iii$_7$ of Ex. 4-42 appears in a sequential context, with the roots of the chords a fifth apart. Note that the sequential effect is reinforced by the accompanying non-chord tones of various types.

Ex. 4-42. Verdi: Requiem, *Requiem* and *Kyrie*.

The mediant seventh chord sometimes progresses to the subdominant, as noted here in Ex. 4-43.

Ex. 4-43. Debussy: Ballade. Permission for reprint granted by Editions Jean Jobert, Paris, copyright owner, and Elkan-Vogel Co., Inc., Philadelphia agents.

Both mediant and subdominant sevenths are juxtaposed in Ex. 4-44.

Ex. 4-44. Copland: *Appalachian Spring*. Copyright 1945 by Aaron Copland. Reprinted by permission of Aaron Copland, Copyright Owner, and Boosey & Hawkes, Inc., Sole Licensees.

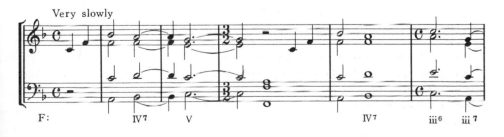

Ex. 4-44 continued.

IV

Other less common resolutions are to the tonic, supertonic, and leading tone chords, and to various secondary dominants. One further example (Ex. 4-45) illustrates the progression III⁷—i⁶₅. As is frequently true in such instances, the III⁷ briefly enacts the role of tonic in a transitory shift to the mediant in a minor key.

Ex. 4-45. Puccini: *La Bohème,* Act IV, "Sono andati."

Ninth Chords

Like the collection of seventh chords studied previously, more complex chords involving intervals of a major or minor ninth have become part of harmonic practice. Though not limited to nineteenth- and twentieth-century works, these chords are most characteristic of works of the past hundred years, and they are congruent with the fuller, richer textures in which they usually appear.

Ex. 4-46 and Ex. 4-47 show several ways in which ninths have been treated as *decorative* pitches. The accompanying reductions (on the third staff) represent the sonorities that are momentarily formed or implied where decorative ninths are heard.

Ex. 4-46. Bach: *Well-tempered Clavier,* Book I, Prelude in F Minor.

Ex. 4-47. Bach: Three-voice Invention in E-flat Major.

In Ex. 4-48 the approach by leap to *g-flat* and the subsequent leap away suggest that it is part of a chord on *f,* i.e., the ninth.

Ex. 4-48. Bach: *Well-tempered Clavier,* Book I, Prelude in F Minor.

In contrast to ninths formed by contrapuntal motion, there are numerous examples which are essentially structural. In such cases the ninth is a colorful member of the chord.

Ex. 4-49. Brahms: Intermezzo, Op. 116, No. 1.

The *f-sharp* in measure 1 of Ex. 4-49 forms the major ninth of an arpeggiated chord built in thirds, whose root is *e*. Since *b* is tonic, the chord is a subdominant ninth chord. A dominant ninth lacking a third appears in Ex. 4-50.

Ex. 4-50. Wagner: *Tristan und Isolde*, Act I.

Ninth chords built on *a* (ii$_9$) and *d* (V$_9$) form the harmonic basis of the passage shown in Ex. 4-51.

Ex. 4-51. Ravel: *Pavane*.

Ninth chords, built in superposed thirds, can be constructed on any scale degree by the same process used to create the full complement of triads and seventh chords. All of the notes of diatonic ninth chords are drawn from the scale members of the prevailing key, as shown in Ex. 4-52.

Ex. 4-52. Diatonic ninth chords.

In constructing ninth chords in minor keys we must be aware of the variability of various scale steps. Compare the different qualities of ninth chords which result from the use of various scale forms, as shown in the group of chords in *c* minor under Ex. 4-52. Many of the chords are virtually foreign to most harmonic practice associated with major-minor composition. For example, iii^9 and vii°_9 seldom occur.

The Dominant Ninth Chord (V_9)

If we regard the dominant ninth chord (V_9) as a "new chord," a harmonic complex to be heard and studied as some sort of innovation, then we will fail to make use of considerable prior information about root relations, chord progression, and resolution. If, however, we see that V_9 is simply V_7 to which a major or minor third is added, then we can anticipate that V_9 is merely a logical addition to the group of dominant functioning chords, as in Ex. 4-53.

Ex. 4-53. Brahms: Intermezzo, Op. 116.

Progressions of V_9—I (i) are illustrated in Ex. 4-55. Like the seventh, the ninth of the chord usually resolves by descending step. However, other resolutions of the ninth by an ascending third or descending fourth can be found.

Ex. 4-54. Typical resolution of V_9.

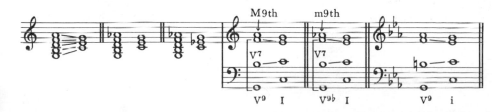

Mutation occurs often in the use of V_9 chords, as composers have freely used either the major or minor ninth (or both) in the V_9—I relation in major keys. In minor keys such freedom does not prevail, and we seldom find a V_9 with a major ninth directly preceding a minor tonic triad. The V_9 with a minor ninth prevails in minor keys.

Ex. 4-55. Minor ninth chord.

A V_9 in *B-flat* occurs over a dominant pedal in Ex. 4-57. The ninth, approached and resolved by step, heightens the tension of the prevailing V_7 chord.

Ex. 4-56. Beethoven: Symphony No. 9, I.

The dominant minor ninth chord (M3rd, m7, m9) occurs as an accented chord in Ex. 4-57. Its resolution is to I_6 in *B-flat*. The ninth of the chord, *g-flat*, represents a mutation of the diatonic *g-natural*.

Ex. 4-57. Ibid.

Now note how the same chord type is used in Ex. 4-58.

Ex. 4-58. Wagner: *Tristan und Isolde*.

The ninth of the V_9, *e-flat* in measure 5, is approached and left by leaps. The leaps, however, are somewhat balanced by the step-progression formed by the *e-flat* and *d flat* in measure 8. In a broad sense, the *d-flat* of measure 8 is the delayed melodic resolution of the *e-flat*.

The most salient feature of the resolution of major or minor ninths of dominant chords, as exemplified by Ex. 4-56 and Ex. 4-57, is the melodic movement from 6 to 5. (The ninth of V^9 is the submediant scale degree.) As we noted in earlier studies of melody, the submediant is an unstable melodic pitch whose resolution is usually by descending step to the dominant (6-5). The most common resolution of an unstable chord containing 6 coincides with a basic melodic pattern (6-5), and the necessity of viewing chord resolution as a confirmation of melodic impulses cannot be overstressed.

The 6-5 resolution of the ninth of the chord may be found along with a change of root, or as a lessening of tension before the change of root, e.g., V_9—V_7—I, as in Ex. 4-59.

Ex. 4-59. 6-5 resolutions

Deceptive resolutions of V_9 to vi are rare, since the ninth of V_9 is identical with the root of vi, and the progression V_9—vi (or VI) would prohibit the normal 6-5

resolution of the ninth. When V_9 is resolved deceptively to vi or VI, as in Ex. 4-60, 6-5 melodic movement generally results in a lessening of harmonic tension *before* the change of chord to vi.

Ex. 4-60. Deceptive resolutions of V_9.

In Ex. 4-61 a V_9 in *c* minor is heard in measure 3 over a rearticulated dominant pedal. The resolution of the ninth (6-5) occurs as a slackening of tension in measure 4, whereas the dominant root is maintained. In this excerpt the ninth has the character of a protracted suspension, resolved a measure late.

Ex. 4-61. Schubert: Symphony No. 4 in C Minor (*Tragic*), I (Piano Reduction).

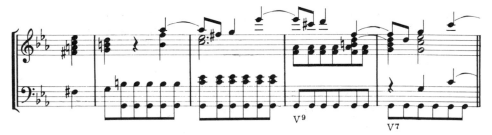

The harmonic approaches to V_9 are virtually identical to the basic harmonic approaches to V or V_7. The same root relations prevail, and V_9 is generally found in relatively weak metric positions, like the simpler dominant chords, preceding metrically stronger assertions of more stable chords (specifically tonic).

Several common approaches to V_9 are illustrated in the group of excerpts under Ex. 4-62 and Ex. 4-63. Play them.

Ex. 4-62. Approaches to V^9.

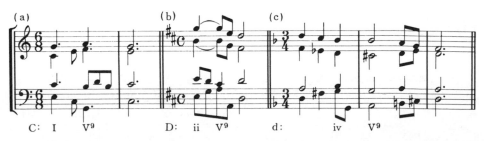

Ex. 4-63. Ibid.

Inversions of V_9

Root position is by far the most frequent arrangement of V_9 (or any other ninth chord), and produces the intervals $\frac{9}{7}_{(3)}^{5}$ above the base. The third, seventh, and ninth above the root are generally present in four-voice arrangements of the chord. As in V_7, the fifth is the most frequently omitted chord member. *First inversions* of V_9 are quite common, resulting in a $\frac{7}{6}_{(3)}^{5}$ distribution above the bass (the third of the chord). It is shown in Ex. 4-64.

Ex. 4-64. Schuman: Symphony No. 2, Adagio. Reprinted by permission of the copyright owner, G. Schirmer, Inc.

In Ex. 4-65 the fifth is present in a first inversion of V_9. The upper voice touches both the ninth and seventh of the chord. The second inversion of V_9 $\frac{(5)}{4}_3$ is rare, but both first and second inversions are found in Ex. 4-65.

Ex. 4-65. Beethoven: Piano Sonata in E-flat, Op. 31, No. 3.

Although third and fourth inversions of ninth chords occur, their use is so infrequent that they will not be dealt with in this chapter.

The ninth most often occurs in the top part of the ninth chord. The chord is rarely distributed so that a second occurs between the root and the ninth. The ninth is virtually never found below the root,[2] since such an arrangement would obscure the most characteristic interval of the chord, the major or minor ninth. A variety of spacings of ninth chords, in four or five parts, is shown in Ex. 4-66.

Ex. 4-66. Spacings of ninth chords.

Briefly, the principles of spacing, doubling, and voice leading that are generally applicable to V_9 chords include the following:

1. The ninth, which usually occurs in the soprano or alto part, is always separated from the root by the interval of a major or minor ninth or more.
2. The fifth of the chord is most often omitted in four-voice texture; it is generally present in five.
3. No doubling normally occurs in four-voice textures. In fuller textures the root is usually doubled.
4. In inversions of the chord, the interval of a ninth is maintained between the root and the ninth.
5. The ninth generally resolves by descending step (6-5).
6. The tritone that occurs between the third and seventh resolves according to the established principles.

Study the examples of V_9 resolutions shown in Ex. 4-67.

Ex. 4-67. Typical resolutions of V_9.

---

[2] There are important exceptions to this in works of Stravinsky and others appearing in the opening years of this century; e.g.,

Like V_7, V_9 is susceptible to an enormous variety of resolutions. Composers have not limited their use of the chord to dominant-tonic relations, as a study of the various progressions shown in Ex. 4-68 will reveal. Play the illustrations and experiment with other resolutions of V_9.

Ex. 4-68. Other resolutions of V_9.

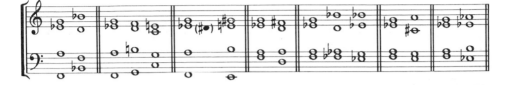

Nondominant Ninth Chords

The mmM ninth chord, comprised of a root, m3, (p5), m7, and M9, occurs as ii_9 and vi_9 in major keys, as i_9 and iv_9 in minor.

Ex. 4-69. Different arrangements of ii_9 (mmM) in C.

As attractive as these sonorities may be, they had only a nominal role until the twentieth century. Where they do occur in earlier music, the ninth (and seventh too) are most often heard as leaning tones or suspensions. Unlike the V_9, these chords, particularly the mmM9 and the MMM9 discussed below, contain *no tritone*, and occur generally within the phrase rather than as a part of the cadence.

In Ex. 4-70 the ii_9 precedes V_7. The root pattern of the closing measure, which contains the ii_9, is 2—5 1.

Ex. 4-70. Hugo Wolf: *Spanish Songbook.*

A more contrapuntal treatment of a mmM9th chord (iv$_9$) is found in Ex. 4-71. The ninth and seventh are treated as suspensions which form a part of a sequential pattern beginning in measure 2. Predominantly contrary motion between the outer voices leads to the cadence. Through a continuation of the sequence, the Neapolitan resolves to °$_7$/VI, evading the anticipated V$_7$ until the fourth beat of measure 3.

Ex. 4-71. Mahler: *Songs of a Wayfarer*, No. 1.

Adding a minor third above the seventh of a major-major seventh chord produces the MMM ninth chord (root, M3, M7, and M9). Again, the fifth is omitted from four-voice arrangements of the chord. The MMM9th chord is usually built on tonic or subdominant in major keys, and can occur as III^9 or VI^9 in minor.

Ex. 4-72. MMM Ninth Chords.

Leaps to and from ninths occur on the first beats of the first two measures in Ex. 4-73. The same notes, *g* and *f*, which within the harmonic context create iv^9 and III^9 chords, are treated in the accompaniment as a leaning tone and a suspension.

Ex. 4-73. Schumann: Symphony No. 2, II.

Where the MMM9th is found, it usually occurs as the result of melodic activity and is heard as a non-chord embellishment of a simpler triad or seventh chord. A comparison of Ex. 4-74 and Ex. 4-75 will show the sonority as a double suspension in the former and as a cadential tonic ninth chord in the latter. The two treatments are a musical world apart.

Ex. 4-74. Bach: *Well-tempered Clavier,* Book I, Prelude in E-flat.

The sonority heard on the first beat of measure 2 is a MMM ninth. However, the brief duration of the seventh and ninth, coupled with the clear suspension patterns which form them, preclude regarding the chord as a true MMM ninth chord. It should be explained as ii$_6$ in *E-flat,* embellished by a double suspension figure.

In contrast to Ex. 4-74, the cadential chord of Ex. 4-75 is a full fledged tonic ninth chord (I$_9$).

Ex. 4-75. Ravel: *Le Tombeau de Couperin.* Permission for reprint granted by Durand et Cie., Paris, copyright owners, and Elkan-Vogel Co., Inc., Philadelphia, agents.

The ninth (*f-sharp*) of the chord in measure 2 of Ex. 4-76 has been "prepared" melodically in the first measure.

Ex. 4-76. Wagner: *Tristan und Isolde,* Prelude to Act I.

In measure 2 the ninth occurs within a harmonic context as a repetition of the preceding motive, and the V_9 in *a* minor resolves deceptively to VI. The whole passage seems to spring from the semitone motive of measure 1, since both the prevailing melodic intervals and the root relation of E—F (V_9—VI) constitute developments of the same interval, the second. Harmonic and melodic activity are virtually inseparable in examples such as this, as they are in Ex. 4-77.

Ex. 4-77. Beethoven: Piano Sonata, Op. 81a, I.

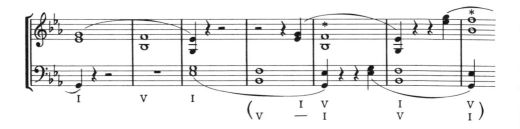

Exercises

For more detailed assignments see *Materials and Structure of Music II, Workbook,* Chapter 4.

1. Spell various types of seventh chords (nondominant) from the bass up, and identify them as to chord type and as to function in various major and minor keys.
2. Considering *d* as the root, third, fifth, and seventh, respectively, of different non-dominant seventh chords, spell various types (mm^7, MM^6_5, $°^4_3$, $°_7$, etc.) and indicate the function of each in the major and/or minor keys in which they might appear as diatonic chords.
3. Indicate the chord quality and function of each of the *seventh* and *ninth* chords appearing in Exx. 4-59 and 4-62.
4. Sing (from the bass up) various types of nondominant seventh chords (root position and inverted).
5. Make two different four-part settings of each of the following:
   a. $ii°_7$—V   b. ii^6_5—I^6_4—V   c. $ii°^4_3$—V^7 d. ii^4_2—V^6_5 e. $ii°^6_5$—i_6—V
   f. $ii°^4_2$—V^7/iv—iv   g. $ii°^6_5$—VI—i^6_4—V

6. Construct a two-phrase period per the following specifications:
   a. Employ at least 4 of the following in typical progressions:
      ii$^6_5$, ii$^4_3$, ii$_7$, V$^4_3$/vi, V$^4_2$/IV
   b. Write in open score for string quartet.
7. Analyze several of the following, indicating keys, chords, and non-chord tones:
   a. Beethoven: *Piano Sonata*, Op. 2, No. 3, I (5-8)
   b. Brahms: *Symphony No. III*, Op. 90, III (1-8)
   c. Chopin. *Mazurka*, Op. 30, No. 1 (5-8)
      Nocturne, Op. 37, No. 1 (33-40)
      Nocturne, Op. 48, No. 1 (25-32)
   d. Franck: *Symphonic Variations*, Allegro non troppo
   e. Mozart: *Piano Sonata in D major*, K. 311, III (23-26)
   f. Schubert: *Symphony No. V*, III (1-18)
   g. Sibelius: *Symphony No. II*, Op. 43, III (Trio) (1-4)
8. Find other examples containing supertonic seventh chords, particularly in the music for your own instrument.
9. Build ninth chords on the various scale degrees of *F* major and *f* minor, indicating the quality of each resulting chord.
10. Build and resolve dominant ninth chords in several keys, major and minor.
11. Compose short examples for various combinations of four voices or instruments which contain typical illustrations of V$_9$ resolving to I.
12. Compose a vocalise which illustrates melodically outlined seventh and ninth chords on different scale degrees.
13. Listen to a recording of the first principal section of Ravel's *Pavane to a Dead Princess* and identify the ninth chords that occur.
14. Play major triads on the piano and superpose ninths and sevenths above each triad vocally.
15. Make harmonic reductions of the chordal sections of Bach's *E-flat* Prelude, Book I, *Well-tempered Clavier*, noting particularly the use of ninths as decorative pitches.

5

EMBELLISHING
DIMINISHED CHORDS

We turn now to chords whose basic sonority is formed by the diminished triad, and whose usual harmonic function is that of chromatic embellishment of diatonic chords. In Chapters 22 and 23 of Volume I we discussed the way a basically diatonic scheme of chords can be enriched by embellishing secondary dominants. Our present concern is with other *nondiatonic* chords whose main structural link with any established key is a *secondary leading-tone* relationship with a diatonic chord. The diminished triad ($^{\circ}{}^5_3$), the fully diminished seventh chord ($^{\circ}{}_7$), and the half- diminished seventh chord ($^{\varnothing}{}_7$) perform this function more frequently than any other sonority types[1] in the music of 1700–1900.

The structures of the diminished triad and the fully diminished seventh chord make them well suited as embellishing chords, for as we noted in Chapter 3, their intervallic contents create no root effect; they are not stable chords by comparison with major and minor triads. Since they lack the simple intervals that could create a root effect, we shall refer to the chord member that lies at the bottom of their fundamental position as the "prime."

Ex. 5-1. Intervals of diminished chords.

It is the secondary leading-tone relation that forms the link with the chord it embellishes. In *function* the diminished triad and diminished seventh chord perform the same role as secondary dominants, and it should be clear that they share three pitches in common with the Mm7th that embellishes as a secondary dominant.

---

[1]We shall refer to the secondary diminished function in a way that is consistent with our analysis of the secondary dominant function. Thus °/V represents a secondary diminished embellishment of V, while °$_6$, etc. refer to inversions of this chord type.

Ex. 5-2. Similar structure of Mm$_7$ and diminished chords.

Because of this strong identity between secondary diminished chords and secondary dominants, a separation of the two types in terms of *harmonic function* is misleading. It is only the absence of the root relation by fifth, in the progression of the secondary diminished chord to its successor chord, that warrants separate identification.

Embellishing Diminished Triads

The only difference between the diminished triad and the diminished seventh chord is that of sonority; the triadic form lacks the richer sound of the four-note structure. The one could replace the other in any musical context except in passages where limitation of voices or characteristic melodic patterns preclude the use of the fourth member of the seventh chord. The passage shown in Ex. 5-3 illustrates the latter kind of limitation, for here a descending line of triplets demands triadic outlines (some of which are spelled enharmonically).

Ex. 5-3. Bach: *Well-tempered Clavier*, Book I, Prelude No. 6 in D Minor.

The more typical function of secondary diminished chords is as a chromatic sonority directly succeeded by a diatonic chord. In Ex. 5-3 the string of outlined triads served to suspend the tonality, each followed by still another nondiatonic diminished pattern. In contrast, Ex. 5-4 shows the usual °$_7$ chords as they relate directly to diatonic triads in a major and minor key.

Ex. 5-4. °₇ chords as embellishing chords.

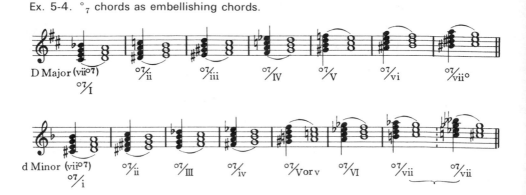

Notice that the °₇ chord built on the leading tone of the minor scale is a diatonic chord, but in major it contains a mutation (flatted sixth degree) of the diatonic vii°₇ (which in D major would be *c-sharp—e—g—b*). All of the other chords are nondiatonic.

In Ex. 5-5 the dominant chord is reinforced by the $^{\circ}_6$/V that immediately precedes it in a weak metric position. The diminished chord is further subordinated by the constant presence of the pedal on the dominant *C.*

Ex. 5-5. Beethoven: Symphony No. 6, I.

Further typical embellishing roles are portrayed by the diminished triads in Ex. 5-6. Here the ii and V chords are preceded by their secondary diminished triads related by lower leading tones. Notice that the V chord and its diminished embellishment are momentarily separated by I$^6_4$.

Ex. 5-6. Mozart: Piano Sonata, K. 330, III.

The basic harmonic structure of this passage would not be altered if the texture were thickened by the addition of sevenths to each of the embellishing triads. Mozart might well have done this had he not preferred the thinner three-voice texture that typifies this passage. But in terms of *function*, the four-note chords could replace the simpler triads.

Because of this identical function of the two sonorities, we shall regard the two as interchangeable, the only differentiation being the sonority. Everything said about secondary °₇ chords in terms of contextual harmonic role is equally true about the diminished embellishing triad.

Embellishing °₇ Chords

It is the absence of root orientation that establishes the ° triad and the °₇ chord as indeterminate, rendering them void of the stability that is required to create (removed from a musical context) any definite sense of pitch focus. And yet, it is just this instability that makes the chord one of the most interesting of music, particularly music in which diatonic chords are paramount.

It is significant that the °₇ chord depends upon notation for its functional identity. The same set of actual pitches which constitute the fully diminished sonority can be spelled in many different ways and still form a notationally "correct" °₇ chord. Ex. 5-7 shows the three basic sets of notes that form all available diminished seventh chords within the twelve-note scale system. Notice that each basic chord is subject to at least the four other notated versions shown, not to mention the many other enharmonic possibilities.

Ex. 5-7. °₇ chords, enharmonic spellings.

Unlike major and minor triads and Mm7th chords, the *sound* of the isolated °₇ chord cannot imply inversion. If chord (x) of Ex. 5-8 is played at the piano, the listener has no reason to assume that he is not hearing the "inverted" forms of (y) or (z).

Ex. 5-8. Ibid.

The most common secondary $°_7$ chord embellishes the dominant, usually as a lower leading tone resolving up to the root of the V chord.

Ex. 5-9. Schumann: Op. 15, No. 1.

In Ex. 5-9 the arrival of the V in measure 2 is made more probable by the appearance of the $°_7$ on the second beat of measure 1. Aside from the inherent instability of the $°$ sonority, the linear implications are imposing: the *g—c-sharp* tritone of the bass line (following the stable *G* major triad) suggests a resolution to *d* of the bass line; and the *b—b-flat* step-progression of the middle voice clearly sets up the logical chromatic continuation to *a* (the fifth of the V chord).

This Schumann passage also demonstrates the usual voice leading in the resolution of the $°_7$; the notation clearly shows the secondary leading-tone function and resolves as such.

Ex. 5-10. Resolution of $°_7$.

Since the $°_7$ chord includes two tritones, both do not always resolve in the way prescribed for the single tritone. One of these intervals frequently bypasses the usual expansion or contraction resolution; this is generally the tritone that *does not contain the secondary leading-tone relation with the subsequent chord.* In Ex. 5-11 the (a) resolution is more typical than the (b) or (c).

Ex. 5-11. Ibid.

However, when the leading-tone member is not also the bass tone and the resolution is to a V_7 chord, the leading tone frequently resolves down by step to the seventh of the V_7. As Ex. 5-12 shows, the third of the $°_7$ varies in resolution, moving up or down by step as demanded by the particular melodic patterns of the context.

Ex. 5-12. Ibid.

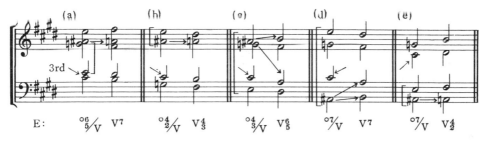

The resolutions of (c) and (d) are problematic because of the cross relations formed when the secondary leading tone does not step down to the seventh of the subsequent chord.

Extension of the leading-tone relation to other degrees of a major or minor scale identifies additional $°_7$ functions, so that any chord within a diatonic set might be embellished by a $°_7$ chord. Ex. 5-13 contains four such chords, each bearing a leading-tone relation to a diatonic chord of F major.

Ex. 5-13. Schumann: *Nachtstücke*, Op. 23, No. 2.

It is important to pause here and concentrate on the aural effect of this rapid succession of mixed chromatic and diatonic chords. Although every eighth note in some of these measures carries a different complete chord, the total result is more that of interesting harmonic motion *between* some structurally important tonal landmarks.

The tonality of the passage is not vague; if anything, the embellishing $°_7$ chords have strengthened the resolution chords, heightening their functions *within* the tonality of *F*. The upper line's contour from f^2 down to f^1 and the bass motion within f^1—*C* both establish the structural framework of the passage with clarity.

In contrast, the embellishing $°_7$ chord can momentarily wrench our attention to its resolution chord as a potential tonic if its duration and phrase location (such as at a cadence) make it more prominent. In Ex. 5-14, the two-measure units of the phrase structure focus our attention on the $°_7/vi$—vi cadence, thereby creating a fleeting emphasis on the relative minor tonic.

Ex. 5-14. Beethoven: Setting of "God Save the King."

The embellishing diminished sonority is not always relegated to a position of metric and durational insignificance by virtue of its "secondary" harmonic role. In subsequent examples we shall see the embellishing function manifested by chords whose durations are as great as those of their chord of resolution. As a matter of fact, musical styles which emphasize appoggiatura patterns create as a by-product embellishing sonorities whose durations are relatively great. For instance, the durational relations in measure 2 of Ex. 5-15 are typical of this reversal of durational stress; here the $°_7$ chord occurs on a strong beat, and its duration is four times greater than its resolution chord.

Ex. 5-15. Reger: String Quartet, Op. 109, I.

Our discussion thus far has dealt exclusively with the diminished sonority as a secondary *lower* leading-tone embellishment of diatonic chords. In addition, the $°_7$ and $°$ triad sometimes appear in contexts which demand an explanation as *upper* leading-tone embellishments.

Ex. 5-16. $°_7$ as lower and upper leading-tone embellishment.

Within a musical passage the dual embellishment by $°_7$ chords might represent a prolonged linking of two diatonic chords within a clear tonality framework. Note the linking of IV and V in this way in Ex. 5-17.

Ex. 5-17. Bach: *Well-tempered Clavier*, Book I, Prelude No. 1 in C Major.

It is important to recognize that although the chords of measures 2 and 3 in Ex. 5-17 are formed by different tones, they are both exemplars of the same sonority ($°_7$), and they both perform the same function, i.e., the chromatic embellishment of the dominant. For this reason they are represented by the same analytical symbol, $°_7/V$, with the addition of directional arrows to indicate leading-tone direction ($\uparrow°_7/V$ and $\downarrow°_7/V$). A similar condition is shown in the next excerpt.

Ex. 5-18. Mozart: String Quartet in B-flat, K. 458, III.

In making harmonic analyses it is not essential to employ arrows, denoting upper or lower leading-tone embellishment, as we have shown here, although precision would in some cases demand this additional indication.

Irregular Resolutions of °₇ Chords

In accordance with the leading-tone function of the secondary °₇, its "regular" resolution entails that the leading-tone relation, above or below, progress directly to a chord whose root "resolves" the leading tone. In the light of such a classification, the (a) resolution in Ex. 5-19 is regular, whereas (b) is irregular.

Ex. 5-19. Resolutions of °₇ Chords.

When the °₇ resolves as in Ex. 5-19b, it no longer functions as a secondary leading-tone chord in the usual sense. Rather, its embellishing role is fulfilled as a *collection of tendency tones*, some of which are not diatonic; it frequently operates as such between two positions of the same chord, as in Ex. 5-20. Since the subsequent chord is I rather than V, it is a deceptive resolution.

Ex. 5-20. Brahms: Symphony No. 3, I.

In this irregular resolution the common note between the °$_7$ and the following chord represents a point of stability; the remaining notes are unstable members which move by step to members of the resolution chord. The usual tritone resolution is still operative in such a scheme, °5 contracting, +4 expanding.

Ex. 5-21. Irregular resolutions of °$_7$ chords.

The same irregular resolution can be found where the °$_7$ does not link different distributions of the same chord. Again, the common note and attendant linear tendencies represent the most salient features of this relation. In Ex. 5-22 the °$_7$/V stands between the ii$^6_5$—I$^6_4$ cadence. The *g-flats* of the °$_7$ could as well have been notated as *f-sharps*, thereby revealing more clearly the obvious parallel sixth progression that frames the passage.

Ex. 5-22. Beethoven: Piano Sonata, Op. 31, No. 3, I.

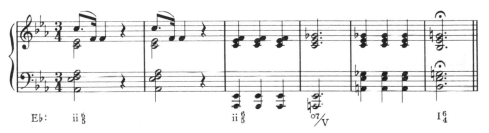

The same harmonic type of irregular resolution occurs in Ex. 5-23, but here the embellished chord is VI (in *b* minor) rather than tonic. Since the °$_7$ formed on the first beat of the second measure is the diatonic vii°$_7$ (as vii$^o_2^4$), the progression is similar to the deceptive cadence, V—vi in minor.

Ex. 5-23. Chopin: Prelude, Op. 28, No. 6.

In Ex. 5-24 the vii°$_7$ in g minor functions as $\overset{\circ}{4}_2$/III; the a of the °$_7$ here represents the leading-tone link between the two chords.

Ex. 5-24. Rameau: *La Poule*.

The °$_7$ Chord as an Agent of Tonal Instability

All of our discussion thus far has centered on the °$_7$ chord as a chromatic sonority once removed from the diatonic set of harmonic possibilities, its functional identity determined wholly by the chord that follows. This is by no means its exclusive function as a nondiatonic chord in traditional music. Its lack of inherent stability makes it an effective modulatory pivot, and this same ambiguity also makes it a useful source of tonal indefiniteness within any context.

The passage of Ex. 5-25 contains a vii$\overset{\circ}{4}_3$ that moves directly to another °$_7$ chord. Obviously, no immediate resolution occurs, and the lack of stability created by the succession heightens the listener's anticipation of resolution with some forth-coming chord. This return to stability does not occur until the eighth measure, when i$^6_4$ appears as part of a cadential pattern.

Ex. 5-25. Schubert: Symphony in B-flat, III.

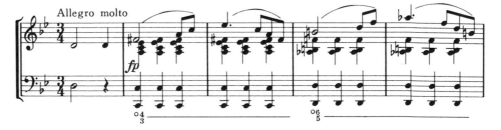

A similar passage, marked by ambiguity but again bounded by clear tonality, is shown in Ex. 5-26. *F* major is clearly established at beginning and end, but the progression from measure 6 through measure 8 unfolds a quite foreign set of harmonies that resolve momentarily with the *e-flat* minor triad of measure 7. The two $°_7$ chords resolve irregularly, forming the same linear resolutions as shown in Ex. 5-22.

Ex. 5-26. Mozart: Piano Sonata, K. 533, II.

In Ex. 5-27 a rearticulated suspension adds harmonic color to the passage, in which vii$°_7$ is linked with what appears to be $°_7$/V but never resolves as such. If the section immediately preceding this passage had not already established *E-flat* as tonic, the first two-and-one-half measures of the excerpt would be tonally vague. Within the excerpt, delineation of tonic appears only in the third and fourth measures with the *e-flat* minor triad and the cadence that ends with V$_7$.

Ex. 5-27. Franck: Praeludium, Chorale and Fugue for Organ.

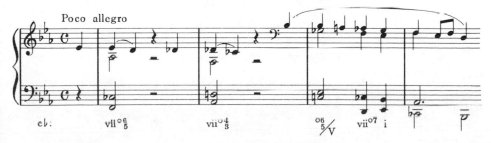

Since the $°_7$ chord can be tonally disruptive, the composer's wish to create an extended passage in which tonality is vague might well be realized by a succession of such sonorities, none of which resolves to a more stable chord for momentary pause. This procedure was followed by many late nineteenth-century composers for precisely this purpose.

The sense of tonal orientation provided by the *F-sharp* triad in the fifth measure of the next excerpt is especially gratifying because of the tonal ambiguity of the previous measures.

Ex. 5-28. Liszt: Piano Concerto in E-flat, I.

The $°_7$ Chord as Modulatory Pivot

The potential leading-tone function of the $°_7$ chord and its inherent lack of tonal stability make it an obvious potential link for the process of modulation. Subject, as it is, to wholesale variations of spellings, any $°_7$ can be accommodated easily into any key. This potentiality of notational transfer can be seen more readily by reviewing the four enharmonic spellings of a single $°_7$ chord and the possible vii$°_7$ function of each.

Ex. 5-29. Enharmonic spellings of $°_7$.

By making enharmonic changes of the members shown in Ex. 5-29 further resolution possibilities appear. Such an implied enharmonic shift is illustrated in Ex. 5-30 in a phrase modulation. Here the pivotal $°_7$ is immediately spelled within the new scale relationship rather than the old. Parentheses set off the "correct" spelling as it could have functioned within the former key of *d* minor, presumably as $°_3^4/V$).

Ex. 5-30. Mozart: Piano Sonata, K. 332, I.

Composers of the eighteenth and nineteenth centuries capitalized on this ambiguity of the $°_7$ within schemes of rapidly shifting keys. Ex. 5-31 announces each shift of tonic by unexpected appearances of $°_7$, which progress to one of the alternative chords of resolution. In each brief section the listener accommodates the particular $°_7$ within the established key, realizing that a new tonic probably is forthcoming, but never knowing exactly *which tonic* it might be.[2]

---

[2] The chords enclosed in parentheses in the example show an enharmonic spelling of the $°_7$ chord that relates it more readily (in terms of notation) to the next chord.

Ex. 5-31. Schubert: String Quartet in A Minor, I.

a: vii°⁷   Eb: ↓°⁴₃/V   V⁴₂   I⁶

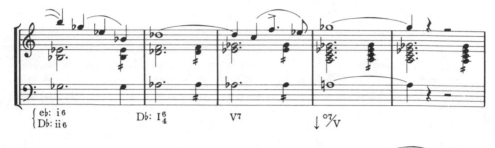

{ eb: i⁶
{ Db: ii⁶   Db: I⁶₄   V⁷   ↓°⁷/V

E: ↓°⁷/V   V⁴₂   V⁶₅   I⁶

A similar psychological state is induced by the passage shown in Ex. 5-32. Here successions of secondary °₇ chords, secondary dominants, and their respective resolutions establish a passage of kaleidoscopic change. After the beginning in *C* major, the section passes through a series of temporary points of stability, each embellished by its attendant °₇ or secondary dominant. The passage reaches a more settled area of tonal focus in the *b* minor statement where the excerpt ends.

Ex. 5-32. Haydn: Piano Sonata in E Minor, I.

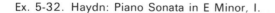

C: V⁷————————   I————————   V⁴₃————

Passages such as this paved the way for the more fluid, less definite tonal focus of late nineteenth- and early twentieth-century music. Similar passages, in which relatively unstable sonorities follow one another in extended progression, made chromaticism an end within itself for some composers, so that tonality sometimes resulted more as a fortuitous by-product of chords than as an established basis for total pitch organization.

The °$_7$ Chord

Like the °$_7$ chord, the °$_7$ (or dm$_7$ or "half-diminished" seventh chord) frequently appears as an embellishment of a diatonic chord, but it also occurs in some contexts solely for its contribution to the overall harmonic color, devoid of strong relationship to the prevailing tonality. As discussed in Chapter 4, the °$_7$ sonority occurs as a diatonic chord within the minor scale as ii°$_7$, in major as vii°$_7$.

As an isolated sonority the °$_7$ presents a fascinating case study of harmonic root, for its notational spelling does not reveal its important structural characteristics. If we reduce the chord to its simplest notation of stacked thirds, the bottom note appears to be the root. However, the pitch in this position suffers the same intervallic weakness as the lowest member of the notated °$_7$ chord, for it is a member of a tritone. We shall refer to this member as the *prime* rather than the *root*.

Ex. 5-33. $^{\circ}_{7}$.

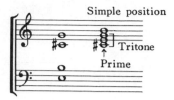

The simplest interval in the $^{\circ}_{7}$ is formed between the third and the seventh (represented by *e—b* in Ex. 5-33). It is a perfect fifth or, when inverted, a perfect fourth. This interval is the most stable unit of the whole sonority, and its root is the root—albeit a tenuous one—for the whole chord.

It is interesting to note that as a collection of intervals the $^{\circ}_{7}$ has a strong similarity to the Mm7th chord; its interval complement is the exact inversion of that sonority.

Ex. 5-34. Comparison of $^{\circ}_{7}$ and Mm$_7$.

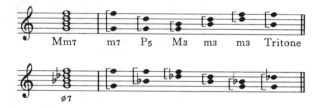

Since the presence of the perfect fifth (or fourth) lends an element of stability to the $^{\circ}_{7}$, one arrangement of the chord appears in rare instances as a tonic sonority. This function is the same as that performed by the mm$_7$ chord in first inversion—the "added sixth chord"—that we discussed in Chapter 3. The $^{\circ 6}_{5}$ version gives the effect of a major sixth added to a basic minor triad.

Ex. 5-35. $^{\circ}_{7}$.

Both of the excerpts in Ex. 5-36 and Ex. 5-37 contain the $^{\circ}_{7}$ chord serving the tonic function. In each case the chord appears in first inversion, the root of the chord's fifth serving as tonic for the passage.

Ex. 5-36. Debussy: Danse.

Ex. 5-37. Gershwin: Prelude for Piano, No. 3. Copyright 1927 by New World Music Corporation. Used by permission.

These are unusual and isolated instances, for the °7 normally commands a much less imposing structural role. It is shown here at the beginning of our discussion primarily to accentuate this somewhat improbable use of a slightly ambiguous chord functioning as a structural unit of harmony—even tonic.

As a secondary embellishing chord the °7 manifests the chromatic tendency tones that are typical of the secondary °7. It is found frequently as a chromatic embellishment of V in a major key. In Ex. 5-38 its embellishing role is clarified by its appearance above a *dominant pedal* as well as preceding the *dominant chord.* Note also the embellishment of the dominant from above (*A-flat*) in the previous measure.

Ex. 5-38. Schubert: *Die Schöne Müllerin,* "Morgengrüss."

In more typical fashion, the $°_7$/V in Ex. 5-39 occurs on a weak beat followed by the dominant. This particular passage contains suspensions which delay the full realization of dominant sonority; in some instances the tonic $^6_4$ separates the $°_7$ and the full dominant chord.

Ex. 5-39. Wagner: *Die Meistersinger*, Act I.

The cross relation present between the $°_7$/V and i in a minor key makes this relationship most improbable.

Ex. 5-40. Cross relation between $°_7$/V and minor tonic.

As with the fully diminished seventh chord, the function of the $°_7$ as an embellishing sonority is not determined by its root; on the contrary, it is usually established by reference to a member of the tritone that serves as a secondary leading tone (above or below) to the root of its chord of resolution. Even though the third member of the $°_7$ must be regarded as its "acoustical root" (rather than the prime of the chord in its fundamental position), it is the secondary leading-tone action from the one chord to the next that defines the chord's harmonic role.

Ex. 5-41. The leading tone in $°_7$ chords.

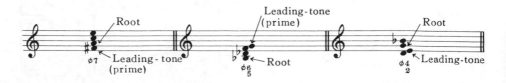

In the passage of Ex. 5-42, the first chord is not a diatonic member of the *A-flat* tonality. But its prime, *d*, bears a leading-tone relation to the root, *e-flat*, of the dominant chord that follows. For this reason, the °₇ is denoted as an embellishment of the diatonic V chord.

Ex. 5-42. Wagner: *Siegfried,* Act III.

Since melodic progression frequently affects a composer's notation, the spellings of the °₇, as with the °₇, are not always trustworthy guides to harmonic function. Ex. 5-43 contains three different °₇ chords, each of which embellishes a dominant-representative of three separate tonal regions. But these chords are not *notated* as if they were of the same type, nor do they each bear the same leading-tone relationship with the chord they embellish. In (a) and (b) it is the prime of the chord that serves as the leading-tone link, but in (c) it is the seventh. In all three cases the composer's notation reveals more concern for linear motion than for chord spelling.

Ex. 5-43. Wagner: *Tristan und Isolde,* Prelude to Act I.

Ex. 5-43 continued.

If we respell these chords in order to make their identity as $^{\circ}{}_{7}$ chords more clear, the following result:

Ex. 5-44. Enharmonic respellings of $^{\circ}{}_{7}$ chords of Ex. 5-43.

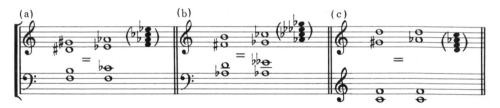

In this passage the three $^{\circ}{}_{7}$ chords are not parallel in structure, for in (c) the chord's seventh is in the bass. It is significant, however, that the semitone step down to the root of each of the temporary dominants does project a pattern of harmonic sequence.

Ex. 5-45. Embellishing functions of three $^{\circ}{}_{7}$ chords.

Embellishing E   Embellishing G   Embellishing B

The Wagner excerpt reveals more clearly than any other single passage how the grip of diatonic notation, as it had evolved from the major-minor key schemes, was loosened by many late nineteenth-century composers. The chromatic melodic lines that bear much of the organizing burden in such music demanded notational procedures that were free from the traditional spellings of superposed thirds.

Some composers of the late nineteenth and early twentieth centuries, whose music still maintained strong ties to a functional system of harmonic relationships, adopted the $°_7$ as a sonority useful primarily for its own sound, aside from its immediate relation to a diatonic scheme. Its rich sound became a frequent sonorous image within the harmonic palettes of those composers who, like Strauss, Debussy, and Ravel, occasionally strived for an effect of "suspended tonality" in order to achieve dramatic musical ends.

Ex. 5-46. Debussy, *Pelléas et Melisande,* Act. IV

Ex. 5-47 contains a passage in which $°_7$ and $°_7$ chords, almost to the exclusion of any other sonority types, make the harmonic image a striking contrast to the sharply delineated tonal schemes of most earlier music.

Ex. 5-47. Debussy: *Blessed Damozel.*

Later in the same score a $°_7$ acts as the cadential chord for the entire section, in this case the final utterance of the principal soloist of the composition.

Ex. 5-48. Ibid.

We have seen the $°_7$ as a diatonic chord (as ii$°_7$ and as vii$°_7$); in other contexts as a secondary embellishing chord (as $°_7$/V); again as the most important harmonic function within the pitch structure (as tonic in the form of i$°{}^6_5$ in minor); as a chromatic chord related by leading tone (upper or lower) between some member to a member of the subsequent chord; and finally as a purely coloristic sonority whose partial ambiguity adds harmonic spice. It should not surprise us to find a single chord type acting in such different ways; many words in our language derive their meanings exclusively from the contexts in which they occur, and some—such as the word "to" ("two," "too") retain the same spoken sound but derive both meaning and spelling from functional relations within written speech. In this sense the $°_7$ chord, more than any other sonority type, is a "tonal homonym," its musical meaning derived exclusively from the relation it bears to its harmonic neighborhood.

Exercises

For more detailed assignments see *Materials and Structure of Music II, Workbook,* Chapter 5.

1. Mentally trace through the notes of any major or minor scale. For each scale degree, spell the $°_7$ chords whose primes are related as upper and lower leading tones. Write out each chord for SATB voices and resolve to its regular chord of resolution.
2. Write a passage for solo instrument and piano based on the following chord scheme. (Use a simple block chord style for the piano part.)

G major, $\frac{3}{4}$:

3. Plot a chord progression that modulates to a distant-related key through a diminished seventh chord that is enharmonically relatable to the second key. Write a texture for SATB (using the syllable "ah" as text) based on this progression.

4. Play a note at the piano that is in comfortable voice range. Immediately sing the $°_7$ chord whose prime is the leading tone for this pitch.

Example:

5. Explore the embellishing possibilities for the $°_7$ chord *d—f—a—c* in several different major and minor keys. Keep in mind the possibility of any of its four members as a potential "leading-tone" relationship to a diatonic chord.

6. Write a simple work for piano that utilizes the $°_7$ as an embellishment of V, as in the following chord scheme:

7. At the piano, establish a key with I—V—I. Then play a $°_7$ or $°_7$ and immediately resolve to a logical chord that is diatonic to the established key.

Example:

6

CANTUS FIRMUS TECHNIQUE: THE CHORALE PRELUDE

On many occasions composers have used pre-existent melodies as the basis for extended compositions. The procedure is psychologically effective for the listener—particularly if the melody is a familiar one—because it can provide a thread of continuity for the whole composition. The listener is better able to assimilate and respond to the less familiar tone combinations that have been created by the composer, for the known tune provides a focal point of familiarity.

The same procedure can be effective even if the basic tune is not a familiar one to the listener. The composition from which Ex. 6-1 is taken consists of an elaborate contrapuntal texture built around a melody that was well known during the composer's day; even though the average listener of today does not know the tune, the successive entries of its phrases establish a framework that makes the total composition more unified.

Ex. 6-1a. *L'Homme Armé* (popular song of medieval Europe).

Ex. 6-1b. Dufay: Mass based on *L'Homme Armé,* Kyrie, I.

(L'homme armé tune in tenor voice)

Compositions that used German chorale tunes as their foundation melodies (or as a *cantus firmus*) became significant in the Lutheran Church service of the Baroque period. These compositions used various techniques of thematic and textural elaboration integrated with the chosen chorale melody, and they were called *chorale preludes*.

The same name frequently is used as a blanket term to denote any composition that makes use of the same cantus firmus procedures. Thus a popular song (as in Ex. 6-1), a folksong, a religious hymn, or a patriotic song might serve as the melodic basis and that work still be called a "chorale prelude."

There are many approaches a composer might follow in writing a composition based on a pre-existent melody. Some of these fall more in the domain of the *variation forms* that we shall discuss in Chapter 8. Our attention for the present will center on two important chorale prelude types, both of which use a complete melody in relatively unaltered form.

The Imitative (or "Fugal") Chorale Prelude

One of the most interesting treatments combines a contrapuntal texture with the successive phrases of the selected tune. This type begins with an exposition section much like the *invention*, to which is added, at an appropriate moment, the basic tune in relatively long note values. The previous texture continues as an accompanying web, thus forming continuity with the imitative opening. Ex. 6-2 shows the chorale tune "Vater Unser im Himmelreich" ("Our Father in Heaven") and the opening section of a chorale prelude based on it.

Ex. 6-2a. German Chorale, *Vater Unser im Himmelreich*.

Ex. 6-2b. Telemann: Chorale Prelude, *Vater Unser im Himmelreich*.

As in most chorale preludes of this type, the initial motive is derived by diminution from the first few notes of the chosen melody, thereby creating a preview of the melody before its formal entry. Although the answering part here is a perfect fourth above the leader, many such beginnings are an octave apart, as in the inventions discussed in Chapter 9.

The preview section is sometimes called *vorimitation*, meaning "imitation before" the appearance of that which is imitated. A similar procedure introduces each new section of the chorale prelude, each time anticipating the next phrase of the melody. The excerpt of Ex. 6-3 begins where Ex. 6-2b ended. Notice that the motivic answer in the *vorimitation* lies a sixth above the leader's statement.

Ex. 6-3. Continuation, *Vater Unser im Himmelreich*.

The successive phrases of the *cantus firmus* (*C.F.*) form the sectional organization of the complete chorale prelude. The length of the work is related, then, to the number of phrases of the melodic basis and their respective lengths. Since the chorale illustrated in Ex. 6-2b contains six phrases, this particular chorale prelude is organized into six sections, each of which begins with a brief section of vorimitation.

The total composition could be expanded considerably if the sections of vorimitation were developed to greater lengths. Obviously, the composer gauges the extensiveness of these bridge sections to fit the scale of the composition he wishes to create, so aside from the phrase structure of the original tune, this variability of length can be controlled by other means.

Although the listener expects important melodic utterances to appear in the higher parts of a texture, the *C.F.* appears in the lowest part in some examples, in the middle in others. In the work whose beginning section appears in Ex. 6-4, the *C.F.* is placed at the bottom.

Ex. 6-4. Telemann: Chorale Prelude, *Herzlich tut mich verlangen*.

In many chorale preludes the melodic pattern introduced at the beginning of the piece is not derived from the *C.F.*; it is used as the motivic basis for each bridge section, thus forming a monothematic basis as in the invention. This technique creates a more tightly unified composition, but it sacrifices the advantage of phrase-by-phrase variety that results from the vorimitation procedure.

Ex. 6-5 shows excerpts from a chorale prelude in which a single pattern is the motivic accompaniment for all statements of the *cantus firmus* phrases. It is not derived from the *C.F.* (except for its first three pitches, *e, f-sharp, g*), and thus it acts as a free contrapuntal accompaniment that frames and enhances the delayed unfoldings of the entire melody.

Ex. 6-5. Bach: Chorale Prelude, *Wo soll ich fliehen hin.*

last phrase, C.F.

In this chorale prelude the accompanying parts alone would constitute a full two-part invention, its key scheme founded in the cadential plan dictated by the phrase endings implied by the tune. The composer has some freedom in manipulating these cadences to tonalities of his choice. The second phrase of the chorale tune in Ex. 6-5 ends with an *f-sharp* that could imply a cadence in *D* major. But Bach shifts the accompanying parts so that V_u/V in *e* minor becomes the basic harmony; this introduces a modulation (measures 11–14) to the key of *B* minor, thus injecting an element of tonal variety.

In some chorale preludes written for organ the notation of the *C.F.* in the pedal part appears to fix that voice in the bottom of the texture. However, organ registration that places the bottom voice one or two octaves higher than notated is used frequently. This places the voice within the middle or at the top of the texture. The organist can engage a so-called "4-foot stop"[1] for the pedal that

---

[1] Familiar to organists, this expression designates the pitch level of a sounding pipe: 8′ stop equals pitch as notated, 16′ equals one octave lower, 4′ equals one octave higher, and 2′ equals two octaves higher.

produces the actual sound of Ex. 6-6b, as opposed to the original notation shown as Ex. 6-6a.

Ex. 6-6a. Bach: *Nun Komm, der Heiden Heiland*, as notated.

Ex. 6-6b. Ibid., as sounded.

A mixture of "free motive" (i.e., not derived from the *cantus firmus*) and derived motive appears in the accompanying texture of some chorale preludes. In such instances the two melodic patterns might be introduced as a kind of *motive* and *counter-motive* within the opening statement. The work from which Ex. 6-7 is taken incorporates this bi-thematic arrangement, both patterns appearing in combination as *vorimitation* for each new phrase of the chorale tune.

Ex. 6-7. Telemann: Chorale Prelude, *Christ lag in Todesbanden*.

In some Baroque chorale preludes the chorale tune itself is ornamented so that
the resultant composition is much like a *melodic variation*. The application of decorative overlay is an effective means of variation from the listener's point of view
only if the *C.F.* is well known. (This was a fundamental assumption for Bach in
regard to the melodies of his Lutheran Church service.)

The chorale "Nun Komm, der Heiden Heiland" ("Now come, Savior of the
Gentiles") is shown in Ex. 6-8a, followed by the first section of a chorale prelude
that incorporates an embellished version of it as *C.F.* (Ex. 6-8b). Notice that the
main motive of the imitative accompaniment in measures 3 and 4 is derived from
the first five notes of the chorale.

Ex. 6-8a. Chorale Tune, *Nun Komm, der Heiden Heiland.*

Ex. 6-8b. Bach: Chorale Prelude, *Nun Komm, der Heiden Heiland.*

Whatever the relation between the accompanimental motivic material and the
C.F., or between the original tune and its appearance in the resultant composition,

the sectioning of the chorale prelude is determined by the phrase structure of the original tune. The contrapuntal texture built around this tune accomplishes approximately the same end as the frame around a painting; it establishes an appropriate context, and it focuses attention on the primary element, the *cantus firmus* melody itself.

The Embellished Chorale

Another notable setting composers have developed for the presentation of a pre-existent melody is essentially more homophonic than the imitative chorale prelude. By fusing several voices into a tonal fabric that weaves through the chords implied by a given melody, an activated harmonic accompaniment can be created that sets the main line in relief and adds a dimension of interest that is not present in a bare "harmonization."

It is impossible to draw a precise line of distinction between the embellished setting and the simple harmonic—or "familiar style"—setting of a chorale tune. However, the examples that follow in this section reveal the gist of what constitutes the embellished type. Again, the chorale preludes of Baroque composers are ideal examples; many of them served as models for later composers who have utilized this *cantus firmus* organizational plan for brief works.

Ex. 6-9 shows excerpts from two settings by J.S. Bach of the chorale "Christ lag in Todesbanden" ("Christ lay in the bonds of death"). The first is a straightforward *harmonization;* the second shows the more active voices that characterize the *embellished chorale prelude.*

Ex. 6-9a. Bach: *Christ lag in Todesbanden,* harmonized version.

Ex. 6-9b. Ibid., embellished version.

These two settings of the same melody make an apt comparison, for the harmonic progressions are almost duplicates. The basic difference lies in the more active nature of the participating voices in the embellished version. In this respect, note that a subdivision of the basic duration, the quarter note, occurs on each beat in the embellished setting, except at the cadence on *d* of the second phrase. (The only other slackening of motion occurs at the final cadence.)

In at least one respect the embellished chorale prelude is similar to the fugal chorale prelude: it also frequently contains a motivic unit that functions as a thread of continuity. In the setting of Ex. 6-9b, this motive is the sixteenth-note group

(♪♪♪♪). It usually appears with a pitch contour similar to its first statement,

in the tenor voice,

When a motive is used as a common feature, the composer's problem is to weave this motive into each voice at one location or another to create thematic units. This procedure usually leads to imitative relations between voices, but without the vorimitation of phrases that is a feature of the fugal chorale prelude. In some of Bach's embellished settings the motive lends itself to a predominantly imitative style, the overlapping of "active-passive" patterns between voices creating a forward propulsion in a texture that otherwise could be rhythmically static.

Ex. 6-10. Bach: *Christ ist Erstanden*.

The same continuous motivic imitation persists in Ex. 6-11, which is an excerpt of an embellished setting of "Christ lag in Todesbanden." Another setting of the same kind appeared earlier in Ex. 6-9.

Ex. 6-11. Dupré: Chorale Prelude, Op. 28, *Christ lag in Todesbanden*. Copyright 1932 by The H. W. Gray Co., Inc. Used by permission.

An unusual example of a two-voice embellished setting, also illustrative of motivic organization, was made by Bach's contemporary, Telemann. Compare the harmonic progression of Ex. 6-12 with the first two phrases of Ex. 6-9 and Ex. 6-11.

Ex. 6-12. Telemann: Chorale Prelude, *Christ lag in Todesbanden*.

Ex. 6-13a uses a single rhythmic motive. A powerful monorhythmic piano accompaniment has been added to the simple chorale melody played by the trumpet, which lies within the middle and upper regions of the piano texture. A more contrapuntal and rhythmically intricate setting by Bach of the same tune is shown for a comparison of techniques.

Ex. 6-13a. Hindemith: Trumpet Sonata, III. © 1936 by B. Schott's Soehne, Mainz. Renewed 1963. Reprinted by permission.

Ex. 6-13b. Bach: Chorale Prelude, *Alle Menschen müssen sterben*.

Some examples of the embellished type contain episodic fragments between phrases of the cantus. These extend the composition beyond what its length could be if strict adherence to phrases of the original tune were maintained. Ex. 6-14 shows episodes in the form of double echoes of preceding cadence patterns.

Ex. 6-14. Brahms: Chorale Prelude, *O Welt, Ich muss dich lassen*.

A quite different setting, but of the same type, makes use of an obbligato line that is more prominent than the other parts. In Ex. 6-15 the hymn-tune *C.F.* is presented in mid-texture, then with an obbligato line above, these two voices supported by a very simple bass line.

Ex. 6-15. Barber: Variations on the hymn *Wondrous Love*, Variation No. 3.
      Reprinted by permission of the copyright owner, G. Schirmer, Inc.

Some tunes can be set against themselves in canon, so that the embellished type is further enhanced by canonic statements of the melody. This procedure was often used by Bach when the chorale melody was amenable to such treatment. Ex. 6-16 is an excerpt in which the top and bottom voices state the tune at a measure's separation, the two inner parts filling out the harmonic structure with characteristic patterns.

Ex. 6-16. Bach: Chorale Prelude, *Gotte, durch deine Güte.*

An even more unified composition results when a double canon is created from *C.F.* and accompanying line, as illustrated in Ex. 6-17.

Ex. 6-17. Bach: Chorale Prelude, *In Dulci Jubilo*.

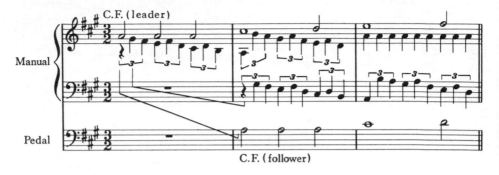

Exercises

For more detailed assignments see *Materials and Structure of Music II, Workbook*, Chapter 6.

1. In class (or in private) play through several chorale preludes by record or at the piano or organ. Direct attention to the following:
   a. thematic elements, chorale prelude type
   b. vorimitation sections (if present), thematic basis;
   c. key scheme; any deviations from tonic if present;
   d. relation of *C.F.* to original tune: phrase structure, alterations of rhythm or meter, pitch alterations, decorative patterns.
2. Write a fugal chorale prelude for three voices that is based on a selected *C.F.* Use vorimitation that is derived from the *C.F.* for each section.
3. Write an embellished chorale prelude for four voices that is based on a chosen *C.F.* Begin by making a sketch of a simple harmonic setting of the chosen melody, then decorate the accompanying lines to create a contrapuntal texture that is consistent with the embellished type.
4. Find multiple settings of a single chorale (or hymn tune) as a *C.F.* basis. Compare the results and contrast the techniques of accompaniment used.
   (Collections of organ music are most rewarding for examples of chorale preludes. For Bach examples look in the *Orgelbüchlein* and the *Clavierübung*.)

7

NEAPOLITAN AND
AUGMENTED SIXTH CHORDS

The chromatic chords discussed in earlier chapters of this book and its predecessor have all resembled in some way dominant harmony and have been described as "secondary"—i.e., their role is defined by their *relationship* to another chord. Generally, this relationship has consisted of a chord (major or diminished triad; major-minor, diminished, or half-diminished seventh chord; or more complex dominant chord) embellishing a diatonic scale step. Their characteristic is the use of leading tones.

The chords that form the subject matter for this chapter, while they, too, are characterized by the use of leading-tone relationships (upper and lower), have more of an independent existence and distinctive tonal personalities that possess great potential for piquant harmonic color, melodic force, and emotional expressiveness.

Although it is difficult to generalize about two harmonic phenomena that differ substantially from one another, one can readily see the double leading-tone action that is their trademark. The Neapolitan chord[1] arises when this relationship is exploited melodically; augmented sixth chords appear when both leading tones are aligned vertically.

Ex. 7-1. Leading tone relationships, upper and lower.

Realized melodically   Realized vertically

And further, the following statements apply equally to Neapolitan and augmented sixth chords: their most frequent tonal role is as *approach* chords to dominant (the Neapolitan, in particular, has a strong subdominant flavor). Originating in

---

[1] The name derives, most likely, from its use in the works of a school of eighteenth-century composers thought to have originated in Naples. However, it appears in many works before and after that time.

the late Renaissance, they became part of common harmonic practice by the mid-seventeenth century, appearing only in minor keys at first but later (in the early nineteenth century) in major keys as well. Each has at times been explained as a survival of melodic tendencies associated with the Phrygian mode, particularly the descending half-step: flat 2 to 1 or flat 6 to 5.

The Neapolitan Chord

Put in simplest terms, the Neapolitan chord is a major triad on flat 2 of the scale and appears most often in first inversion (hence the common use of the term Neapolitan "sixth"). The following example suggests a probable evolution of the N_6 in successive stages of harmonic practice: originating as a melodic elaboration of the subdominant and eventually harmonized as a separate chord.

Ex. 7-2. Melodic evolution of the N_6.

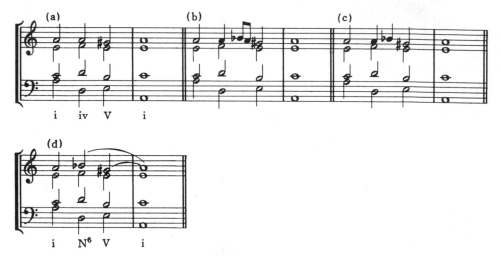

The same melodic action appears in Ex. 7-3, characterized by the interval of the diminished third (*b-flat* to *g-sharp*), which serves to focus attention on the tonic through the converging of the two leading tones.

Ex. 7-3. Beethoven: Bagatelle, Op. 119, No. 9.

Most melodic contexts using this melodic pattern do so in a less direct way, as in Ex. 7-4. Here the strong downward pull of the upper leading tone (*a-flat*) is not fully resolved until a full measure later.

Ex. 7-4. Schubert: "Der Müller und der Bach" (*Die Schöne Müllerin*).

The following illustrations show typical doublings and voice motion in common progressions involving N_6: characteristic are the doubling of the subdominant tone, the descending melodic motion of the line with the chromatic tone, and the stepwise voice motion throughout.

Ex. 7-5. Typical doubling and voice motion in progressions with N_6.

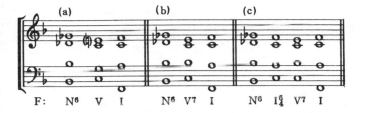

Uses of the Neapolitan "Sixth"

In cadences, the N_6 is a frequent substitute for subdominant or supertonic chords, resolving to V or V_7. The colorful tritone root relation is formed when the Neapolitan moves to the dominant, and a cross relation may occur between the Neapolitan's root and the fifth of the dominant chord.

Often, in an effort to avoid such cross relations, composers have resolved N_6 to a tonic six-four as in Ex. 7-6. This progression also avoids the characteristic melodic diminished third and results in smooth stepwise motion in all voices. The gain in melodic smoothness compensates for the loss of harmonic color.

Ex. 7-6. Beethoven: Sonata in C-sharp Minor, Op. 27, No. 2, III.

A similar use of the N_6 appears in Ex. 7-7, although here within the context of a major key. The Neapolitan follows ii_6, and consequently the flatted second and sixth scale degrees make the progression more conspicuous.

Ex. 7-7. Brahms: *Ein deutsches Requiem*, Op. 45, "Denn alles Fleisch."

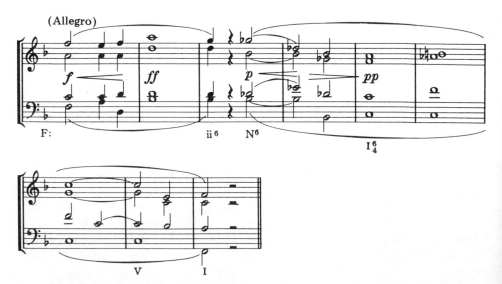

Ex. 7-8 shows a striking use of the Neapolitan sixth in a plagal cadence, substituting for the subdominant and resolving directly to tonic.

Ex. 7-8. Brahms: Quartet, Op. 51, No. 1, I.

In the fourth measure of Ex. 7-9 Schubert has achieved a highly unpredictable cadential effect by setting the Neapolitan sixth as the goal of a deceptive resolution, replacing the expected tonic chord. This colorful passage reminds us that blandness and suave voice motion are not always the objectives of harmony: certain progressions exist in part for their "shock value," the element of unpredictability that can add spice to an otherwise unexciting passage.

Ex. 7-9. Schubert: Sonata in B-flat Major, Op. Posth., I.

Turning to other harmonic uses, we find the N_6 in frequent use for passages of extended parallel motion as in the two following examples. In Ex. 7-11, the more elaborate of the two, N_6 is combined with extensive chromaticism in a particularly striking setting.

Ex. 7-10. Haydn: Sonata in E Minor, I.

Ex. 7-11. Beethoven: Sonata in D Minor, Op. 31, No. 2, I.

The Root Position Neapolitan Chord

Although less frequent than the N_6, the Neapolitan triad is effectively used in root position. When resolving to dominant, as in Ex. 7-12, the tritone root relationship is dramatically exposed in the bass line. In this context the chord's root is generally doubled.

Ex. 7-12. Chopin: Prelude in C Minor, Op. 28, No. 20.

In Ex. 7-13 the tonic and Neapolitan triads alternate as the basis for an extended cadence. The contrary motion in the outer voices conceals the basically parallel nature of the progression.

Ex. 7-13. Kabalevsky: "Novelette" from *Fifteen Children's Pieces*, Op. 27, Book 1.
© Copyright MCMXLVI by Leeds Music Corporation, New York, N.Y.
Used by permission. All rights reserved.

Other Forms and Uses of the Neapolitan

The appearance of the Neapolitan triad in six-four position is extremely rare. One such passage is quoted in Ex. 7-14 in which the progression N_4^6-V_7 resembles a Phrygian cadence.

Ex. 7-14. Handel: *Messiah*, "Rejoice Greatly"

Ex. 7-15 presents a more complex situation: the N_4^6 is used to embellish a mutated submediant ($^\flat$VI) and sounds more like a subdominant chord in the region of *B-flat* major. All this harmonic activity is part of an elaborate preparation for the half cadence that concludes this excerpt.

Ex. 7-15. Schubert: Mass in G, *Sanctus*.

Ex. 7-16 contains an extremely effective resolution of N_6, using the bass note as preparation of the seventh of the dominant seventh chord.

Ex. 7-16. Bach: Prelude in E-flat Minor, W.T.C., Book I.

Ex. 7-16 continued.

The Neapolitan is used in connection with the tonic pedal in Ex. 7-17, both as a vertical sonority and (later) as melodic arpeggiation. The Phrygian modal color that permeates this excerpt is a characteristic of the entire movement from which this excerpt is taken.

Ex. 7-17. Brahms: Symphony No. 4, II.

The Neapolitan triad can also function as a pivot chord in modulations. Since it originates as a chromatic chord in the original key, two possibilities for pivot chord relationships exist: (1) becoming a diatonic chord in the new key, or (2) becoming a chromatic chord in the new key.

The first of these processes is illustrated in Ex. 7-18: N_6 is the pivot chord connecting *C* minor and *A-flat* major; i.e., the *chromatic* N_6 becomes the *diatonic* IV_6 in the new key.

Ex. 7-18. Schubert: Quartet in C Minor, I.

In the pivot chord modulation of Ex. 7-19 (from *A* major to *D* major), *both* roles of the pivot triad are as chromatic chords: the result is a temporary moment of tonal ambiguity which is seemingly unrelated both to the previous key and to the goal of the progression. In both of these processes, the Neapolitan is extremely effective as an agent of modulation.

Ex. 7-19. Wagner: *Lohengrin*, Prelude to Act I.

The Neapolitan is frequently preceded by its own dominant, as in Ex. 7-20. When this harmonic relationship is emphasized or prolonged, as in later examples, the lowered second scale degree is established as tonic of a Neapolitan region.

Ex. 7-20. Chopin: Mazurka, Op. 7, No. 2.

The Neapolitan is established even more firmly as a temporary tonic in Ex. 7-21, first in measures 4 and 5 and later in measures 7 and 8. The use of secondary diminished seventh chords serves to focus attention upon the Neapolitan scale degree.

Ex. 7-21. Schumann: Symphony No. 2, III.

The Neapolitan Key Relationship

The Neapolitan relationship may be an integral part of the key scheme of a composition. We have seen how the Neapolitan chord might be the tonic of a tonal region. On a larger scale, a key a minor second higher (a *Neapolitan relation*) than the original key might be used to provide variety as well as to mark off formal units.

Ex. 7-22 contains such a Neapolitan relationship to provide dramatic tonal contrast to the initial thematic statement. Such a usage of the Neapolitan key in sequence following the tonic is a characteristic of Beethoven's style.

Ex. 7-22. Beethoven: Quartet in E Minor, Op. 59, No. 2, I.

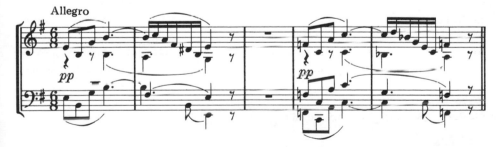

Nineteenth century composers expanded the use of Neapolitan key relationships between large formal divisions of their compositions. In place of the diatonic pivot chord process of modulation, which served so effectively to connect closely-related keys, composers turned to more chromatic modulatory procedures and enharmonicism. Ex. 7-23 contains such a passage in which a Neapolitan region (*E* major) is set within the context of a larger section in *E-flat* major. Both modulations involve the use of an enharmonic pivot chord.

Ex. 7-23. Wagner: *Lohengrin*, Act II, Scene 4, Procession.

The Neapolitan key relationship may extend to the various movements of a multimovement work, as in Ex. 7-24. The key of the second movement (*E* major-enharmonically *F-flat* major) forms the equivalent of the Neapolitan of *E-flat*, the tonic of the first and third movements. This relationship, not common in composers of Haydn's generation, became more frequent in the nineteenth century.

Ex. 7-24. Haydn: Sonata in E-flat Major.

Augmented Sixth Chords

Despite the origin of the Neapolitan chord in melodic activity, as shown at the beginning of the present chapter, its role in music has been primarily a *harmonic* one; few linear considerations are involved. In approaching the study of augmented sixth chords, however, we come to a family of chords that are intensely linear, almost totally melodic we might say, in their development and use in compositional practice.

Their most characteristic feature is the presence of the augmented sixth (or its inversion, the diminished third) *as a vertical interval*. This pair of complementary intervals, illustrated below, embodies the leading tone relationships (upper and lower) shown in Ex. 7-1. One of the most unstable of all intervals, the augmented sixth gives this entire family of chords a unique harmonic color and sense of melodic "urgency."

Ex. 7-25. The augmented sixth and diminished third.

The chords that arise from this interval are, statistically, quite infrequent: their typical use, as seen in subsequent examples, is as approach chords to cadences or other important structural points. They possess, furthermore, a high potential effectiveness for modulation, a potential that became fully realized by nineteenth-century composers.

The linear origin and interval structure of augmented sixth chords is best shown through an examination of the two-voice cadence. Of the various two-voice cadential patterns, perhaps the most frequent is the $\frac{7-8}{2-1}$ form, approaching the final octave in contrary motion by step both from above and below.

Ex. 7-26. Cadence resolution to the octave $\frac{7}{2}-\frac{8}{1}$.

The size of the melodic seconds (which constitute the $\frac{7}{2}-\frac{8}{1}$ pattern) is variable and depends upon the prevailing mode. Three cadence possibilities are illustrated in Ex. 7-27: Dorian, Lydian, and Phrygian. Note that in the Dorian cadence only major seconds occur; in each of the others, one voice moves by a major second, the other by a minor second. We might say that each of the latter demonstrates the leading tone-tonic relationship. (Lydian featuring the *lower* leading tone, Phrygian the *upper* leading tone.)

Ex. 7-27. Resolution in Dorian, Lydian, and Phrygian modes.

In the fourteenth, fifteenth, and sixteenth centuries it was customary for performers to insert leading tones in such cadences, although these frequently were not indicated in the music. Such a practice may have led to the emergence of the augmented sixth interval in the two-voice cadence. Ex. 7-28 illustrates the same cadences with leading tones added, upper and/or lower as the case may be.

Ex. 7-28. Cadences with leading tones added.

This characteristic contrary motion by minor seconds to an octave is the most important feature of augmented sixth chords. Ex. 7-29 illustrates various forms of the augmented sixth in three and in four voices.

Ex. 7-29. Augmented sixth chords.

All of the common types of augmented sixth chords share the same basic three-voice structure: to the augmented sixth interval a third voice is added, a major third above the bass. In thicker textures other tones are often added, as in Ex. 7-29. Note the step motion of all members of these chords in their resolutions.

The fourth member that can be added to this basic three-part structure is variable in that it can form a major third, a tritone, or a perfect fifth above the bass. These chords are traditionally identified with the geographical labels *Italian, French,* or *German* for reasons that remain obscure. Since the use of this terminology is widespread, we shall retain it, but we shall indicate the intervallic structure of the chords with abbreviated symbols such as It_{+6} (Italian sixth); Fr_{3}^{+6} (French six-four-three); and Gr_{5}^{+6} (German six-five).

There is disagreement as to the roots of these chords. If we follow the traditional notational means of determining roots, we arrive at the following fundamental tones for the chords in Ex. 7-29. *C-sharp* for both It_{+6} and Gr_{5}^{+6}; *A* for the Fr_{3}^{+6}. Aurally, however, this may seem a questionable choice, since to many ears the lowest tone of each of these (*E-flat*) appears to be a more stable tonal foundation. This apparent contradiction between notation and sound makes the question of root determination in augmented sixth chords problematic. For the moment it is more profitable to measure the intervals solely from the bass. The figured bass symbols are used to indicate intervals above the bass note.

Resolutions of Augmented Sixth Chords

The tonal placement of these chords is significant, since they are clearly embellishing or ornamental chords that are closely tied to a diatonic resolution chord. In almost all cases the augmented sixth interval expands by steps to the octave (*root*) of the following chord, usually the dominant. Since they usually function as approach chords to the dominant, their role is similar to that of ii and IV. Ex. 7-30 illustrates this usage: the It_{+6} in *G* minor resolves to V.

Ex. 7-30. Haydn: Quartet, Op. 74, No. 3, III.

Several points should be kept in mind when employing augmented sixth chords:

1. The augmented sixth interval is formed by the upper and lower leading tones of the dominant (the raised fourth and lowered sixth scale degrees in major, the raised fourth and diatonic sixth scale degrees in minor).
2. This interval resolves in contrary motion to the octave on the dominant.
3. A major third appears above the bass.
4. Another voice may appear either a major third, tritone, or perfect fifth above the bass.
5. Each of these tones resolves by step to the nearest tone of the chord of resolution.

When augmented sixth chords appear within a strongly defined tonality, their resolution possibilities are few in number. Since the resolution tendencies of the characteristic interval are so intense, the resolution tends to be predictable. Approach possibilities, though, are more numerous: any chord that might appropriately precede ii or iv serves well. The context of the augmented sixth chords in Ex. 7-31 (two obvious augmented sixth chords and one that is implied) illustrates several possible approaches—from i_4^6, ii_3^4, and iv. Dominant and submediant chords are equally effective in such a context.

Ex. 7-31. Beethoven: Quartet in C Minor, Op. 18, No. 4, IV.

Examples 7-32 through 7-34 contain characteristic uses of the Italian, French, and German augmented sixth chords in various contexts and in combination with different non-chord tones.

Ex. 7-32. Mozart: Piano Concerto in D Minor, K. 466, III.

Ex. 7-33. Bruckner: Mass in F Minor, *Crucifixus*

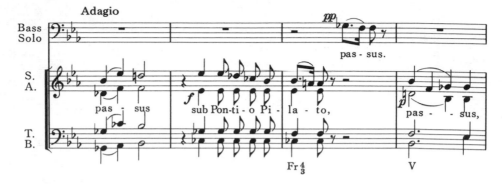

Ex. 7-34. Chopin: Sonata in C Minor, IV.

Augmented sixth chords resolve to the tonic six-four almost as frequently as to V. Compare Ex. 7-35 (which illustrates this procedure) to Ex. 7-29. The motion in each voice is generally by step, and the resolution still emphasizes the octave of the dominant (although it is now the fifth instead of the root of the resolution chord).

Ex. 7-35. Resolution to i$^6_4$.

Ex. 7-36 and 7-37 illustrate the Gr_5^{+6} in typical resolutions to V and i_4^6. In the first of these examples, Haydn has avoided the parallel fifths that frequently result from this progression (cf. Ex. 7-29). The Schubert example is particularly striking in its prolonging of the Gr_5^{+6} over several measures.

Ex. 7-36. Haydn: Quartet in E-flat Major, Op. 76, No. 6, I.

Ex. 7-37. Schubert: *Die Winterreise,* "Rast."

Ex. 7-37 continued.

re - gen.

"Inverted" Augmented Sixth Chords

The effect of augmented sixth chords is not greatly altered when the sonority is rearranged so that the lower note of the characteristic interval is no longer in the bass. Ex. 7-38 contains a sampling of some of the possibilities, many of which will appear in subsequent examples.

Ex. 7-38. Inverted augmented sixth chords.

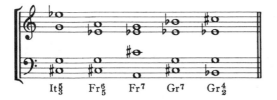

In the first four of the above chords, the interval of the augmented sixth has been inverted to a diminished third. Thus the typical melodic action of the interval is likewise inverted, i.e., converging upon a unison instead of expanding to an octave.

Ex. 7-39 is particularly rich in inverted augmented sixth chords. In this highly chromatic and complex harmonic idiom, augmented sixth chords are basic members of the harmonic vocabulary, lending a unique color and opulence to the progression. One can also observe the tendency for voice motion to become more and more conjunct in intensely chromatic music: as chromaticism increases in music, the part motion narrows until most or all voices move primarily by semitones.

Ex. 7-39. Mussorgsky: *Songs and Dances of Death,* IV.

Still another arrangement of the French sonority appears in Ex. 7-40. Again the characteristic interval has been inverted to form a diminished third which converges upon the root of the resolution chord.

Ex. 7-40. Bruckner: Mass in F Minor, *Sanctus*.

The Gr^{+6}_5 sonority is often inverted, as in the following examples. The first of these, Ex. 7-41, displays clearly the resolution of the Gr_{+7} (compare its resolution to that of the $°_7$ built on the same pitch). In Ex. 7-42 the Gr_{+7} that is reached in measure 3 evolves gradually through linear activity in all four parts, emphasizing the chord's contrapuntal origins: each of the four parts progresses by half-step, culminating in the B major six-four chord which is the apparent goal of the progression.

Ex. 7-41. Chopin: Sonata in B-flat Minor, I.

Ex. 7-42. Liszt: Sonata in B Minor.

The Gr$^{+6}_{5}$ and Enharmonic Uses

The Gr$^{+6}_{5}$ displays some peculiar properties. Its common notational spelling obscures the fact that its structure is the same as that of the major-minor seventh chord. Out of context it might well be heard as this more familiar chord; only within a context can its identity as an augmented sixth chord become apparent. Because of this ambiguity, the modulatory possibilities of the Gr$^{+6}_{5}$ are numerous. As Ex. 7-43 illustrates, the It$_{+6}$ shares this enharmonic potentiality with the German type, since it is indistinguishable (as an isolated sonority) from an incomplete major-minor seventh chord.

Ex. 7-43. Enharmonic forms of German and Italian sixths.

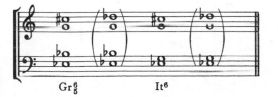

Gr$^{6}_{5}$ It^{6}

The enharmonic resolution of the Gr$^{+6}_{5}$ has been fully exploited by composers in the last two hundred years. The possibility of a sudden shift of key coupled with smooth melodic progressions made this an attractive modulatory device for composers who were seeking out chromatic tone relations. The procedure is simple: any major-minor seventh chord can be interpreted enharmonically as a Gr^{+6}_5 and resolved accordingly.

Ex. 7-44. Enharmonic resolution of augmented sixth chord.

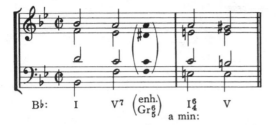

This process can, of course, be reversed. When we consider that any dominant seventh or secondary dominant seventh can assume this tonal guise, we see how varied are the possibilities.

This extended type of "common chord" modulatory technique is exhibited in Ex. 7-45. For several measures Beethoven has prepared for the tonic "arrival" in *G* major by a dominant pedal point. In the measures before the *fermata* the It_{+6} is used as a neighboring chord to V. At the *fermata*, however, another member is added, and the chord is here notated as a major-minor seventh chord. Nonetheless, the previous context leads the listener to expect a resolution to a structural chord in *G*, thus, in retrospect, making the chord in question a Gr^{+6}_5. Considerable musical surprise results when the chord resolves as V_7 of *A-flat* major. (A few measures later the key of *G* major is restored.)

Ex. 7-45. Beethoven: Quartet, Op. 18, No. 2, Finale.

Occasionally the Gr^{+6}_5 is spelled with a doubly-augmented fourth, the usual perfect fifth above the bass being replaced by its enharmonic equivalent. Ex. 7-46 contains a progression that illustrates this notational deviation. In major keys the enharmonic spelling more clearly suggests the resolution of the upper note of this interval.

Ex. 7-46. Schubert: *Am Meer.*

Ex. 7-46 continued.

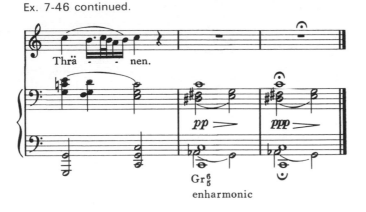

Thrä - - nen.

$pp >$ $ppp >$

Gr^6_5
enharmonic

Many composers have remained indifferent to this linear aspect, spelling the chord as the common Gr^{+6}_5 regardless of its resolution. In Ex. 7-47 the composer used the spelling *D* in preference to *C-double sharp*—even though the latter would have revealed more clearly the leading-tone function to its *D-sharp* resolution.

Ex. 7-47. Verdi: *Otello*, Act III.

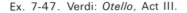

Andante
Otello
p

Gra - zie ma-don - na,   da - te-mi la vos-tra e-bur-nea ma - o

p +6   dominant 8^{ve}

B: V^4_3/V Gr^6_5 I^6_4

A similar lack of concern for the linear motion of the inflected tones of the Gr^{+6}_5 occurs in an early example of the use of this chord. The major-minor seventh chords in measures 1 and 4 are revealed in their resolutions as enharmonic German augmented sixth chords.

Ex. 7-48. Gesualdo: "Io pur respiro."

Deh   mor - - te

Deh mor - - te
enh. Gr^6_5 (enh. Gr^7)

In the harmonic analysis of nineteenth-century music, every seemingly distant chordal succession involving a major-minor seventh chord should be considered potentially as a Gr^{+6}_5 or V_7. Composers (especially Schubert) frequently used this means of modulation when moving up or down a minor second.

Spelling reveals the enharmonic dual relationship in Ex. 7-49. The fourth measure contains a chord with the dual function of V_7/IV in *E-flat* major and Gr^{+6}_5 in *G* major.

Ex. 7-49. Haydn: Quartet, Op. 76, No. 3, I.

Augmented Sixth Chord as Related to Tonic

Since the interval of the augmented sixth, as a dual set of leading tones, imparts great emphasis to its resolution tones, it is inevitable that the chords characterized by this interval should embellish the *tonic* as well as the dominant. The resolution of the augmented sixth to tonic octave establishes a relationship similar to that of dominant-to-tonic, but somewhat more intense in resolution effect because of the greater number of leading tones. In this relationship the lower tone of the augmented sixth interval corresponds with the lowered *supertonic* of the major and minor scales—the *Neapolitan relation.*

Ex. 7-50, which we have seen earlier in this chapter, contains a typical progression from It_{+6} to I.

Ex. 7-50. Schumann: Symphony No. 2, III.

The $\frac{7\text{-}8}{2\text{-}1}$ progression of the outer voices clearly indicates the lines of progression from the two-voice cadence formulae illustrated earlier in the chapter. If we compare this cadence to its diatonic equivalent, we see that it differs by only one note from the imperfect authentic cadence, vii°_6—I. It is interesting to observe that the *D-flat* is prepared earlier in the measure as the root of the Neapolitan chord, demonstrating the obvious identity of function of these chords. The entire measure is characterized by its harmonic relation as a chord whose root is the upper leading tone to tonic.

The $Fr^{+6}_{\;\;4\;3}$ appears more frequently in this context than either of the two other augmented sixth chords, possibly because it contains the dominant pitch. Most examples of augmented sixth chords related directly to tonic resolve to the major tonic triad rather than minor, although this is not essential. Ex. 7-51 illustrates the $Fr^{+6}_{\;\;4\;3}$ in this role.

Ex. 7-51. Brahms: Symphony No. 4, Finale (Theme).

Augmented Sixth Chords in Other Relationships

Augmented sixth chords sometimes resolve to chords other than dominant and tonic; nineteenth-century examples that are associated with other scale degrees are fairly common. In Ex. 7-52 an It_{+6} serves as an embellishment of the supertonic, resolving to V/V.

Ex. 7-52. Brahms: Symphony No. 1, I.

In Ex. 7-53 and Ex. 7-54 the relation of the augmented sixth chord to the prevailing tonality again is not completely clear at the moment it occurs. Ex. 7-53 contains a prolonged $Fr\,{}^{+6}_{\,\,\,\,3}$ in a context that is eventually revealed as *E-flat* major.

Ex. 7-53. Mahler: Symphony No. 8, Finale.

Even more remote is the augmented sixth in Ex. 7-54, built on the subdominant and resolving to V/vi. Despite this apparent remoteness from the tonic, the tonal center is never really in doubt.

Ex. 7-54. Beethoven: Quartet, Op. 18, No. 5, III.

Although twentieth-century composers have generally discarded the traditional augmented sixth sonorities as described in this chapter, they have retained one of their characteristic features—the cadence upon a unison or octave approached in contrary motion by double leading tones, as in Ex. 7-55.

Ex. 7-55. Diminished third as double leading-tone cadence.

But, despite the appearance of isolated examples of the above, augmented sixth sonorities are of little significance in twentieth-century harmonic practice. They are, at best, peripheral features even in the harmonic idiom of the eighteenth and nineteenth centuries. As fashions of dress change, so do fashions in sonority. In many respects the emergence of these chords as significant harmonic elements in late nineteenth-century styles was symptomatic of the growing chromaticism that was superimposed over an essentially diatonic system.

Exercises

For more detailed assignments see *Materials and Structure of Music II, Workbook,* Chapter 7.

1. Practice spelling the Neapolitan chord in all major and minor keys.
2. Practice spelling drills related to augmented sixth chords as follows:
   a. Locate rapidly both the upper and lower leading tones of:
      F-sharp, A, D, G-flat, B, E-flat, C-sharp, A-flat, F.
   b. Spell augmented sixths on the following pitches:
      G-flat, F, B, D-flat, A-flat, C, E-flat, G.
   c. Spell, from the bass note, the following:
      an It$_{+6}$ on *B-flat*
      a Gr$^{+6}_{5}$ on *G*
      a Fr$^{+4}_{3}$ on *D-flat*
      an It$_{+6}$ in the key of *E-flat* minor
      a Gr$^{+6}_{5}$ in the key of *C-sharp* minor
      a Fr$^{+4}_{3}$ in the key of *F* minor
3. Make an analysis of the first movement of Beethoven's Sonata, Op. 31, No. 2. Locate as many different Neapolitan chords as possible, note how they are approached and left, and state how the Neapolitan participates in modulation.
4. Spell a Gr$^{+6}_{5}$ in any major or minor key, then convert enharmonically into a dominant seventh chord and resolve accordingly. Write a short melody that utilizes this harmonic scheme for modulation.
5. Write melodies using the following sequential harmonic pattern: a phrase clearly delineating the tonic key followed by a sequential phrase in the region of the Neapolitan (cf. Ex. 7-22 for a model).
6. Experiment with short passages using the N$_6$ (or N) and augmented sixth chords as the basis for modulation. Then study the second movement of Schubert's *Unfinished Symphony* (Exposition, second theme group) as a brilliant example of enharmonic modulation using Gr$_{+6}$ chords.
7. Spell:
   a. three different Gr$^{+6}_{5}$'s in each of the following keys:
      D major, *A-flat* major, *F* minor, (and spell the resolution chord of each).
   b. the tonic-embellishing Fr$^{+4}_{3}$ in each of the following keys:
      C-sharp minor, *A* minor, *F* minor.
   c. an It$_{+6}$ resolving to vi in *E* major; in *D-flat* major.
   d. the Gr$_{+7}$ in *D* minor; in *F-sharp* minor; in *A* major.
   e. the Fr$_{+7}$ in *F-sharp* minor that embellishes the tonic.

8

VARIATION FORMS

The principle of variation occurs in music at many different levels of organization; even in the simple, straightforward folksong, a succession of altered versions—or "variants"—of a brief motive sometimes serves to spin out the total song.

Ex. 8-1. Spanish Folksong.

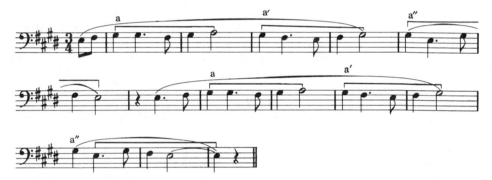

Successive variation of a given pattern offers a solution to the problem of musical continuation, for it represents the simultaneous incorporation of unity and variety; the *varied* aspect affords variety—the difference, whereas the prototype—the common link—establishes continuing unity. For this reason, the variation principle is a fundamental ingredient, in one way or another, in most music.

In view of this rich potentiality as a musical technique, it is easy to understand why composers have developed large-scale forms that exploit variation procedures. These can be found in a multitude of designs, all of which correspond to one of the two main variation types that we shall study here.

A common trait of all variation procedures is the use of some fundamental pattern—melody or chord succession—that can be traced as a guiding force throughout an entire work or a section within a larger work. When this pattern is retained intact within a series of continuously varied textures, as in the chorale prelude discussed in Chapter 6, it is known as a *cantus firmus*. In the strictest sense

172

cantus firmus means "fixed chant"; however, our use will embrace melodic patterns and harmonic patterns as well. This term, as used in connection with variation procedures, denotes the unchanging (or *firm*) incorporation of the basic pattern, the results of which are known as *cantus firmus variations*. If, on the other hand, the basic pattern is subjected to transformations which result in musical ideas quite different from the original, then the result is *independent variations*. In this second type, the successive variations are usually separated one from another so that they are independent, self-sufficient little compositions in their own right, in spite of their debt of origin to the initial *theme*.

Other common names for these two kinds of variation forms are "continuous variations" (in place of *cantus firmus variations*) and "sectional variations" (rather than *independent variations*). There are many subtypes within these main categories, the foremost of which we shall discuss subsequently.

Cantus Firmus Variation Types

The variation employing a *cantus firmus* is unique in that the musical pattern on which it is based is not itself subjected to extensive alterations (if any). It is classified as a variation type because of the continuously varied textures and thematic references that accompany the repetitions of the *cantus firmus*, whether that *cantus firmus* be a melodic, harmonic, or phrase-pattern foundation, and not because of variation of the *cantus firmus* itself.

The most common unifier in this type is a brief melody. Thus the composer incorporates into each variant section the restatement (exact or, more rarely, slightly modified) of the melodic *theme*. This melody serves as a thematic backbone for the composition, while each restatement is couched in a fresh setting made different by the rhythmic, harmonic, textural, and melodic reshapings of the accompanying materials.

In the *cantus firmus* type the composer has a built-in unifier; his compositional problem consists of shaping each restatement of the theme within a fresh context that is a complementary but, at the same time, varied texture.

Various kinds of *cantus firmus* treatment have been used as design elements in many musical styles. Our discussion of the chorale prelude in Chapter 7 dealt with one kind, in which a pre-existent melody is clothed in elaborate contrapuntal texture. The *cantus firmus* variation constitutes still another treatment, differing from the chorale prelude in certain simple respects. It too is a sectional form, but each section is based on the repetition of the *same* pattern, and not on the successive phrases of a melody. Further, the *cantus firmus* variation type is based on a brief pattern normally no longer than eight measures. And last, this *cantus firmus* need not be a melodic unity; it may be a series of chords.

Because of the brevity of the *cantus firmus*, a sizable number of variations are required to add up to a total continuous form of any size. The *passacaglia*, the *chaconne*, and the *ground* are all compositional designs that fit this multisectional variation procedure.

Disagreement exists about the exact historical differentiation of the three sub-types, at least insofar as the names were used as titles by the first composers to use them. "Chaconne" and "passacaglia" in particular appear to have been used synonymously during the Baroque period.

To be consistent in the use of the three names and their application for forms, we shall follow modern precedent: We shall restrict the meaning of "ground" to any piece in which a particularly short melodic bass pattern is repeated throughout the course of the work. The restriction of this pattern to the bass voice is significant, as we shall see later when we discuss the passacaglia.

Ex. 8-2 shows parts of a composition based on a ground; a four-measure pattern serves as the melodic substructure for each of the continuing variations. There are twenty-one appearances of the cantus, two of which (numbers 12 and 13) are transposed to the dominant (*g* minor).

Ex. 8-2. Purcell: *Dido and Aeneas*, "Ah! Belinda." Copyright 1961 by Hawkes & Son (London) Ltd. Realization by Britten. Reprinted by permission of Boosey & Hawkes, Inc.

peace___ and I   are stran - girs__ grown

peace_____ and   I

In contrast to the *ground*, the *passacaglia* is usually a more highly developed composition based on a longer, more tunefully "melodic" pattern, usually from six to eight measures long. As in the ground, the passacaglia cantus (*C.F.*) is first stated in the bass voice, where it remains during most of the composition. However, the pattern frequently is moved up into the middle and top regions of the texture at some point during the variations, normally around the middle portion.

The passacaglia is in a triple meter, either written in a triple-simple notation such as $\frac{3}{4}$ or $\frac{3}{2}$, or in some instances, as the compound meter of $\frac{6}{8}$ or $\frac{12}{8}$. This affinity for triple meter is apparently a vestige of the form's origins as a dance.

The three variations appearing in Ex. 8-3 have been extracted from a powerful work for organ. A study of the entire work through listening, combined with a careful reading of the score, will give a more accurate picture of the magnificent structure created around this simple eight-measure theme.

Ex. 8-3. Bach: Passacaglia for Organ in C Minor.

Manual

Pedal

Passacaglia cantus firmus

Ex. 8-3 continued.

A number of recent composers have shown interest in the organizational strength of the *cantus firmus* forms, and the *passacaglia* has been a favored framework. In some instances the basic design incorporated by Bach—a triple-meter theme of eight measures relegated to the bass, subsequent variations of texture woven above this recurring pattern—has been followed rather faithfully. But some composers occasionally have overhauled the technique to suit their immediate musical needs.

A passacaglia section that bears most of the earmarks of the "standard" outline appears toward the end of Barber's First Symphony (Ex. 8-4). This section opens with a six-measure theme in the bass followed by the usual textural growth over the repeated theme. The example shows excerpts of this work that reveal the theme in varied contexts. The total passacaglia section encompasses twelve statements of the *C.F.*, followed by an extension that makes a fitting close for the whole.

Ex. 8-4. Barber: Symphony No. 1, Final Section. Reprinted by permission of the copyright owner, G. Schirmer, Inc.

Orchestra

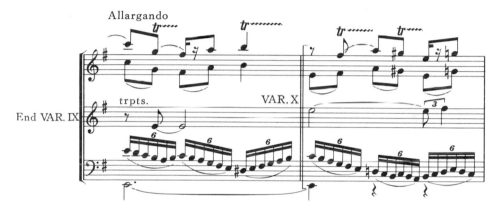

Allargando

End VAR. IX

trpts.

VAR. X

In ways reminiscent of the Bach work of Ex. 8-3, this passacaglia makes use of rudimentary alterations of the theme, which is shifted from the bass to a higher register during the middle part of the development. (It returns to the bass in the twelfth variation.)

The *chaconne* has come to be regarded as a series of variations based on a recurrent harmonic scheme, as opposed to the purely melodic *C.F.* of the ground and the passacaglia. It is not restricted to triple meters, appearing frequently in duple-simple schemes.

In the chaconne a set group of chords (or a linear pattern too simple to be termed *melodic*) forms a harmonic substructure above which a series of variations is woven. A clear example of the whole process can be heard in the series of instrumental variations played by a group of jazz performers when no pre-established melody (such as a popular tune) is the point of departure for their improvisations. In this sense, the innumerable jazz renditions of the basic "blues" progression could all be regarded as chaconnes. Each makes use of a series of chords—the *cantus firmus* as a harmonic scheme—to which are appended free melodic variations. In the blues progression a pattern of slow harmonic rhythm runs through a twelve-measure phrase-form.

Ex. 8-5. Basic "blues" progression.

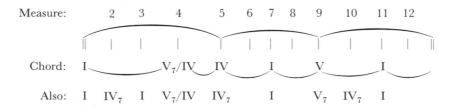

A more classic example of the chaconne uses a shorter chord series for its harmonic foundation, usually a four- or six-measure unit.

As we mentioned earlier, a lack of conformity persisted in the application of names for these three *cantus firmus* types during the Baroque period, and one of the clearest, simplest examples of what we now call "chaconne" was titled "passacaille" by its composer, Handel. Ex. 8-6 contains the four-measure *C.F.* of this piece, followed by excerpts from five of the fifteen variations.

Ex. 8-6. Handel: Passacaille ("Chaconne").

The alterations of harmony that occur within the later variants (only in number 11 here) are negligible changes made for the sake of variety once the basic pattern has been thoroughly established (as it certainly has been). Following deviations of this kind, the progression usually resumes its original form, as is the case in this composition.

A modern adaptation of the same principle forms the basis for the chaconne illustrated in Ex. 8-7. In this piece the *C.F.* is a pattern devoid of the motion necessary to be called "melodic"; it consists of a series of three chromatic steps upward in a static rhythm of four dotted half notes. This unyielding little pattern pervades the whole movement, giving rise to thirty statements of the four-measure sequence, all clothed in rich orchestral textures. As an example of *cantus firmus* variation, the almost constant reiteration of the four-measure figure makes a rigid basis for the varied instrumental tracings built around it. Note that the pattern is transposed to different pitch levels in later variations.

Ex. 8-7. Dello Joio: Variations, Chaconne, and Finale, Chaconne. Copyright 1950 by Carl Fischer, Inc. Reprinted by permission.

Independent Variations

A somewhat freer variation technique appeared as an incipient formal design within the Baroque period and grew into a variation type favored by such composers as Haydn, Mozart, and Beethoven. This second type, along with the *cantus firmus* variations, has been passed on to later composers as another basic approach to the organization of large-scale variation forms.

In this less rigid approach, a theme of somewhat greater dimensions initiates a series of independent variations, all of which take root in some characteristic that is peculiar to the parent theme. The listener hears these fresh, separate, minute compositions as individual statements which, in spite of their separation from the theme proper and from one another, nonetheless grow from a common origin and thus share some trait or traits in common with it.

In this form the composer chooses those aspects of his theme which he will retain as a common bond between it and its offspring, so that the listener can recognize the kinship of the two. This relation of *theme* and *variation* is made more obvious by some composers than by others; the first hearing of some sets of independent variations is not always successful in making clear the common bonds between all parts of the work.

Many sets of *theme and variations* are similar to the *cantus firmus* type in that they retain the thematic element in a relatively unaltered state through each section. Most Baroque variations illustrate this type. However, they differ from the *cantus firmus* variation procedure in at least two important respects: (1) each separate variation is a self-sufficient part of the overall design; and/or (2) the basic pattern is never relegated exclusively to the bass of the texture. (This latter does not mean, of course, that the theme cannot appear in the bass within one or more variations.)

The variations from which the excerpts in Ex. 8-8 were taken illustrate in simple terms the textural, harmonic, and rhythmic changes that might be applied in this kind of variation procedure.

Ex. 8-8. Scheidt: Variations on a German song, "Ei, du feiner Reiter."

VARIATION II (two - voice, contrapuntal)

VARIATION IV (meter change, imitative texture)

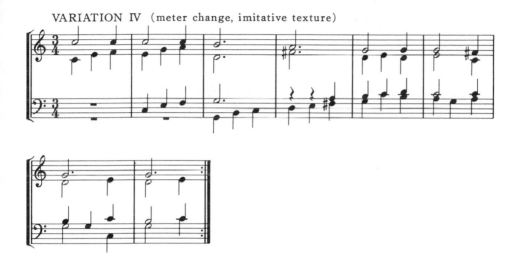

In other theme and variation compositions the variation procedure is rooted in elaborations or distillations of the melody, creating a decorative technique that ushers in all manner of melodic variety. One distinguishing element, then, is the degree of transformation undergone by the theme. In many such variations the original pitch line is so camouflaged that the probability of immediate recognition is reduced. Ex. 8-9a follows its melodic prototype in a uniform way, while Ex. 8-9b departs from its parent drastically, utilizing only its basic pitches as a framework.

Ex. 8-9a. Handel: Klavier Suite No. 5, "Air with Variations."

THEME
Andantino

Ex. 8-9a continued.

VARIATION I
Un poco più animato

Ex. 8-9b. Dello Joio: Piano Sonata No. 3, I. Copyright 1948 by Carl Fischer, Inc. Reprinted by permission.

THEME

VARIATION I (♩.= 80)

The theme of the independent variation type usually possesses a complete formal plan that enables it to stand alone as a separate and satisfactory musical statement. Each variation is shaped according to the same or quite similar dimensions, thereby maintaining the formal outline as well as some of the theme's most salient melodic, harmonic, and rhythmic characteristics.

The set of Variations illustrated in Ex. 8-10 is a clear example of this self-contained formal design, as it appears in both the theme and its subsequent five variations. Each of the variants is a replica of the form of the theme, each incorporating the   A   A   B   A   design.

Ex. 8-10. Mozart: Piano Sonata, K. 331, I.

Andante grazioso
A section

Ex. 8-10 continued.

Var. I
Section A beginning

Section B

Section A return

Maggiore

A careful study of each variation of this first movement will reveal how Mozart retained the basic pitch line of the original theme as a melodic scaffolding. Each section represents a new departure in style, a reorientation of textural combinations which create a distinct musical statement, a unique mood or character. Each is closely affiliated with the theme, although independent from it.

In most melodic variations the pitch line is preserved in a way that clearly reveals its origins. But it is possible to organize a variation that, although derived exclusively from the theme, is so drastically changed in other ways that even the original theme's pitch line is not apparent to the listener. Ex. 8-11 contains excerpts from a work in which the original melody of the theme is entrenched as a *cantus firmus* in the truest sense of the term, but the octave displacements and rhythmic shifts have hidden the original from all but the most perceptive ears.

Ex. 8-11. Hindemith: Theme and Four Variations. © 1947 by B. Schott's Soehne, Mainz. Reprinted by permission.

Still another approach to the variation procedure depends less rigidly upon pitch-line duplications by using the theme as a kind of melodic springboard. Each of the variations' patterns is derived from some unique characteristic of the theme rather than from wholesale pitch repetitions.

Ex. 8-12 shows this method as it occurs in two variations from a large work. In the first variation an imitative texture is built out of the first fragment of the theme's melody, this texture leading to a cadence that duplicates the original thematic organization. In the second variation the first five pitches of the original theme are the melodic basis of an *antecedent-consequence* phrase grouping.

Ex. 8-12. Beethoven: String Quartet, Op. 18, No. 5, III.

Ex. 8-12 continued.

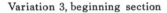
Variation 3, beginning section

A motive can be shaped from fragments of the original theme and the variation spun out by the developmental processes applied to these units. Ex. 8-13 shows an excerpt from a variation that has been created from the abbreviation and rhythmic reshaping of patterns from the original theme.

Ex. 8-13. Dello Joio: Piano Sonata No. 3, I. Copyright 1948 by Carl Fischer,
         Inc. Reprinted by permission.

The point of departure for any such variation might be a conspicuous rhythm,
a unique pitch contour, or as in the chaconne, a series of chords that is typical
in some way of the theme. Any (or several or all) could establish the link of
continuity between theme and variant.

One of the distinguishing features of the theme in the *Variations* partially illustrated below is the after-beat beginning that veils the meter during the first few
measures. Beethoven capitalizes on this feature by stressing after-beat patterns
within each of the variations that follows.

Ex. 8-14. Beethoven: String Quartet in C-sharp Minor, Op. 131, IV.

Ex. 8-14 continued.

Variation 2

Variation 3

Ex. 8-14 continued.

In working out his problems of unity and variety within the theme-variations format, the composer might choose one musical factor as a thread of continuity, thereby allowing other factors greater freedom. The *Variations on a Theme of Josef Haydn* by Brahms illustrates this balancing of powers by retaining the theme's phrase structure and harmonic plan intact, but adopting a very liberal attitude toward melodic continuity. This variation procedure is usually called "harmonic variations" because it is the theme's harmonic plan that forms the common element for each variation.

In this work the tonality (of *B-flat*), harmonic succession, phrase lengths, and subsidiary figures (such as pedal points) all form a thread of continuity within which the ensuing eight variations and Finale are firmly entrenched. Melodic strands in many sections of the variations are clearly *related* to the original theme, but passages in which exact melodic duplications appear are rare and fragmentary.

Ex. 8-15 shows the complete reduced score for the theme and the first variation of this work. It is evident that Brahms has not followed the same procedure of pitch-line decoration as Mozart did in the *A* major theme and variations discussed earlier. Here the theme is nowhere in evidence *as a melody,* except as an occasional pattern that creeps in to suggest a similarity with the original theme.

Ex. 8-15. Brahms: *Variations on a Theme by Haydn,* Theme and Variation I.

Ex. 8-15 continued.

VARIATION I

Andante con moto

However, the following similarities are imposing: (1) tonic of *B-flat*; (2) duplication of phrase structure; (3) duplication of harmonic progression (and cadence patterns); and (4) duplication of overall formal structure of A A B A codetta.

The same spirit of kinship pervades each of the succeeding variations, some of which contain more concrete thematic references to the original theme. But in each variation the same basic phrase plan has been retained, the same fundamental chord progression forms the harmonic basis, and the same tonic unifies the whole, even when shifts to the minor mode are made.

Ex. 8-16. Brahms: *Variations on a Theme by Haydn,* Variation II.

Ex. 8-16 continued.

A rather obvious but significant stepchild of the classic theme and variations design incorporates more than a single melodic prototype within the theme. In its simplest manifestation, two themes of contrasting nature (but of comparable length and importance) appear successively within the theme section. The succeeding variations take both of these melodies as their points of departure, each serving as the basis for a separate variation section. In this schematic order it is natural that fewer variations of a single theme occur, since there are more themes to be varied.

Some of the simplest examples of this bi-thematic variation type can be found in works by Haydn, who was probably the first to develop the plan. Ex. 8-17 shows the first parts of two themes of a theme section, the first in *G* major, the second in parallel minor, that serves as the basis for only three variations, two of the "A" theme, one of the "B." The design of the total movement is diagrammed below the two themes.

Ex. 8-17a. Haydn: Piano Sonata in G Major, I, themes and form plan.

THEME "A"

Allegretto innocente

THEME "B"

Ex. 8-17b. Formal plan of total movement.

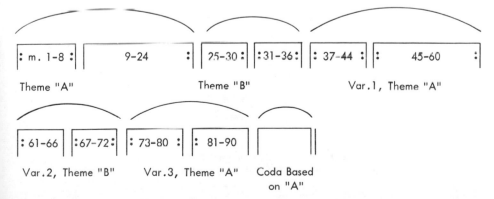

The excerpts in Ex. 8-18 can be matched with the organization illustrated in Ex. 8-17 to gain a more vivid idea of the process incorporated within this movement.

Ex. 8-18. Ibid., opening of Variation I, Variation II, and Variation III.

Var. 1 Theme A (beginning)

Var. 2 Theme B

Var. 3 Theme A

Beethoven wrote some variations that parallel rather faithfully this bi-thematic principle. A particularly interesting sample appears in the slow movement of his Piano Trio in E-flat, Op. 70, No. 2. It is perhaps through Beethoven that the idea was passed on to contemporary composers, particularly Paul Hindemith, whose *Theme and Four Variations* has a theme of three distinct sections—each of which contrasts in a marked way with its associates.

In Hindemith's work, each of the four variations[1] is also a three-part design, each separate section of which is derived from its respective "theme." Ex. 8-19 illustrates the three themes and their incorporation into the first two variations of the work.

---

[1] The subtitles of the Variations are drawn from the medieval classification of the bodily humors, which establish the *affection,* or mood, as it shifts from one variation to the next. In order, they are: *melancholic, sanguine, phlegmatic,* and *choleric.*

Ex. 8-19. Hindemith: Theme and Four Variations, Three Themes. ⓒ 1947 by
B. Schott's Soehne, Mainz. Reprinted by permission.

Ex. 8-19 continued.

Theme C

Variation 2
Theme A

Theme B

This tri-thematic basis results in a total plan that is considerably more complex than the *theme-variations* title normally implies. Here each variation is in reality a set of three sections, all of which total twelve variation-parts. The principle is remarkably sound. The composer has at his disposal the element of unity, through each variant's common bond with its respective theme; but variety is an inherent feature as well, through the contrasts afforded by the succession of three themes as they are couched within each variation.

An even more fascinating accommodation of the theme and variations format can be heard in a number of works by living composers in which melody and harmony, in the traditional sense, play no part. In György Ligeti's *Atmospheres*, for example, the "theme" is a brief sound event whose main characteristic is a sense of motionlessness. This static blob of complex sound provides the point of departure for a set of twenty-one "variations," all of which—in twenty-one different ways—replicate a sense of stasis, or "non-motion." In works such as this a *musical condition or state* is the theme rather than a single musical property such as harmony or melody or form.

Exercises

For more detailed assignments see *Materials and Structure of Music II, Workbook,* Chapter 8.

1. Study one or more of the following works, listening to a recording (with score in hand), paying particular attention to the following points:
   a. Variation type (*cantus firmus* or *independent*)
   b. Variation techniques: What is the "theme" or elemental unit?
      How is *variation* accomplished? How is unity incorporated within each variation?
   c. What is the overall plan of the work?
Works:
   Beethoven: *Thirty-two Variations in c minor*
   Brahms: *Variations on a Theme by Handel*
   Haydn: *String Quartet,* Op. 55, No. 2, I.
   Bach: *B minor Mass,* Crucifixus
   Ralph Vaughan-Williams: *Symphony No. 5,* Finale
   Hindemith: *String Quartet in E-flat,* III.
   Beethoven: *Symphony No. 5,* II.
           Symphony No. 9, III.

Schubert: *D-minor Quartet* ("Death and the Maiden"), II.
Reger: *Variations on a Theme by Mozart* (Same theme illustrated in Ex. 8-10)
Hindemith: *Nobilissima Visione,* "Passacaglia"
Wm. Schuman: *Symphony No. 3,* "Passacaglia" (1st Section of Part I)
Ligeti: *Atmospheres*
(Or any of the works quoted in this chapter.)

2. Add a series of, say, four variations to a short *ground* pattern.

3. Using the same procedure illustrated by Hindemith in the *Theme and Four Variations* discussed in this chapter, devise six different variations of varying meters and rhythmic style based on a chosen theme. (Only the single line variant is required, although further time might be taken to complete the variations by adding appropriate textures to the single lines.)

4. Write two variations for a chosen theme that are of a consistent harmonic and melodic style with that theme. (For an interesting study, choose a theme for which another composer has written variations and compare your results with his.)

5. Plan a chord progression of six to eight measures. Write a series of simple distinct textures, each of which fits the progression. Incorporate one dominant melodic idea in each of the variations.

6. Plan a chord progression as in Exercise No. 5 (or use the same chord series). Play the progression at the piano or organ until you know it thoroughly. Subject to your limitations as a performer at the keyboard, improvise simple melodic patterns to this set progression. (You might play the basic progression in the left hand, the melodic improvisation in the right.) Start with the most rudimentary and easy patterns, repeat and perfect until they can be fitted together into a fluent variation.

7. Plan a progression as in Exercise Nos. 5 and 6. Learn the progression thoroughly. While a friend plays the progression at the piano, improvise melodic patterns that fit this chord series on your major instrument. Decide upon a main rhythmic pattern that can be utilized as the basis for most of your melodic improvisations.

9

THEMATIC DEVELOPMENT
IN TWO-VOICE
COUNTERPOINT

One of the solutions used by composers to achieve musical coherence and continuity in extended forms stems from the continuous imitative combinations of two or more parts. A melodic idea is announced successively by the participating voices, these announcements constantly shifting into a variety of contrapuntal contexts that create a developmental atmosphere. The *invention* is one of these formal procedures that is rooted in a basically imitative style.

A broad description of what might occur in an invention, in terms of musical structure, might include any process in which a musical idea is stated, then progressively developed. This musical idea conceivably could be merely a rhythmic pattern, a series of chords, a pitch pattern, or even a single tonality. Inventions have been written in which each of these has served as the nucleus of a musical creation.

Our interest will focus on the invention type in which a brief melodic theme, or *subject*, forms the embryonic topic of musical development. For this reason our models will be the two-part inventions of J. S. Bach, which exemplify musical unfolding through a process of thematic development. As an introduction to this study, listen to performances of several of these miniature works, played by recording or by a fellow student. Or best, play through them yourself.

General Characteristics

The invention is a brief work in any tempo, usually lasting no more than forty to sixty seconds. In terms of actual measures, an invention might run twenty or fifty measures, depending upon the meter notation: a $\frac{12}{8}$ work might consist of only twenty measures, while one notated in $\frac{3}{8}$ might well consume considerably more.

The invention is a sectional piece in which key is one of the main formal determinants.[1] Generally, each section has a tonic different from its immediate

---

[1]An invention could very well be atonal, in which case key would not be a relevant structural factor.

207

predecessor, but all are grouped in relation to a common tonic that begins and ends the form. Each section contains a reworking of the basic melodic material, the *subject*, in a variety of melodic and harmonic environments.

The Two-part Invention in d minor of Bach, reproduced as Ex. 9-1, is a clear example of the features that normally appear in the whole invention.

Ex. 9-1. Bach: Two-part Invention in D Minor.

The most obvious characteristic of this piece (and of other inventions as well) is its total incorporation of the melodic subject first announced at the beginning. With the exception of measures 17, 37, 48, 51, and 52, every measure of the piece is in some way devoted to the continued exploitation of this simple scalar pattern. And even these exceptional measures consist of a common cadential formula that, by its repetition, adds unity to the whole design.

As a scheme of keys, this Invention follows the broad outline of

d − − − F − − − a − − − d − − − ‖
  (m.18) (26–27) (44)

Each main section is delineated by a separate tonic and, in two instances, scale basis (major-minor).

The developmental procedures of this model invention can best be summarized in an outline that refers to measure numbers.

> 1–6 Announcement of subject in each voice, first statement solo.
>
> 7–17 Slight alteration of motive contour, sequential repetitions, cadence that confirms *F* major.
>
> 18–21 Sequential statements of subject in major key.
>
> 22–25 Sequential statement of subject in contrary motion (melodic inversion).
>
> 26–37 Development within *a* minor; measures 29–33 a free textural inversion and expansion of measures 19–21.
>
> 38–44 Continued imitative statements of subject, now undergoing modulation to *d* minor.
>
> 44–48 Reprise of subject in original key, simple accompanying voice.
>
> 49–52 Coda built from subject in contrary motion.

In summary, the following four techniques of development are applied to the restatements of the subject: (1) contrary motion (as at measure 22); (2) pitch alteration (as at measure 7); (3) shift to a new position within the tonality framework (as in measure 30 where subject begins on the 3rd of *a* minor rather than on the original tonic); and (4) change of key (occurring throughout). We will observe other means of development in the remaining inventions of Bach, but these are the most prominent in all.

Other unifying elements are present within the parts which contain the subject. For example, the simple rhythm in the top voice of measures 3 and 4 (♩ ♩ ♩) plays a prominent accompanying role throughout the whole work. It can be called a *countersubject* because of its major role as a melodic foil to the statements of the subject.

Further accompanimental patterns are derived from the subject itself. The figure of the top voice in measure 11 is constructed from fragments of the subject, as illustrated in Ex. 9-2.

Ex. 9-2. Bach: Two-part Invention in D Minor, original motive.

Derived pattern
(Fragmentation)

This derivative method represents still another way Bach has gleaned material from his original melodic pattern. The technique of *fragmentation* is, then, a fifth means of subject development incorporated in this one invention.

It is important to recognize the equal significance of each of the two voices in this invention, for here lies one of the main characteristics. The whole texture is permeated by a give-and-take contrapuntal relation between the two participants, each contributing to the development of the material at hand, and both outlining simple harmonic progressions which create a unified counterpoint.

Since the single subject dominates the entire invention, it must be a pattern that is definite in contour, clear in tonality, and generally worth hearing repeatedly. The Bach examples fulfill each of these requirements. Each subject delineates the tonic chord of the whole piece, and each is a "catchy" melodic utterance that makes a definite, forthright impression on the listener.

With few exceptions, subjects of predominantly conjunct motion adhere to the mode of the piece, thus establishing immediately the pitch basis for what is to follow. When disjunct patterns form the subject, its skips almost always outline the tonic triad. The rudimentary analyses that accompany Ex. 9-3 reveal the structural causes of clear tonality.

Ex. 9-3. Tonal frameworks of invention subjects.

Invention No. 3

D Major

Invention No. 8

e Minor

Invention No. 14

Bb Major

Similarly, the subject establishes the metric framework with clear articulations of basic beats. A majority of the Bach examples begin with an upbeat figure that propels the subject forward. An accompanying pattern can establish clearly the metric structure, as Ex. 9-4 illustrates.

Ex. 9-4. Bach: Two-part Invention in B Minor, No. 15.

Most inventions have a brief subject. (Most of the Bach examples begin with a subject no longer than two measures.) Imitative entries between parts are generally more forceful if the leading voice does not run for a long time before it is answered by the follower. If the subject is longer, the total pattern consists of smaller units which are repeated to fill in the whole. For instance, the opening subject of the Invention in f minor (No. 9) consists of one measure repeated sequentially, thus reducing the actual number of motive patterns.

Ex. 9-5. Bach: Two-part Invention in F Minor, No. 9.

Most of the subjects are more succinct than that of Ex. 9-5, many lasting no more than a few beats.

Ex. 9-6. Subjects of Inventions No. 10, No. 13, and No. 1.

Beginning Section of the Invention

The opening statements of the subject expose the melodic material of the whole piece. As a by-product of this exposition certain other matters are established: the basic key is introduced; the metric rhythmic units are posed; and the accompanimental patterns are first set in combination with the subject in ways that set the scene for subsequent combinations.

These goals are met within the invention's first section by successive imitative statements by the participating voices. From this point forward the two parts are usually heard together for the duration of the work.

In most of the Bach Inventions both voices make their first statements in the tonic key. The second part thus repeats the subject an octave lower than the first. The D major Invention, No. 3, illustrates this normal arrangement of entrances.

Ex. 9-7. Bach: Two-part Invention in D Major, No. 3.

In some inventions the subject is stated more than once by each voice during the opening section. It is heard twice in each part during the first two measures of Invention No. 13, after which derivations of the subject are pitted one against another in imitative fashion.

Ex. 9-8. Bach: Two-part Invention in A Minor, No. 13.

The leader-follower plan adhered to in the opening section presents the possibility of a canonic relationship between voices—the follower duplicating the leader exactly. Although none of the Bach Inventions maintains this exact duplication throughout, some do contain sections that are *canonic*. Invention No. 8 is strictly canonic through its first seven measures, and then a shift of harmony disrupts the exact duplication in measure 8. At that point the lower voice duplicates the upper at the interval of a ninth below.

Ex. 9-9. Bach: Two-part Invention in F Major, No. 8.

Ex. 9-9 continued.

Invention No. 2 contains a canonic relationship to the first beat of measure 11, and then another long section of exact duplication begins when, in measure 13, the top voice states an answer to the pattern that began in the bottom voice at measure 11. Only the first two notes of the subject are not duplicated exactly.

Ex. 9-10. Bach: Two-part Invention in C Minor, No. 2.

This section of canonic relation continues for eight measures, breaking off into free counterpoint at measure 21.

The invention usually is less rigidly controlled by part-duplications; inexact imitations are found even in the initial statements. For example, Invention No. 10 is exceptional in that its lower part sounds the answer at the dominant scale level and, in so doing, presents a pitch alteration that keeps this first section solidly entrenched in the tonic key. (This minor change is not enough to change the character of the subject.)

Ex. 9-11. Bach: Two-part Invention in G Major, No. 10.

Although the lower voice commonly answers the upper immediately, some inventions reveal a wider separation of entries. Invention No. 14 begins with three statements of the subject (at different pitch levels) followed by a two-measure episode that bridges the gap between this introductory statement and the complete version of the subject in the second voice. This particular episode is built from the imitative echoes of a fragment of the subject.

Ex. 9-12. Bach: Two-part Invention in B-flat Major, No. 14.

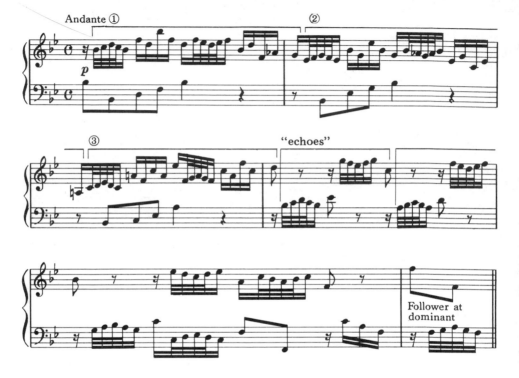

One of the most interesting of all the Bach Inventions, No. 6, makes extended use of textural inversion or *double counterpoint*. In this passage a section is turned upside down so that an original upper part now becomes the lower, and vice versa. The first eight measures of this invention are derived from this simple but effective process. Note that this kind of inversion of parts *in relation to each other* is not the same as *melodic inversion*.

Ex. 9-13. Bach: Two-part Invention in E Major, No. 6.

Textural inversion is so successful here that Bach incorporates it as the main developmental procedure throughout the remaining sections of this invention.

Developmental Sections

The heart of the invention lies in those sections which follow the expository statements, in which the subject is developed through several keys and combined with new contrapuntal associations.

We noted earlier how Bach used *contrary motion, pitch alterations, sequential tonal shifts within a single key, fragmentation, modal change,* and *changes of key* in shaping the many variants of the basic subject. All of these procedures and a few more play an important role in the sections of the invention that follow the opening.

For a composition no longer than the invention, the developmental sections cannot be extensive. The Bach examples generally fall into a division of four units of approximately equal length. The key scheme for such a plan is relatively flexible, and it is dependent upon the structure of the subject and upon whether it is in major or minor. The following diagrams show usual characteristics of key outlines in the Bach Inventions.

Section:	I	II	III	IV
Key:	I(major)	V(major)	vi(minor)	I(major)

or:

Section:	I	II	III	IV
Key:	i	v	VII	i

or:

Section:	I	II	III	IV
Key:	i	III	v	i

or:

Section:	I	II	III	IV
Key:	I	V	ii	I

Each of these fragmentary sketches must be regarded as a generalization, because the developmental character of the middle sections sometimes precludes strict adherence to a single clear tonality; in some cases it is impossible to say what the tonic is in a particular measure, a modulatory condition prevailing.

The section following the exposition usually begins like a re-exposition in the new key that has been established by a strong cadence. In some inventions the voice that acted as *follower* in the exposition now assumes the role of *leader,* as Ex. 9-14 illustrates.

Ex. 9-14. Bach: Two-part Invention in C Major, No. 1.

The peculiarities of a subject may require rhythm or pitch changes to sustain the forward motion at the junction between sections. To fulfill this need, the subject might be given a decorative addition such as Bach made at the beginning of the second section of Invention No. 3.

Ex. 9-15. Bach: Two-part Invention in D Major, No. 3.

In this Invention Bach added three notes at the beginning of the subject, causing it to span the two-beat vacuum that otherwise would lie between the first-beat cadence and the third-beat pickup of the subject. He retains this revised version of the subject through the remainder of the Invention.

The invention's second section normally is imitative, each voice tossing the subject or variants of the subject back and forth in successive statements. This is also the logical location for the appearance of developmental alterations of the subject, although these might have figured prominently in the earlier expository statements.

Variation of the subject can occur within the first few measures of an invention. It appears in the first four measures of Invention No. 1 and Invention No. 13, but such examples are rare.

Ex. 9-16. Bach: Inventions No. 1 and No. 13, subject variants.

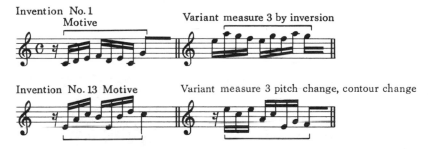

A different kind of developmental technique appears in No. 7. Here successive fragmentations of the subject are spun out in a modulation that leads to a re-exposition in both voices beginning in the relative major key.

Ex. 9-17. Bach: Two-part Invention in E Minor, No. 7.

Still another kind of development is used in No. 6. Here the second large section (following a repetition of the exposition) forms the second part of a *binary* form. The initial eight measures in the key of the dominant (*B* major) are a textural inversion of the first eight measures of the exposition section.

Ex. 9-18. Bach: Two-part Invention No. 6, double counterpoint.

A final illustration of developmental procedures can be seen in Invention No. 5. The top voice states the main pattern of the subject three times in a modulatory sequence. This is answered by a full statement of the subject in the bottom voice. The accompanying line for the subject appearances in the top voice is derived from the *countersubject* carried by the lower voice at the beginning of the exposition.

Ex. 9-19. Bach: Two-part Invention in E-flat Major, No. 5.

Whatever the particular departure made within the interior sections of the invention, their common function is to carry the subject through a series of developmental stages that are interestingly varied, but are always linked by rhythmic and harmonic relations with what has gone before. This linkage is effected by a careful planning of large sections, returning always to the tonic key as an aspect of formal close. In this sense the invention can be regarded as a form that begins with a statement of an idea in a particular key, then runs through a series of transformations—thematic and tonal and textural—and then returns to the original tonality for its eventual resolution.

Closing Section

None of Bach's Inventions ends with a subject statement that exactly parallels the initial statement of the exposition. However, most of the Inventions do imply a return to something akin to the first thematic statements. This kinship is brought about by similarities of texture, range, harmony, and rhythm with the opening section, as well as by the return to tonic key. A glance at some of the final sections of the Bach models should make clear how this effect of return separates the final statements from the preceding developmental sections.

A clear "reprise" occurs in Invention No. 3. In measure 43 there is a complete contrast of texture in a return to the single voice that began the Invention. This sets into relief the return of the subject in the original tonic key and at the original pitch level. Only the duplet anacrusis has been altered in order to continue the descending scale line that leads into this section.

Ex. 9-20. Bach: Two-part Invention in D Major, No. 3, last section.

The final section of Invention No. 2 is forcefully signaled by a strong V—I cadence to the original tonic in measures 22–23. The entire subject is stated by the upper voice in measures 23–24 for the first time in the tonic key since the exposition of measures 1–4. The bass voice counters with the last statement that ends the Invention, measures 25–26. The combination of original key (and pitch level beginnings on c^2) and the accompanying figure in the bass that served as a counterpart within the third and fourth measures of the exposition are strong indications that the formal circle is closing.

Ex. 9-21. Bach: Two-part Invention in C Minor, No. 2, beginning of the reprise.

Invention No. 15 uses a similar method of closure, but here it is the bottom voice that leads with the first restatement of the subject in the tonic (*b* minor). The answer in the upper voice confirms the significance of this return to the original key. A curious feature of this passage is the way the answer of the top voice begins before the bottom voice has completed the subject. This thematic "dovetail," or *stretto*, is a significant feature of the *fugue*, which will be studied in Chapters 10 and 11.

Ex. 9-22. Bach: Two-part Invention in B Minor, No. 15, stretto imitation.

Ex. 9-22 continued.

In a more dramatic setting, stretto relation marks the beginning of the final section of Invention No. 14, where the second entry of the subject is piled abruptly onto the first.

Ex. 9-23. Bach: Two-part Invention in B-flat Major, No. 14, stretto imitation.

It is interesting to see in this excerpt how Bach alters the subject in the top voice at the third beat of measure 2 so that the two parts will join as effective counterpoint.

The element of return in simple A   B   A fashion is not essential to the invention, and it does not occur as a clear aspect of the design in some of the Bach models. Invention No. 8 ends without a strong restatement of the original subject, although the pattern is present *at different pitch levels* within the tonic key toward the end.

Ex. 9-24. Bach: Two-part Invention in F Major, No. 8, final section.

The closing portion of Invention No. 7 utilizes the basic sixteenth-note pattern of the subject in sequential successions that lie within the tonic key, but the bold restatements made in some of the Inventions do not appear here.

Ex. 9-25. Bach: Two-part Invention in E Minor, No. 7, final section.

Final section tonic key

Contrapuntal Association

The Inventions are tightly knit in that they incorporate a bare minimum of melodic patterns. A glance at any page of the Bach collection will show that the same rhythmic units are used repeatedly in the sections directly based on the respective subject and those free of the subject proper.

Invention No. 1 is a masterpiece of thematic unity since every pattern can be traced back to the initial subject. Even the most prominent accompanimental pattern is itself the rhythmic augmentation of the first four notes of the motive. Ex. 9-26 shows the way Bach combined the original subject in contrary motion with the rhythmic magnification of the same pattern in its original ascending contour.

Ex. 9-26. Bach: Two-part Invention No. 1, augmentation in contrary motion.

When the first statement of the subject is accompanied, the same associative pattern is normally used in later passages as a countersubject. These later appearances occasionally appear slightly altered or elaborated; at other times they are exact duplications of the original pattern. The motive of Invention No. 9 is constantly combined with its countersubject.

Ex. 9-27. Bach: Two-part Invention in F Minor, No. 9, contrapuntal association.

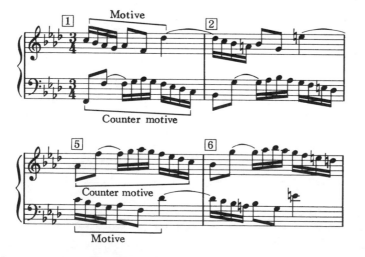

A more ingenious use is made of the countersubject in No. 15 when in subsequent sections it returns in elaborately decorated form along with the motive.

Ex. 9-28. Bach: Two-part Invention No. 15, use of countersubject.

The countersubject of Invention No. 13 appears first in measure 1 as the logical continuation of the subject line in the top voice. It returns in a variety of pitch modifications with every subsequent statement, both as a contrapuntal foil for the subject proper, and combined (in fragmented form) with parts of the subject.

Ex. 9-29. Bach: Two-part Invention in A Minor, No. 13, subject variants.

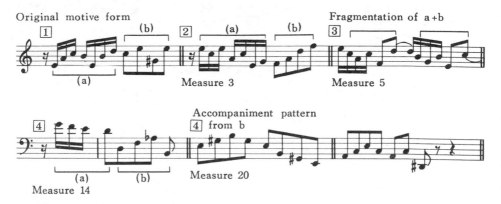

Invention No. 11 also incorporates a contrapuntal associate that combines as a rhythmic complement with several statements of the subject. It appears both in its original form and in contrary motion. Ex. 9-30 shows the reworking of the two forms in various contexts within the Invention.

Ex. 9-30. Bach: Two-part Invention No. 11, countersubject development.

In spite of these numerous instances of extreme thematic homogeneity, the invention can effectively introduce patterns that are unrelated to the main subject—material that serves as episodic "filler" between successive treatments of the subject proper. The sequential chordal patterns of Invention No. 8—first introduced as an accompaniment to the subject—serve this function.

Ex. 9-31. Bach: Two-part Invention in F Major, No. 8, episode.

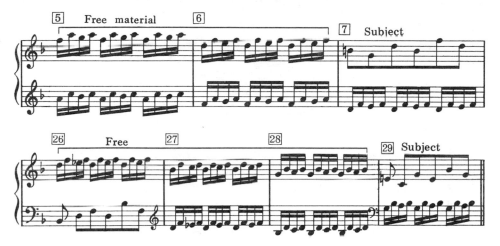

Use of a pedal note (usually trilled in the Bach Inventions to sustain the keyboard tone) is an obvious accompanimental pattern that is unrelated to the subject of the Invention. Its use in the Bach examples is restricted to developmental sections in which the motive goes through sequential patterns in one voice.

Ex. 9-32. Bach: Two-part Invention No. 7, trilled pedal.

The texture that contains the pedal figure is frequently inverted, so that the formerly static voice becomes the active partner. In Ex. 9-33 the "answer" version to Ex. 9-32 is shown, the upper voice now providing the melodic interest.

Ex. 9-33. Ibid., trilled pedal inverted.

The same static accompanying technique occurs in Invention No. 3, but in this case the pedal figure is a rearticulated octave pattern rather than the more common trill.

Ex. 9-34. Bach: Two-part Invention No. 3, activated pedal.

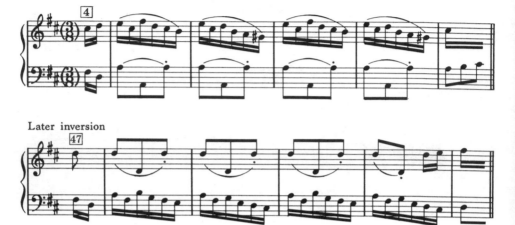

These figures that are unrelated to the main subject and independent of the countermotive are less common than those connected with motive material. This rigid single-mindedness of melodic organization is more in keeping with the compositional "inventiveness" implied within the very name *invention*.

Exercises

For more detailed exercises see *Materials and Structure of Music II, Workbook,* Chapter 9.

1. Make a detailed study of the use of the subject in Invention No. 1 in C Major. Note all developmental techniques applied throughout this Invention.
2. Write a subject that would be suitable for an invention. Apply every one of the developmental techniques discussed in this chapter to a separate section that develops this subject.
3. As a listening project, play recordings of the Inventions (or have a friend play them for you) and mark on a premeasured slip of paper the following information:
    a. Locations of strong formal junctions;
    b. Location of any significant contrapuntal features such as stretto or inverted textures;
    c. Location of a reprise section if present, or return of a hint of reprise and the original tonality; then
    d. Trace the key relations in the Invention without checking with the score.
4. Make an analysis of the chord relations outlined or implied by the voices in any of the Bach Two-part Inventions.
5. Write an invention (of about the same length as the Bach examples) in which the subject is developed mainly through sequential passages of its original form and its inversion.

10

FUGUE

The imitative two-voice works discussed in Chapter 9—the invention in particular—show most of the characteristics of the fugue. It would be accurate to describe Bach's Inventions as fugues for a keyboard instrument. The developmental techniques applied to motives and the imitative textures of inventions are similar to those seen in most fugues. In this chapter we shall be concerned primarily with the gross details of fugues, turning our attention to smaller details in Chapter 11.

At the outset we must distinguish between a number of similar terms: *fugal, fugue, fugato,* and *fughetta. Fugal* is the key word, for it describes the imitative style that is common to works denoted by the other three: they all refer to textures that are "fugal."

For example, a *fugue* is a complete single-movement work that follows broadly predictable procedures, the most important of which we shall discuss in this and the following chapter. By definition, its most important feature is a contrapuntal texture of a rather formalized imitative style. As a distinction, *fughetta* refers to any relatively brief fugue, implying a diminutive example of the bigger, more highly developed form.

On the other hand, a *fugato* is a fugal section within a larger work that, as a whole, is not a fugue. It is an extended passage that incorporates fugal procedures as a means of thematic statement or development. As an illustration of this interpolated fugal texture, Ex. 10-1 shows a passage from a composition that is not a fugue. Since the imitative theme statements set it apart from its immediate context as *fugal*, the entire section (all of which is not quoted) is a *fugato*.

Ex. 10-1. Bernhard Heiden: Sonata for Piano, Four Hands, I. © 1953 by Associated Music Publishers, Inc., New York. Reprinted by permission.

Ex. 10-1 continued.

Since the fugue is the principal form incorporating all of the procedures that characterize these other related imitative styles, our attention will be centered upon its features.

There is no set "plan" that can faithfully represent "the fugue form." The fugue is, rather, a composition that embraces a combination of usual ingredients, all of which are blended into a contrapuntal texture whose chief aim is the development of a single melodic idea and subsidiary patterns associated with that idea.

Exposition

The core element that most clearly stamps a composition as *fugal* is the imitative principle. The content of a fugue is delineated by a series of sections in which the topic melodic idea, the *subject,* is stated by each participating voice in a series of imitative statements. The first of these sections is called the *exposition;* as in the invention, this section contains the first presentation of the melodic strands that will form the basis of all subsequent sections.

Ex. 10-2. Bach: *Well-tempered Clavier*, Book I, Fugue No. 19 in A Major.

Ex. 10-3. Giannini: *A Canticle of Christmas* (Fugue section based on "Come all ye faithful"). © 1959 by G. Ricordi & Co., New York. By permission of Franco Colombo, Inc., New York.

The number of statements in the exposition is almost always restricted by the number of participating voices in the whole fugue.[1] Thus a "four-voice fugue" begins with an exposition of the subject by each of four parts, a cumulative texture gradually being built up by their successive entrances. The exposition proper is finished with the end of the statement made by the final voice.

Ex. 10-4. Bach: *Well-tempered Clavier*, Book I, Fugue No. 10 (two-voice exposition).

Ex. 10-5. Hindemith: *Ludus Tonalis,* Fuga Secunda in G (three-voice exposition).
ⓒ 1943 by Schott & Co., Ltd., London. Reprinted by permission.

---

[1] This cannot be understood as a literal guide to orchestral or keyboard fugues. While in those combinations the participating "voices" are normally limited to no more than four or five, the texture may at some points contain more simultaneous tones, or parts, than that number.

As Ex. 10-5 illustrates, the exposition does not consist of successive statements of the subject in a strict additive order. In this particular exposition a three-measure bridge stands between the second and third statements. Here, as in most bridges of fugue expositions, the total subject is not present.

Similar bridge passages appear in the three-and four-voice expositions quoted earlier in Ex. 10-1, Ex. 10-2, and Ex. 10-3. These "nonsubject" passages serve a twofold purpose: they help to avoid the monotony of strictly successive entries, and they also prepare for subsequent statements in terms of key, rhythmic contrast, and textural emphasis. Each of these three factors is utilized in the bridge (or "episode") passage of Ex. 10-6 that spotlights the entrance of the subject in the bass voice.

Ex. 10-6. Bach: Three-part Invention in F Minor.

Subject (3rd statement)

A fundamental characteristic of the fugue exposition is the tonality contrast that is built into the successive subject statements. In fugues written before the twentieth century, tonic-dominant interplay is usually established between the expository entrances of the separate voices. When applied to a four-voice exposition this arrangement would yield the scheme of *tonic-dominant-tonic-dominant*, or in some less common examples, *tonic-dominant-dominant-tonic*. Many fugues written during the present century also follow one of these tonal plans, but the less restrictive key schemes of recent music have led to more flexible arrangements of entrances.[2]

The tonality contrasts typical of the second and fourth voice statements led to the common application of the names *subject—answer* to the relation of the successive statements. But this distinction is not altogether helpful in fugues which do not expose the subject in the simple two-level order of *tonic-dominant-tonic-dominant*, etc. The fugue exposition from which Ex. 10-7 is taken contains a succession of seven subject statements, each a semitone higher than its predecessor. The first three appear in this excerpt.

Ex. 10-7. William Schuman: Symphony No. 3, Fugue. Reprinted by permission of the copyright owner, G. Schirmer, Inc.

[2] The distinction between "real" and "tonal" answers will be discussed in Chapter 11.

Developmental Sections

It is dangerous to generalize about what happens in the fugue after the exposition section. As indicated earlier, the fugue is more a set of probable ingredients than it is a defined formal design. However, the basic ingredients, as well as some elemental procedures, can be established for all fugues, even though their manifestations in particular examples do not follow any pat formula.

In most fugues the post-exposition sections are similar to the initial exposition in that they are molded from imitative restatements of the subject. But the composer's goal following the exposition is to create thematic, textural, and harmonic transformations of the original subject matter; in a restricted sense, the unfolding of the fugue consists of continuous variations of the initial exposition.

We can illustrate this developmental nature of the subsequent sections by quoting an entire fugue here. It should be performed at the keyboard or heard in a recorded performance several times before pursuing the discussion that follows.

Ex. 10-8. Bach: *Well-tempered Clavier*, Book I, Fugue No. II in F Major.

Ex. 10-8 continued.

As indicated in the score, this fugue falls into six large sections, some of which can be divided into still smaller groups as noted. We can itemize the most salient features of each section.

Section.   Description.

I   Exposition of subject, voice order 2 (middle), 1 (top), and 3 (bottom). Last statement ends at measure 13, the subsequent four measures bridge this section to the next, II. (Pitch structure of answer that does not duplicate interval structure of subject will be discussed in Chapter 11.)

II   Essentially another exposition containing the same order of keys (*F-C-F*) but with the different voice order of 1-2-3. Because of this basic similarity of technique and tonality arrangement, this section is called a *counterexposition*. Ends with slightly abbreviated statement in the middle voice that is in stretto with the bass (measures 27–30).

III   Section is marked by change of mode to minor and by stretto statements of subject, voice order 1–2–3.

IV   Divided from Section III by decisive V-I cadence in measure 45. Section is a kind of "answer" in that same stretto relations are formed, but now in *g* minor and following opposing orders of entries, 3–2–1.

V   Punctuated by same cadential form as measure 45, this section leads back to original tonality of *F* major. Similar to bridge passage in section II (measures 31–35). Again, thematic material derived from subject's first measure (in contrary motion) in patterns of rising eighth notes.

VI   Camouflaged return to subject in top voice, imposed on continuation of pattern that dominated section V. As reprise, most obvious feature is reestablishment of initial key, *F* major.

A summary of the resources used in the organization of the total fugue follows: (1) dominance of the subject as melodic source; (2) key change as element of variety (*F, d, g, F*), (3) modal variation of subject (in this fugue from major to minor); (4) fragmentation as a developmental procedure; (5) stretto as a developmental procedure; and (6) melodic elaboration as a developmental procedure (as applied to the subject in measures 64–68).

We shall be concerned with a more thorough investigation of some of these fugal ingredients in the following chapter. For the present we must observe some of the developmental procedures that are commonly applied to the subject in the developmental sections.

Ex. 10-8 illustrated three techniques prominent in the inventions discussed in Chapter 9: *fragmentation, melodic elaboration,* and *change of mode.* The full roster of procedures used in the invention can be found in fugues, with the addition of a few others which we shall discuss presently.

Inversion is one of the most common variants of the fugue subject. It is an effective means of thematic variation because the rhythm pattern is preserved and the conjunct-disjunct nature of the subject remains, even though the directions of pitch movement are reversed. Ex. 10-9 and Ex. 10-10 each show a fugue subject and accompanying passages that draw upon contrary motion as a source of development.

Ex. 10-9. Hindemith: *Ludus Tonalis,* Fuga Quarta in A Major. © 1943 by Schott & Co., Ltd., London. Reprinted by permission.

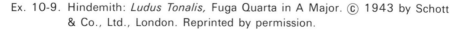

Ex. 10-10. Shostakovitch: Twenty-four Preludes and Fugues, Fugue No. 9.

An interesting texture results from a combination of the subject in its original form and in its contrary motion version. In Ex. 10-11 the two appear in a stretto.

Ex. 10-11. Bach: *Well-tempered Clavier*, Book I, Fugue No. 6 in D Minor.

Modifications of pitches within a subject usually retain the main contoural features of the original; skips and steps duplicated in the variant preserve the basic outline. Amplifying a characteristic skip by means of a wider interval plays a prominent role in the development of a motive fragment of the Invention shown in Ex. 10-12. Here the skip-step pattern is preserved intact, even though the exact interval sizes of this relation are altered considerably.

Ex. 10-12. Bach: Three-part Invention in F Minor.

Ex. 10-12 continued.

Three variant procedures that occur, though infrequently, in the fugue are *augmentation, diminution,* and *retrogression.* The first two are rhythmic alterations through which the durations of a subject can be proportionately stretched or shrunk. Both usually occur only within a two-level scheme, an original pattern made twice as long (by augmentation) or half as long (by diminution) by a simple process of durational multiplication or division.

Ex. 10-13. Bach: *Well-tempered Clavier*, Book II, Fugue No. 2 in C Minor.

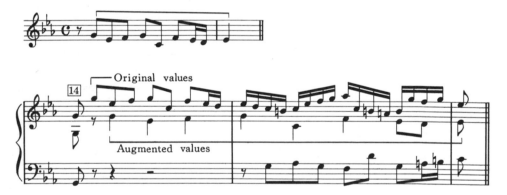

Ex. 10-14. Schönberg: Suite for String Orchestra, Fugue. Reprinted by permission of the copyright owner, G. Schirmer, Inc.

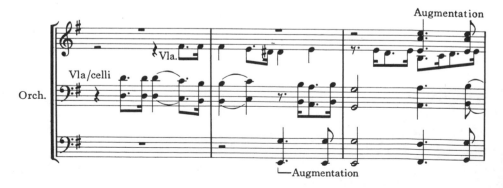

But greater scales of proportion have not been overlooked by composers.

Ex. 10-15. Bartók: Concerto for Orchestra, Finale. Copyright 1946 by Hawkes & Son (London) Ltd. Reprinted by permission of Boosey & Hawkes, Inc.

Melodic *retrogression*[3] consists of the total reversal of a pattern, so that its last pitch becomes its first and vice versa. This compositional "trick" appears within the developmental sections of some fugues, even though the effectiveness of the process is questionable as a means of thematic transformation. Its validity is relative to the structure of the subject so ordered; a short, rhythmically simple pattern might well be recognized in its retrograde version. Ex. 10-16 shows a subject and its reversal that seems to represent favorably the latter set of conditions.

Ex. 10-16. Hindemith: *Ludus Tonalis*, Fuga Tertia in F Major. © 1943 by Schott & Co., Ltd., London. Reprinted by permission.

---

[3] Also known as *cancrizans*.

The structure of Ex. 10-17 (which is not from a fugue) is less easy to recognize as a retrograde version of its original form.

Ex. 10-17. Honegger: Symphony No. 5, II. © 1951 by Editions Salabert, Paris, by permission of Franco Colombo, Inc., New York.

Many composers have regarded the fugue as a vehicle for plying their "bag of contrapuntal tricks," so it is not surprising that the listener's recognition of retrogression has not been regarded as a crucial test of acceptability.

The most common developmental process within the fugue is *stretto*. This is not a technique of melodic variation, for the subject usually occurs in almost exact duplication within the stretto to achieve an effect of imitative compression.

As we noted in our discussion of the invention in Chapter 9, the composer might, by virtue of the structure of his motive, be able to use several different spans of imitation, thereby achieving greater and lesser degrees of compression within stretto sections. The fugue from which Ex. 10-18 is taken contains many different spans; the entire fugue is organized by means of successive sections of stretto among the four participating voices.

Ex. 10-18. Bach: *Well-tempered Clavier*, Book I, Fugue No. 1 in C Major.

Stretto relation 1

Stretto relation 2, 3, and 4

Most fugues do not exhibit such a wealth of stretto possibilities as this example, and most fugue subjects are not amenable to this multiplicity of overlapping combinations. One of the composer's chief problems in writing an effective fugue subject is to accommodate stretto relations in at least one span of imitation.

One flexibility inherent to stretto lies in the intervallic relation between the overlapped imitations. The usual relation is the octave, because without pitch modifications of the subject, this relation most readily avoids chromaticism that could undermine tonality. But granted the possibility of "tonal" imitations that produce pitch modifications, other interval relations may be accommodated into a simple key framework.

Ex. 10-19. Bach: *Well-tempered Clavier*, Book I, Fugue No. 6 in D Minor.

For subject see example 12

Even when the stretto relations occur at the octave (the same note names in different pitch registers), alterations of the original subject usually appear after the first statement. A composer might reshape the subject drastically to make it fit a series of stretto announcements within a single passage. Ex. 10-20 and Ex. 10-21 illustrate such changes.

Ex. 10-20. Bach: *Well-tempered Clavier*, Book I, Fugue No. 16 in G Minor.

Ex. 10-21. Shostakovitch: Twenty-four Preludes and Fugues, Op. 87, Fugue No. 5.

In more recent fugues that are organized within a less restricted key scheme, stretto relations can be found at any interval gap. The goal of overlapping imitation is still paramount.

Ex. 10-22. Barber: Piano Sonata, IV, "Fuga." Reprinted by permission of the copyright owner, G. Schirmer, Inc.

Ex. 10-23. Hindemith: *Ludus Tonalis*, Fuga Sècunda in G Major. ⓒ 1943 by
Schott & Co., Ltd., London. Reprinted by permission.

Sectional Linkage

The composer must so organize his work that it produces the effect of continuity from the outset until the final chord, without creating a feeling of choppy sectional groupings, of one section merely tacked on to another.

Earlier we noted the bridge sections that link parts of the exposition together into a continuous series of related parts. Similar bridge passages are used elsewhere in most fugues, both as temporary relief from the sections of imitative subject statements and as a procedure of modulation that leads to the key of the next subject statements. The melodic substance of these bridge sections frequently is derived from the subject by fragmentation. In many such passages two fragments are joined together in a contrapuntal association such as that shown in Ex. 10-24.

Ex. 10-24. Bach: *Well-tempered Clavier*, Book I, Fugue No. 2 in C Minor.

This episode bridges the exposition to a statement of the subject in a new key. The sequential pattern drops by steps until the new tonic, *E-flat*, becomes imminent in the last measure of the excerpt. Aside from this linking function between the two sections which contain the full subject, the passage reveals how development can occur in the bridge, here in the form of a dialogue between two voices, each the manipulation of a subject fragment.

Such a fragmented portion of the subject might be taken from any of its parts, but usually favored is a pattern readily perceived as a derivative of the subject. In Ex. 10-25 the fragment is obviously related to the final turn of the subject.

Ex. 10-25. Bach: *Art of the Fugue*, Contrapunctus II.

In a particularly long fugue the bridging role may be expanded to become a section of considerable significance in the whole form. Ex. 10-26 shows the beginning of a ten-measure passage that lasts long enough to be recognized as somewhat more important than a mere bridge. This particular bridge is built from a pattern that first appeared in the exposition of the fugue.

Ex. 10-26. Barber: Piano Sonata, IV, "Fuga." Reprinted by permission of the copyright owner, G Schirmer, Inc.

Episode bassed on counter subject

Sost. ped.

When materials not clearly related to the subject achieve a significant level of formal distinction, it is difficult to justify the usual term "bridge," for this designation implies lesser structural importance. However, this term remains as a way of distinguishing sections based upon imitative development of the subject from those which are independent of the subject.

Bridge sections are not always based on subject-derived materials. They must be similar in rhythm to the subject passages that surround them, but the contrast desired in some such sections may be best achieved by the absence of specific references to the subject. The passage shown in Ex. 10-27 forms a logical continuation of what has preceded, mainly because of the continuing sixteenth-note motion. But it bears no direct melodic relation to the subject as a whole, nor is it a fragmentary derivation. As usual, the organization is sequential.

Ex. 10-27. Bach: *Well-tempered Clavier,* Book I, Fugue No. 10 in E Minor.

Subject

Episode

Subject return

Tonality Relations in the Fugue

Whatever method of development is chosen for a particular fugue, the process always involves shifts of tonality, these shifts in themselves acting as an element of developmental variety. The brief tonality contrasts in the exposition represent an interior kind of shift; the fugue as a whole offers further tonal variety in the form of sectional key contrasts.

It is impossible to set down a prescribed order of keys for the fugue; such a generalization would be contradicted by too many particular fugues. However, most examples written before the present century maintain a set of key orders consistent with the definition of "near relationships" given in Book I. The general rule of "no more than one sharp or one flat removed from tonic key," based on the major-minor key signature system, is an adequate guide. The key schemes illustrated as typical of the invention on page 217 apply to the conventional fugue as well.

The important tonal convention of all fugues is the return to the tonic key for the final statement (or statements) of the subject. In most fugues it is this return to the initial key, usually in conjunction with a clear statement of the subject and a return to a simpler texture, that signals impending closure to the listener.

Space does not permit the quotation of entire fugues here to display the incorporation of all those elements that might produce a sense of formal reprise. However, the brief excerpts and attendant synopses of Ex. 10-28, Ex. 10-29, and Ex. 10-30 will provide a guide for a study of the fugues represented.

Ex. 10-28. Bach: *Well-tempered Clavier*, Book II, Fugue No. 6 in D Minor.

Ex. 10-29. Barber: Piano Sonata IV, Fuga. Reprinted by permission of the copyright owner, G. Schirmer, Inc.

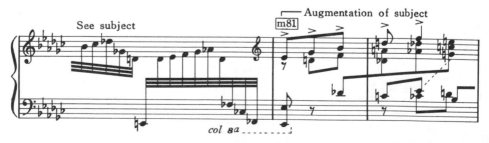

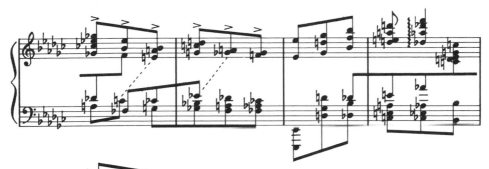

Ex. 10-30. Bach: *Well-tempered Clavier,* Book I, Fugue No. 6 in D Minor.

In some fugues the return to tonic occurs prior to the restatement of the full subject in the tonic. That is, the return of the original key does not always coincide exactly with the final return of the subject. It is when the two factors appear *combined* that a reprise is most strongly implied. In such examples, the beginning of the final section is reinforced by a strong cadence or a textural contrast that marks the junction between what has been developmental and what can be regarded as a closing section. In Ex. 10-31 the extreme contrast of texture that spotlights the bass entrance, in tonic key, forcefully emphasizes the return of the subject in something like its expository form. In this fugue the statement quoted is also the first appearance of the subject in a lower voice since the exposition, thereby reinforcing the formal significance of this statement in tonic.

Ex. 10-31. Bach: *Well-tempered Clavier*, Book I, Fugue No. 14 in F-sharp Minor.

In some fugues the return to tonic at the closing section is accompanied not by the more conventional simplification of texture, but by a stretto that builds these final statements into a climactic fusion of all the voices.

Ex. 10-32. Bach: *Well-tempered Clavier*, Book I, Fugue No. 22 in B-flat Minor.

The composer's selection of the organizational methods used for closing his fugue depends upon the formal order he wishes to establish. If his composition is to move to a climax within an interior section, driving to a pitch of greatest developmental tension there, then the closing section might logically be a return to simple texture, as well as the usual return to tonic and less modified versions of the complete subject.

Exercises

For more detailed assignments see *Materials and Structure of Music II, Workbook*, Chapter 10.

1. Analyze a number of fugue or fugato expositions found in the works of Palestrina, Buxtehude, Bach, Beethoven, Schumann, Shostakovitch, Hindemith, Bartók, Wm. Schuman. Pay particular attention to the following details:
   a. Structure of subject;
   b. Presence or absence of countersubject;
   c. Tonal relations of subject statements;
   d. Order of entries in terms of pitch range;
   e. Presence or absence of episodic links between subject statements; nature of thematic material and contrapuntal devices used herein.
2. Follow the procedures of (1) above with a division of the whole fugue into major sections; then determine the following:
   a. Tonalities embraced by each section;
   b. Developmental techniques applied to subject;
   c. Uses of countersubject if present in the fugue;
   d. Appearances of subject in stretto (if present);
   e. Any uses of earlier material or earlier sections in textural inversion: at 8ve or at 12th or at 10th.
   f. Does final section or some "late section" serve as a clear reprise for the whole fugue, or does the work simply "end" without a return other than in terms of tonality?
3. Listen to a fugue several times, paying particular attention to the broad sections that are formed by tonality, textural, and thematic contrasts. Having heard the fugue several times, plot out in gross terms the basic form of the piece. (Make this in the form of a graphic design on a piece of paper.) Then listen again and in the process perfect your outline. By all means avoid seeing a score before or during this session. Then check the accuracy of your outline with the score.

11

FURTHER DETAILS
OF FUGUE

Our main concern in the previous chapter was the fugue as a total composition and general aspects of "fugal procedure." Our problem now is to focus attention upon some of the formal and contrapuntal features of fugue writing.

Since the exposition section presents the elements that dominate all subsequent sections—number of voices, thematic material, accompanimental patterns, and principal tonality—our first step is to examine the features of the exposition in minute detail.

Fugal Exposition

Any complete melodic figure could be used as the subject of a fugue; there is no singular quality that makes one pattern intrinsically "fugal," another "non-fugal." Certain features, however, do make one melodic pattern more workable within the fugal procedure than others. We can enumerate some significant traits which, when present in a melodic pattern, make it more readily adaptable to the usual fugal procedures.

1. *Closed form:* i.e., a pattern complete in itself rather than fragmentary. For this reason most fugue subjects are several measures long and usually can be divided into small motive fragments. Ex. 11-1, Ex. 11-2, Ex. 11-3, and Ex. 11-4 illustrate this tendency toward melodic completeness as opposed to the fragment-like brevity of the usual invention motive.

Ex. 11-1. Bach: *Well-tempered Clavier*, Book I, Fugue No. 16.

Ex. 11-2. Schumann: Fugue for Piano, Op. 72.

Ex. 11-3. Bartók: Concerto for Orchestra, IV. Copyright 1946 by Hawkes & Son (London) Ltd. Reprinted by permission of Boosey & Hawkes, Inc.

Ex. 11-4. Bach: *Art of the Fugue*.

2. *Rhythmic vitality:* The subject is usually characterized by a unified rhythmic structure that is dynamic rather than static, active rather than passive, projecting forward in a way that lends a propulsion to the fabric of the whole fugue. Many subjects begin with upbeat patterns for this reason.

Ex. 11-5. Böhm: Fugue for Organ.

Ex. 11-6. Shostakovitch: Fugue No. 2 for Piano, Op. 87. © Copyright MCMLV by MCA Music, a division of MCA, Inc., New York. All rights reserved.

Ex. 11-7. Bach: *Well tempered Clavier*, Book I, Fugue No. 11 in F Major.

Ex. 11-8. Harris: Symphony No. 3. Reprinted by permission of the copyright owner, G. Schirmer, Inc.

3. *Clear tonality and meter:* Since the subject is the nucleus from which the total form grows, it usually delineates a tonality from the beginning by emphasis on a single pitch by means of repetition, duration, or intervallic play. For the same reason, it usually establishes a metric frame of reference from the outset.

The subject normally appears solo in its initial statement, although some fugues do begin with an accompanied subject. The effect of cumulative texture is best achieved by the gradual addition of voices, rendering the solo statement the most striking means of initiation. In addition, the uncluttered effect of the solo statement most clearly sets forth the subject for the listener's immediate comprehension.

The second voice usually enters at the end of the statement of the subject by the first voice, though there are exceptions to this rule. Some are interrupted by the answer of the second voice, thus creating a "stretto exposition." It is not always easy to pin down the exact note on which the subject proper ends, but answers that enter before the close of the subject usually produce the stretto effect.

Ex. 11-9. Bach: *Well-tempered Clavier,* Book I, Fugue No. 22.

Ex. 11-10. Bach: *Well-tempered Clavier*, Book II, Fugue No. 3.

The same effect of compression can be expected in expositions that display unusual thematic transformation. This is the main feature of the expositions from which Ex. 11-11 and Ex. 11-12 are taken.

Ex. 11-11. Bach: *Art of the Fugue,* Fugue No. 5.

Ex. 11-12. Bach: *Art of the Fugue*, Fugue No. 6.

An opposite condition, the answer actually delayed after the subject appears to have run its full course, occurs in some expositions. It may happen if the subject seems to close on an interior beat while the answer is best stated beginning with the first beat of the following measure. Ex. 11-13 shows a subject that is actually completed two beats before its answer begins.

Ex. 11-13. Bach: *Well-tempered Clavier*, Book I, Fugue No. 7.

Under similar circumstances, many composers have not hesitated to place the answering voice in mid-measure, even though the preceding subject began at the beginning of a measure.

Ex. 11-14. Bach: *Well-tempered Clavier*, Book II, Fugue No. 9.

Ex. 11-15. Hindemith: *Ludus Tonalis,* Fugue No. 6. © 1943 by Schott & Co., Ltd., London. Reprinted by permission.

This notational offset occurs only when parallel stresses (strong answered by strong, weak answered by weak) are preserved. A subject that begins on a metric stress would not be followed by an answer that begins on a weak beat, for such a relation would obliterate the character of the subject.

Tonal and Real Answers

The answers of a fugue exposition are not always exact pitch duplications of the subject's first statement. The bridging of the initial tonality with the tonality of the second statement is frequently expanded by a *tonal* (inexact) as opposed to a *real* (exact) pitch version of the subject. In fugues of major or minor scale basis this *tonal* form of the subject usually entails only a slight alteration at the beginning of the answer, the remainder of the line coinciding with the exact transposition of the original pattern.

The tonal answer illustrated in Ex. 11-16 is typical of eighteenth-century fugue expositions; subjects whose first few notes dwell on *tonic-dominant* pitches are usually answered by the reverse order of *dominant-tonic.*

Ex. 11-16. Bach: *Well-tempered Clavier,* Book I, Fugue No. 8.

The same reversal is common when *dominant-tonic* is answered by *tonic-dominant.*

Ex. 11-17. Schumann: Fugue for Piano, Op. 72.

Ex. 11-18. Buxtehude: Fugue for Organ.

Notice particularly that the simple changes made in each of these subjects occur within the first few notes. The remainder of the answer is an exact transposition of the subject.

Similar changes occur in some answers after the first few notes, usually to avoid an abrupt contrast of tonality. The alteration that makes the answer of Ex. 11-19 *tonal* appears at the fourth pitch, to avoid an abrupt sounding of the leading tone of the new tonality of *F*.

Ex. 11-19. Hindemith: *Mathis der Maler*, I. © 1934 by B. Schott's Soehne, Mainz. Renewed 1961.

When the subject's length or pitch structure makes the key contrast of the answer less abrupt, the *real* answer form is as likely to be used as the *tonal*. The end of the subject shown in Ex. 11-20 prepares the listener for the dominant key, the *e-natural* implying the shift.

Ex. 11-20. Bach: Fugue for Organ in G Minor.

If this bridging function had not been an integral part of the subject, a tonal version, such as that shown in Ex. 11-21, would have been a logical answer for this subject.

Ex. 11-21. Ibid.

Bach provided this solution for a subject of similar pitch structure but of considerably lesser length.

Ex. 11-22. Bach: *Art of the Fugue*.

If an alteration of the answer is not required to make it fit into the initial tonality, a subject is usually answered by its exact transposition. Most fugues written with a freer tonal basis than the major-minor key system preserve the identity of the subject more precisely by building up the exposition from *real* answers after the initial subject statement.

Order of Voice Entries

The effect of gradual textural accumulation mentioned in several earlier discussions is frequently reinforced by the successive expansion of pitch range in the exposition. This is achieved by an order of entrances that follows a "rule of adjacent voices." That is, the first subject statement is usually answered by a voice adjacent in range above or below (such as alto answered by soprano or by tenor); it in turn is answered by its neighbor, and so on until the full complement of parts and total breadth of texture has been reached.

This neat rule of entrances is encountered more frequently in three-voice than in four- or five-voice fugues, for a consistent tiered ordering of so many statements could become monotonous. However, three-voice fugues whose subjects are introduced by the top or bottom voice normally follow the 1–2–3 or 3–2–1 scheme.

Ex. 11-23. Bach: *Well-tempered Clavier*, Book I, Fugue No. 6.

Ex. 11-24. Hindemith: *Ludus Tonalis*, Fugue No. 2. © 1943 by Schott's Co., Ltd., London. Reprinted by permission.

Less frequently, a fugue that begins in the lowest voice is answered by the highest, creating a vivid contrast of register that is interlocked when the middle voice joins.

Ex. 11-25. Bach: *Well-tempered Clavier*, Book I, Fugue No. 4.

If the first statement occurs in the middle voice, the second and third entries (top and bottom voices) will be separated by a wide spacing. The usual choice of order by composers has been to answer the middle voice by the top, leaving the bottom voice for the final entry. This implies that a more satisfactory arrangement is afforded by leaving the weightiest announcement (in terms of the "tonal weight" of the lowest voice) for the final and most decisive statement of the subject.

Ex. 11-26. Shostakovitch: Fugue No. 4, Op. 87. © Copyright MCMLV by MCA
Music, a division of MCA, Inc., New York. All rights reserved.

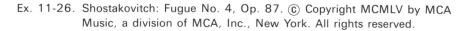

In fugues of more than three voices the entry order usually follows some grouping by adjacent pairs, such as two upper-voice statements paralleled by a similar order in two lower voices (2-1, 4-3), or the two lower voices preceding the two upper voices (3-4, 1-2).

Ex. 11-27. Bartók: String Quartet No. 1, I. Reprinted by permission of Boosey &
Hawkes, Inc., sole agents for "Kultura" (Hungarian Trading Company) in
the U.S.A.

Ex. 11-28. Bach: *Well-tempered Clavier*, Book I, Fugue No. 17.

Only in rare instances is the "rule of adjacency" followed for the entry order of four-voice fugues, producing a successive accumulation from low to high—or high to low   of all voices.

Ex. 11-29. Beethoven: String Quartet, Op. 131, I.

Ex. 11-29 continued.

Other patterns of entries are possible, but they are not as common as the arrangements we have discussed. Ex. 11-30 shows an order that deviates from all of the preceding.

Ex. 11-30. Bach: *Well-tempered Clavier*, Book I, Fugue No. 12.

Tonality Contrasts of Entries

The tonality changes that characterize the exposition were discussed briefly in Chapter 10. As we mentioned there, the tonic-dominant balance of entries in the fugue expositions of seventeenth-, eighteenth-, and nineteenth-century composers does not always govern the subject-answer relation of more recent fugues. The relaxation of this general rule reflects the broader tonal relationships that prevail in all aspects of twentieth-century music. The traditional tonic-dominant relation provides a degree of contrast, but not to the extent of disrupting a principal tonality.

The tonic-dominant order represents a relationship that is consistent with the harmonic vocabulary of seventeenth-, eighteenth-, and nineteenth-century music, which, as a whole, operates within a diatonic pitch framework with emphasis on V—1 as a harmonic basis. In the fugue, the answer's appearance a fifth above its predecessor retains enough tones that are common property of both keys (such as *E* major—*B* major) that the change is readily heard as a smooth shift from one tonal plane to another. The usual brevity of these shifts in the fugue exposition might well be regarded as less than definite modulation, rather more like an elaboration of the dominant *tonal region* of the tonic key.

Ex. 11-31 shows a subject-answer context in which this shift to the key of the dominant can be regarded merely as emphasis on the dominant chord (supported by secondary dominant relations) rather than an actual modulation to the dominant key.

Ex. 11-31. Bach: *Well-tempered Clavier*, Book I, Fugue No. 9.

The *tonal* answer discussed earlier is another means the composer can use to minimize the key contrast of the successive statements, so that each answer is more closely allied in pitch structure to the original key.

As we have noted previously, some music that draws upon a richer set of tonal resources—chromatic scale, complex chords and chord relations—nonetheless retains the simple tonic-dominant contrast as the basis for fugal entries of the exposition.

Ex. 11-32. Wm. Schuman: *American Festival* Overture. Reprinted by permission of the copyright owner, G. Schirmer, Inc.

Ex. 11-33. Barber: Piano Sonata, IV. Reprinted by permission of the copyright owner, G. Schirmer, Inc.

Another manifestation of the fifth relation is present when *subdominant*, rather than dominant, is the key of the answering voice or voices. Although not found in the typical eighteenth-century fugue, this kinship offers another close affiliation that has been exploited in some fugue expositions. (See Ex. 11-29, Ex. 11-34, and Ex. 11-35.)

Ex. 11-34. Bartók: String Quartet No. 1, III. Reprinted by permission of Boosey & Hawkes, Inc., sole agents for "Kultura" (Hungarian Trading Company) in the U.S.A.

(Chord accompaniment of subject omitted)

Ex. 11-35. Hindemith: *Ludus Tonalis*, Fugue No. 1. © 1943 by Schott & Co., Ltd., London. Reprinted by permission.

Contrast by mutation—major subject answered by its relative or parallel minor (or vice versa)—does not appear in the fugue exposition; it is a developmental procedure that alters the character of the subject too distinctly to be expository. It is used in the later sections of the fugue, however, as a means of thematic development.

Tonal patterns which do not adhere to the tonic-dominant or tonic-subdominant plan are usually based on a symmetrical order of one kind or another. Ex. 10-7 shows subject entrances arranged by rising semitones, while Ex. 11-36 shows entries that follow a series of fifths up and down. As a by-product of this latter arrangement, the texture grows with each entry from a thin mid-range strand into a progressively thicker combination that encompasses the string orchestra range.

Ex. 11-36. Bartók: Music for String Instruments, Percussion, and Celesta, I.
Copyright 1937 by Universal Edition; Renewed 1964. Copyright &
Renewal assigned to Boosey & Hawkes, Inc., for U.S.A. and to
Universal Edition for all other countries. Reprinted by permission.

This scheme disregards the traditional pairing by subject-answer-subject-answer that dominated the tonal arrangements of most pre-twentieth-century fugue expositions. And yet, many recent fugues contain the paired order, although not always in the tonic-dominant scheme. In a three-voice fugue the last statement of such a pairing might return to the original note series, suggesting a return to the initial tonality.

Ex. 11-37. Hindemith: *Ludus Tonalis*, Fugue No. 4, © 1943 by Schott & Co., Ltd., London. Reprinted by permission.

In a four-voice texture the pairs of entries can be completed, so that the last entry duplicates the second.

Ex. 11-38. Bartók: String Quartet No. 5, Finale. Copyright 1936 by Universal Edition; Renewed 1963. Copyright & Renewal assigned to Boosey & Hawkes, Inc., for the U.S.A. and to Universal Edition for all other countries of the world. Reprinted by permission.

Ex. 11-38 continued.

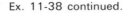

It should be obvious that the composer's choice of tonal relations for subject entries must be determined by the pitch structure of his subject and the harmonic style within which his fugue will be couched. A relatively diatonic subject could well demand the tonally simpler and less disruptive *tonic-dominant* or *tonic-subdominant* scheme, whereas a more chromatic subject might justify a less simple order of entries that follows a nondiatonic relationship.

The Countersubject; Invertible Counterpoint at Twelfth

In addition to a subject, most fugues draw upon another melodic pattern, called *countersubject*, for thematic materials.[1] As in the invention, this pattern usually appears in the exposition as a continuation of the subject along with the second entry.

Ex. 11-39. Schumann: Fugue for Piano, Op. 72.

---

[1] In some fugues several subjects are exposed and developed to an extent that justifies the title *double* or, as the case may be, *triple fugue*. It is beyond the scope of our work here to discuss these significant departures from the monothematic fugue design.

Ex. 11-40. Bach: *Well-tempered Clavier*, Book I, Fugue No. 6.

The countersubject should not be regarded as a full-blown melodic unit like the subject, for it usually does not occur in complete duplications later in the fugue. It is, rather, a characteristic pattern (or group of patterns) that provides accompanimental figures for later appearances of the subject. It also is used in some fugues as a source from which bridge passages are woven.

In some fugues the countersubject can be traced to a motive within the subject, thus unifying further the thematic basis of the whole fugue. The countersubject of Ex. 11-41 clearly originates from the second half of the fugue's subject.

Ex. 11-41. Bach: *Well-tempered Clavier*, Book I, Fugue No. 16.

Ex. 11-41 continued.

A basic requirement of any countersubject is its adaptability to *inversion* (or *double counterpoint*) with the subject. Its continued association with the subject throughout the fugue requires that it form a satisfactory counterpoint above or below. We discussed this requirement of textural inversion in our study of the invention in Chapter 9, where inversion at the octave was cited. In addition to this relation of simple reversal of roles from top to bottom by octave transpositions, composers have occasionally brought about inversions at other intervallic relations. Inversion at the twelfth (fifth plus octave) and the tenth (third plus octave) occur most often.

As a simple illustration of invertible counterpoint at the twelfth, Ex. 11-42 shows two textures; the second is an inversion of the first at the twelfth.

Ex. 11-42. Inversion at twelfth.

Here the top voice of (a) has been transposed down one octave, while the bottom voice has been transposed up a fifth (12th) to create the reversal shown in (b). Notice that the following intervallic changes take place when inversion at the twelfth is used:

Ex. 11-43. Interval inversions at the twelfth.

Original Interval	1	2	3	4	5	6	7	8	9	10	11	12
	12	11	10	9	8	7	6	5	4	3	2	1

The same basic relation results regardless of which voice is transposed from its original note level by the interval of the fifth. The *upper* voice can be lowered a fifth when it moves to the lower part of the texture, or, as in Ex. 12-44, the *lower* can be raised a fifth when it becomes the top. Both procedures yield an inversion "at the twelfth," even though different pitches result.

Ex. 11-44. Interval inversions at the twelfth.

Both versions (y) and (z) are derived from the original (x) by inversion at the twelfth. In (y) the top voice of (x) has been shifted down one octave, the bottom voice up one fifth. Note that (z) contains the same intervals between the parts as (y) (5—3—5), but each contains different pitches—(y) is a perfect fourth below (z).

Transposition of one voice up a fifth or down a fifth (or compounds of these intervals) frequently necessitates pitch alterations to retain the desired tonality or to ensure workable harmonic relations between the two parts. Ex. 11-45 shows negligible pitch alterations of the first version when it is inverted at the twelfth.

Ex. 11-45. Bach: *Art of the Fugue*, Fugue No. 9.

(Parts are omitted which do not participate in the inversion)

In textures of three or more voices, double counterpoint can be combined in two voices while additional "free" voices provide a harmonic foil that clarifies the intended harmonic background.

Ex. 11-46. Brahms: *Variations on a Theme by Haydn*, Variation No. 4.

The inverted texture may appear after an intervening section that separates it from its prototype, but it usually follows the statement of the original immediately, as in Ex. 11-47.

Ex. 11-47. Palestrina: Mass, Dies Sanctificatus, Agnus Dei, I.

Here the original top voice has been dropped a twelfth (compound fifth) while the middle voice (highest of the *inverted texture*) has been raised an octave.

The countersubject of the fugue from which the excerpts of Ex. 11-48 are taken is a clear example of invertible counterpoint. Bach uses it inverted at different interval relations during the course of the whole fugue.

Ex. 11-48. Bach: *Well-tempered Clavier*, Book II, Fugue No. 16.

Inversion at 12th (inner voices of texture omitted)

Also see measures 28-31 of the same fugue

Invertible counterpoint achieves thematic unity. Since the same patterns are involved within the prototype and its inversion, no variety of thematic materials arises unless accompanying parts (which do not participate in the inversion) are altered or replaced. It is only the change of vertical relationships and intervals (harmonic relation) that provides any sense of variety.

Exercises

For more detailed assignments see *Materials and Structure of Music II, Workbook*, Chapter 11.

1. From the literature, select a number of fugues for study. Pay particular attention to the following:
   a. Structure of the subject;
   b. Use of *tonal* or *real* answer and why;
   c. Order of voice entries in exposition and in subsequent expository sections;
   d. Tonality contrasts of subject entries in exposition.
2. With the same works selected for (1) above, study the following:
   a. Overall sectional divisions of the fugue; tonality contrasts;
   b. Developmental and contrapuntal devices applied in the various sections;
   c. Presence or absence of invertible counterpoint;
   d. Presence or absence of stretto; time gaps between voice entries in the stretti; tonal relations of voices.

3. Write a subject or select one from a fugue by one of the composers whose works have been discussed in the foregoing chapter. Add a contrapuntal accompaniment to this subject that is rhythmically complementary and that can be inverted with the subject at the octave. Write the original texture and then write the inverted version below. Follow the same procedure with a counterpoint that is invertible at the twelfth.

4. Write several subjects which seem appropriate for fugues. Write an exposition section for three voices using one of these subjects. (The exposition you write does not have to end with a logical sense of finality; it can merely break off after the third full statement of the subject.) Score the results for three instruments and perform.

5. Derive a brief fragment from the subject used for (4) above and write a two- or three-measure episode that is based on that fragment and that modulates from *tonic* to *relative major* or *minor*. Write another that modulates from tonic to a distant-related key.

6. Using one of the subjects written for (4), determine what kinds of development would work well and write several fragmentary textures based on just these developmental processes.

7. Combine some of the above results into a fugue by adding a logical concluding section.

8. Find examples of inverted textures in the inventions and fugues of Bach. Copy the original measures on manuscript paper and place its inversion directly below so that the relations of the two can be studied clearly.

12

SONATA-ALLEGRO FORM

The *sonata-allegro form*, although basically a three-section form, has its historical roots in the binary (two-section) form. For this reason let us summarize briefly the characteristics of the binary design.

The most obvious feature of this form is its division into two similar sections, the second of which is thematically identifiable with the first. The principal differences are tonal, not thematic. As a matter of fact, contrast *per se* is not characteristic of the binary design which features a basic "sameness" of texture and thematic substance and smooth modulation between closely-related keys.

The opening section of a binary form usually consists chiefly of a modulatory passage from the tonic key to a related tonal area, often the dominant or (when the tonic key is minor) to the relative major. The second section generally exhibits considerable tonal instability at the outset but reaches the tonic key at or near the end of the composition. The two sections then are parallel thematically, but each pursues a different tonal goal: the first *departs* from the tonic—the second *returns* to the tonic.

Each section is "open" tonally, since each begins and ends in a different key. The following diagram graphically illustrates this design:

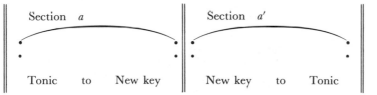

Section *a*	Section *a'*
Tonic to New key	New key to Tonic

Early in the eighteenth century isolated binary movements began to appear containing formal procedures not found in the traditional two-part Baroque dance form. The simplicity of these innovations in no way indicated the impact they were to have upon musical structure in the next several hundred years. To the binary pattern the following two elements were added:

1. A restatement of the opening thematic material near the end of the movement; and
2. The simultaneous arrival of the tonic key.

The coincidence of these two musical events (as in the pattern we call "rounded binary") produces an effect that is proportionately much greater than one might expect from such a simple device. First, the listener is immediately conscious of a third distinct section of the movement, short as this restatement may be. The significance of this exact or partial duplication of the opening musical material can hardly be overstressed. Also, the arrival of the tonic key at the restatement produces an effect of completion and emphasizes it as a structural point for the listener.

It is not far from this simple expansion of the binary design to the sonata-allegro form that we find in the symphony, quartet, and sonata movements of Haydn, Mozart, and their contemporaries. For the present we shall ignore the evolutionary phase of the sonata-allegro and concentrate on its features as they appeared in the second half of the eighteenth century.

The Classical Sonata-Allegro

The overwhelming preference of eighteenth-century composers for the sonata-allegro formal structure testifies eloquently to its psychological soundness and musical effectiveness. This pattern became virtually the inevitable choice for first movements (hence the term "first-movement form" used by many English writers) and was popular for all of the movements in a multi-movement work except when a type of dance movement—minuet or scherzo—was used (usually for a second or third movement). One of the most typical movement groupings is as follows:

Four-movement Symphony, Quartet, or Sonata			
First movement	Second movement	Third movement	Fourth movement
Rarely any but Sonata-allegro	Often S-A in a slower tempo; ternary or theme and variations are frequent alternatives	Minuet (or Scherzo) and Trio	Often S-A; rondo was the most common alternative

Sonata movements from the early eighteenth century to the present display uniformity in general outline—balanced, however, by a wealth of variety in detail. The result is a unique opportunity for the revelation of individual musical ideas within an established framework.

From the most cursory examination of any of the numerous eighteenth-century sonata-allegro movements, it is evident that the pattern outgrew many of its binary characteristics. In the mature compositions of Haydn and Mozart the dimensions of the sections clearly suggest a three-part division. If we compare this to its binary ancestor we see that the second section of the binary design is split into two sections. The start of the final section, of course, corresponds with the restatement of the opening theme and the return of the tonic key.

Another important change also took place: the "sameness" of the older binary design was replaced by two new trends—thematic contrast and development. As the sonata-allegro form evolved, these features became more distinct.

Let us now view sonata-allegro form from a new point of view—as an established three-section form. Each of the three sections has a distinct function to fulfill, contributing to the overall plan. The terminology associated with the following diagram has become a standard part of the musical vocabulary:

Exposition				Development	Recapitulation				Coda
Principal theme	Bridge	Subordinate theme	Closing theme	(sectional)	Principal theme	Bridge	Sub. th.	Cl. th.	(based on previous material)

Exposition

The *exposition* is a series of successive *statements* of the thematic materials which are frequently separated by transition or "bridge" passages (the two terms are synonymous). Most sonata movements feature themes that differ sharply from one another in contour, mood, or general melodic "personality." Although the exact number of themes is variable, the following pattern is the most common: the first or "principal" theme, followed by transitional material (sometimes with considerable thematic substance of its own), followed by a group of themes that often are separated by shorter bridge passages.

Some traditional names given to these themes include "subsidiary" or "subordinate" (used for the first theme in the second group of themes) and "closing" (the final theme of the exposition). This is often an unfortunate choice of terms, since the so-called "subordinate" theme may play a more prominent role than the first theme. Many writers prefer simply to number the themes.

Ex. 12-1 illustrates a typical set of themes appropriate to this form. The contrasts in melodic contour, dynamics, and even articulation emphasize the individuality of each. Not all sonata movements display so vivid a set of contrasting melodic materials.

Ex. 12-1. Beethoven: Piano Sonata in F Minor, Op. 2, No. 1.

Development

The function of the development is likewise indicated by its name, since the primary objective of this section is the "working out" (the development) of the musical ideas of the exposition, displaying them in dramatic juxtapositions, superpositions, etc. Development is a basic part of the process of spinning out musical materials over the framework of a large form; in the development section this process is a primary feature.

Development sections are generally more active (in many ways) than expository sections, and the sequence of musical events moves at a faster pace. Short, terse exclamations often replace the full, sonorous sentences of the exposition. Even the occasional sections of relative repose are short-lived and are often followed by a vigorous return to the previous activity.

Perhaps the most widely-used developmental technique is fragmentation—the breaking up of thematic material into short, incisive motives so that they can be recombined in new and interesting ways, often in a contrapuntal texture. Motives thus derived lend themselves well to sequence, imitative procedures, and all the other familiar methods of extending melodic material.

Not all themes are appropriate for such a process. Ex. 12-2, however, illustrates a theme perfectly suited to fragmentation, since it consists of extremely short, distinct motives. A short segment of the development of the same work, which follows, demonstrates how these motives are combined.

Ex. 12-2. Haydn: Symphony No. 104 (*London*), IV.

Important as it is, fragmentation is but one of a number of effective developmental procedures. The composer's strategy for his development section is greatly
influenced by the character of his themes: long, finely-spun lyrical themes do not
lend themselves to the type of development described above. In treating such
thematic material, composers have preferred to keep the theme more or less intact,
elaborating the melodic line with variations and/or exploring different tonal
regions.

And, in addition, fugato, textural change, dynamic contrast, change of register,
and a number of tonal procedures discussed in earlier chapters (particularly those
on motivic development and fugue) are frequently seen in development sections.

Composers have not followed any general pattern in choosing which themes they
will develop. In one composition each of the themes of the exposition will be
developed in turn; in another the composer will concentrate his entire attention
upon a single theme. Often a seemingly insignificant bridge theme will assume
greater significance in the development until it overshadows the remaining themes.

Many other features are characteristic of the development: the evasion of cadential action, changes in harmonic rhythm, new orchestral combinations, etc. All
of these support the primary role of the development—to serve as a foil for the
exposition and recapitulation, providing variety that helps to emphasize the unity
established by the two outer sections of the formal plan.

Preparing for the recapitulation is the remaining task of the development. Since
the type of preparation depends entirely on the individual composition, few
generalizations are possible about this section. Its role is primarily tonal and, as
such, will be discussed later in this chapter. Some elements, however, are helpful
in creating the anticipation of a significant new musical event: the use of pedal
point, a change in harmonic rhythm, increased rhythmic activity, typical cadential
approach procedures, etc. The development often ends with a strong cadence and
a complete cessation of motion—sometimes even a fermata—before plunging into
the recapitulation.

Recapitulation

The sonata-allegro design is completed by a restatement of the exposition that,
in many respects, exactly balances the earlier section, although it is never a literal
repeat. As regards thematic identification the recapitulation is much like the
exposition, generally displaying the same order of themes, similar transitional
material, similar dimensions, and a similar conclusion.

Psychologically the effect of the recapitulation is of relaxation after the intensity
and unsettling effect of the development. The restatement of the thematic materials
in their original forms aids in restoring the unity that is characteristic of this section.

Coda

A final section is often added to the recapitulation. The coda was relatively
infrequent and of small dimensions prior to Beethoven, but it subsequently began
to assume larger proportions. With Beethoven the coda often turns out to be a

second development section, balancing the first development in the overall formal design. The primary function of a coda, however, is to solidify the completeness of the movement. Often we find material of a fanfare nature at the conclusion of a coda or, as in many of Beethoven's codas, repeated tonic chords, heavily orchestrated and at a high dynamic level, emphasizing the finality of the cadence chord.

The Tonal Design

The tonal organization of the classical sonata-allegro form helps to shape the work as much as does the thematic organization. It is in the realm of tonal relationships that the family resemblances between binary and sonata-allegro are most apparent. The eighteenth-century composer's preference for the dominant and relative major keys in the latter portion of the exposition indicates this relationship to the older form. Let us view the sonata-allegro pattern once again, this time considering the key relationships and other tonal aspects of this form.

A fundamental characteristic of the exposition is a basic contrast between keys, the key of the opening tonic statement and that of the second group of themes. The principal theme generally remains in the tonic key. This is followed, however, by a transition, or bridge, passage that often grows out of the first theme. The tonal function of this passage is to effect a modulation from the tonic key to the key of the second group of themes. The principal theme group of a symphonic first movement appears in Ex. 12-3. The transition between principal and second theme groups demonstrates how thematic material from the first combines with a modulation to effect the transition.

Ex. 12-3. Mozart: Symphony No. 38 (Prague), K. 504, I (piano reduction).

Ex. 12-3 continued.

Several features typical of transition sections are evident in this example. In addition to the obvious modulatory progression (producing temporary tonal instability) and use of motives from the principal theme, we find increased rhythmic drive, important changes of texture, dynamic contrasts, changes of harmonic rhythm, and many of the same procedures we observed in our discussion of development sections. Sequential imitation is particularly prominent in this example.

As in Ex. 12-4, the second theme group of the exposition is often set off by a cadence from the bridge passage preceding it. This cadence is frequently a progressive cadence (to the dominant) or a terminal cadence in the new key. The beginning of this section is usually marked by some change of texture, dynamics, or register. In the Mozart symphony (Ex. 12-3) all of these occur as well as a two-measure interlude that anticipates the upbeat beginning of the subordinate theme.

As a general rule, the key of the second theme group is maintained until the end of the exposition. Viewing the exposition as a whole, the following tonal pattern is established:

Principal theme group — Transition   — Second theme group

stable tonality (tonic) — tonal instability — stable tonality (new key)
                              (modulatory)

This contrast between tonal stability and instability is as much a characteristic of sonata-allegro form as is the contrast in key.

Contrasting keys are further explored in the development section through the juxtaposition of several keys or tonal areas. In the music of the eighteenth century most of these keys are closely-related, although the gradual trend was toward the inclusion of more distant keys. The following diagram presents in comparative form two typical development sections and is clearly representative of the contrasting practices of the Classical (Haydn) and early Romantic (Schubert) composer.

Haydn: Symphony No. 102 in B-flat Major, I.

Keys: *c E-flat* (unstable) *A-flat c d* (unstable) *c C c* (unstable) dom. of *B-flat*

Duration
in
measures: 6   7   9   16 8 9   7   7 7 7   17   10

Schubert: Symphony No. 4 in C Minor (*Tragic*), I.

Keys: (unstable)   *b-flat*   *G-flat*   (unstable)

Duration in
measures: 4   23   8   4

In his tonal plan each of the above composers has included passages of unstable tonality: passages that are modulatory or that do not clearly suggest any single key. Schubert's choice of key features more distantly-related keys than those in the Haydn symphony. It is also noteworthy that Haydn employs a greater number of keys.

Preparation for and Beginning of the Recapitulation

The end of a development section must prepare for the return of the tonic key at the beginning of the recapitulation. This feeling of tonic expectancy can be produced by many means, and its advent may be either obvious or virtually imperceptible. Having avoided the tonic key during the development (so that the effect of its return will be fully realized), the composer's task is now to make its return compelling.

An obvious device for producing this anticipation is the highly elaborated dominant or dominant seventh over a sustained pedal point. In subtler form, however, this section may consist of a sequential treatment of one of the thematic ideas that eventually arrives at the appropriate key without advance warning.

Ex. 12-4 illustrates a relatively simple preparation for the recapitulation. The previous section of development comes to a clear half cadence in *g* minor (measure 3); in measure 4 the dominant of *B-flat* major is introduced and prolonged for the next seven measures. The resolution of this dominant signals the advent of the recapitulation.

Ex. 12-4. Mozart: Sonata in B-flat Major, K. 333, I.

A much different procedure occurs in Ex. 12-5, in which not the tonic key, *D* major, is implied, but rather its mediant, *f-sharp* minor. The final measures of this section preceding the recapitulation at measure 160 merely reiterate the dominant of *F-sharp*, ending with a long, sustained *C-sharp*. In a striking passage this tone becomes the leading tone of *D* major and resolves accordingly, thus accomplishing a return to the tonic key.

Ex. 12-5. Beethoven: Quartet in D Major, Op. 18, No. 3, I.

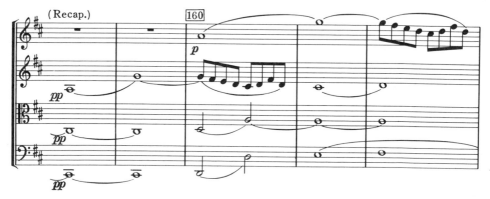

In summary of Classical-period development sections, we quote the entire development of a Mozart sonata as Ex. 12-6. This excerpt contains the typical contrast of tonal stability/instability, exploration of closely-related key areas, and a clear retransition to the tonic key—A major.

Ex. 12-6. Mozart: Sonata for Violin and Piano, K. 526, I.

Ex. 12-6 continued.

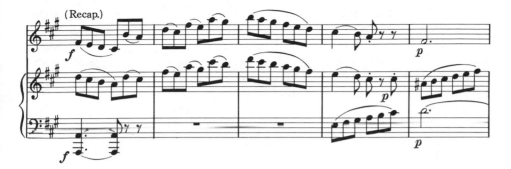

In the recapitulation this contrast of tonal relationships is abandoned, and tonal strategy is usually directed at reaffirming the tonic key as the goal of the whole movement. The key variety of the development gives way to unity of key in this section. The recapitulation's beginning usually parallels closely the beginning of the exposition, since both feature the tonic key.

However, the transition section brings a new problem: where the earlier transition modulated, the later transition's function is to avoid such a modulation so that the second theme group may remain in the tonic key. For this reason, it is precisely in this transition section that recapitulation differs the most from exposition.

Once the second theme group of the recapitulation is reached, the tonic key prevails: tonal unity has taken the place of tonal contrast. Instead of thematic variety and disintegration, we find thematic synthesis and order. Although some slight tonal diversion often occurs near the beginning of the coda, this is of passing significance and serves merely to delay the inevitable drive toward the final cadence. In the concluding sections anything out of the immediate "orbit" of the tonic key is a rarity.

Other Factors Influencing the Perception of Form

The sonata-allegro belongs to a small group of musical patterns featuring an "organic" process of growth and evolution that corresponds to the life process itself. Much of the effect of the form is produced by this gradually emerging, always changing "free-flow" of the musical elements in which the successive sections are closely related to their musical context.

It would be a mistake, however, to assume that this smooth organic evolution is the only goal of sonata-allegro form or the only effect sought by its composers. The perception of *distinct change*—either to a new section or a return to material (as in the recapitulation) suggesting an earlier section—is equally important in understanding musical form.

Composers have formulated many strategies for emphasizing the appearance of what seems to be new material: key change alone is one of the most effective means of delineating the start of a new section. But a host of other possibilities exists—contrast in thematic ideas, contrasting textures, change of register, dynamic change, contrast of timbre (orchestration)—all of these function in an effective way to lead the listener toward the perception of a new formal event.

Ex. 12-7 illustrates this point: using the motive that opens the composition, Brahms has employed several of the devices outlined in the above paragraph to mark the start of successive sections within the development. In contrast to development sections which are cast in a fluid, continuous stream of musical activity, this development clearly demarcates the beginning of each interior section by various tonal, dynamic, and textural means.

Ex. 12-7. Brahms: Quartet in C Minor, Op. 51, No. 1, opening motive.

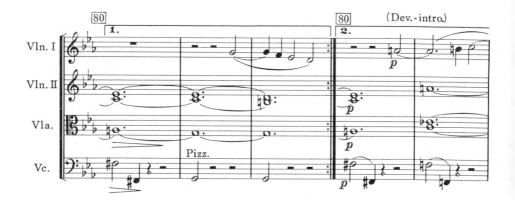

(Section 1)

95

110 (Section 2)

Ex. 12-7 continued.

(Preparation for Recap.)   Recapitulation through
                             augmentation

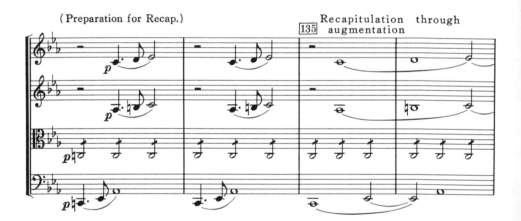

Using very simple means, Ex. 12-8 demonstrates the similar delineation of formal sections: both the individual phrases and the joint between recapitulation/coda are marked by contrasts of register, dynamics, and texture as well as by the use of contrasting material.

Ex. 12-8. Mozart: *Eine kleine Nachtmusik*, K. 525, I.

Ex. 12-8 continued.

135

The Flexibility of the Pattern

Even in the eighteenth century, movements that adhered to the *exact* sequence of events as outlined above were comparatively rare. The most accurate view of sonata-allegro form is as a *general* outline of relationships within which a large number of possible variants exist.

In one variant of sonata-allegro form the development section is missing or is reduced to relatively small dimensions. This reduction of one of the major sections has led to the name *sonatina* (literally a "little sonata") for this form.[1]

Ex. 12-9 illustrates a passage linking the exposition and recapitulation of a Beethoven sonata movement. Because of its brevity, it is difficult to justify the term *development* for this section. Furthermore, the section does not employ developmental procedures to any significant degree, and more than half of its fourteen measures are an obvious transition to the recapitulation.

Ex. 12-9. Beethoven: Sonata in G Major, Op. 49, No. 2, I.

---

[1] Actually this is not too happy a choice of words, since the majority of the Classical sonatinas for piano (written by composers such as Clementi, Kuhlau, etc.) do not bear out this characteristic. Their use of the diminutive term stems more from their brevity than from the absence of a development.

If we take some rare eighteenth-century examples of sonata-allegros as our guides, any or all of the themes in the exposition's second theme group appear to be dispensable. The closing theme of this group is sometimes lacking (the decision whether to call this last theme a "closing theme," "codetta," or "extension of the exposition" is often mere hairsplitting).

Some sonata-allegro movements display a monothematic exposition, avoiding completely any really new thematic material in the passages that follow the first theme. In such compositions the distinction between the sections of the exposition rests primarily upon the difference of keys or tonal areas, as well as textural, harmonic, and instrumental contrasts. The beginning of any subsequent section is unmistakably established by the change of key following the bridge passage. Ex. 12-10 and Ex. 12-11 illustrate this type of exposition in which the same theme serves to open both sections. In comparing the two examples, note the modifications of texture, orchestration, harmonic content (increased chromaticism), and cadence structure that Haydn introduces in the second appearance. The keys are in the conventional eighteenth-century tonic-dominant relationship.

Ex. 12-10. Haydn: Symphony No. 104, I (first section).

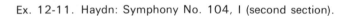

Ex. 12-11. Haydn: Symphony No. 104, I (second section).

Other common deviations from the standard sonata-allegro include the following:

1. A rearrangement of the order of themes in the recapitulation;
2. The omission of one or more themes in the recapitulation;
3. The use of key schemes that differ from conventionalized eighteenth-century practice;
4. The appearance of new thematic material in later sections; and
5. The incorporation of extensive developmental procedures into bridge passages, interior thematic sections, codas, or other formal locations.

The last of these procedures occurs in Ex. 12-12 and was a characteristic of eighteenth-century compositional technique. Short contrapuntal sections of this nature serve a dual purpose—as thematic development and also as interludes between strictly expository sections. In this example a five-voice fugato (based on the principal theme) separates the principal theme from the start of the bridge in the exposition. The contrapuntal texture of this passage contrasts abruptly with the homophonic sections surrounding it.

Ex. 12-12. Mozart: Symphony in C Major (*Jupiter*), K. 551, IV.

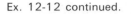

Ex. 12-12 continued.

An amazing developmental section is partially quoted in Ex. 12-13. This passage contains five distinct thematic fragments combined in a tight contrapuntal web.[2] Although several different minor keys are clearly suggested, no one key dominates the section. Only one of the five themes is derived from the exposition; the first violin line beginning in measure 204 duplicates, in a minor key, the second phrase of the principal theme.

---

[2] Since these thematic fragments subsequently appear in several different vertical arrangements, it is apparent that the passage contains quintuple invertible counterpoint.

Ex. 12-13. Brahms: Symphony No. 2, I (development).

Composers have chosen many different solutions to the problem posed by the bridge between theme groups I and II in the recapitulation: how to retain most of the transition material of the exposition and yet avoid the change to the dominant key. One simple solution can be seen in the first movements of Schubert's *Trout* Quintet and Symphony in *B*-flat. His procedure is to begin the recapitulation in the *subdominant* key; this makes it possible to retain the same bridge material as used in the exposition while modulating to the tonic for the final section (*exposition:* tonic to dominant; *recapitulation:* subdominant to tonic). Thus the recapitulation becomes a transposed exposition.

Concerto movements in modified sonata-allegro form reveal a characteristic approach to the initial statement of thematic material in the exposition. The standard pattern in the Classical concerto is a double exposition in which the themes are first stated by the orchestra in the tonic key, then restated by soloist and orchestra, this time proceeding to the conventional dominant or relative major key in the second theme group. (This procedure is clearly illustrated in the first movement of Beethoven's Piano Concerto No. 3, Op. 37, a work that could serve as a model of formal clarity in the concerto idiom.)

The Function of the Introduction

Many sonata-allegro movements contain no introductory material, beginning directly with the exposition. However, a slow introduction frequently precedes the main body of the movement, forming an effective contrast not only of tempo but often of dynamics, thematic content, mood, and texture.

The introduction can serve several purposes. In many symphonies the slow introduction is not related thematically to the ensuing *allegro*. One concept of the introduction in these compositions seems to be a stately "frontispiece" to the main portion of the movement. In all cases the introduction does not participate in the sonata-allegro pattern itself; it generally remains outside of the three-part pattern of exposition-development-recapitulation.

The function of the introduction in Ex. 12-14 is clear: the fragmentary violin figures serve as a gradual "winding up" of motion. One scale degree after another is added until the movement is put "in gear" and moves on its way.

Ex. 12-14. Beethoven: Symphony No. 1, IV.

Introductory material can assume a greater degree of unity with the remainder of the movement, however, when it shares the same thematic material. The common use of thematic material varies, of course, in degree; often the element in common is no more than a short motive that occurs both in the introduction and in the subsequent *allegro*. A more elaborate relationship is shown in Ex. 12-15. Here an entire passage from the introduction is transplanted into a new context and given new rhythmic and textural proportions. The material in the bracketed sections is similar melodically and harmonically.

Ex. 12-15. Brahms: Symphony No. 1, I (excerpts from introduction and *allegro*).

(Allegro)

Sonata-Allegro Form in Twentieth-Century Compositions

If we limited the use of the term "sonata-allegro" to those movements conforming totally to the conventional eighteenth-century mold, we would be forced to conclude that the form is no longer a viable mode of organization for contemporary composers. It is clear that sonata-allegro is one of the least significant structural frameworks for *avant-garde* composers. If we argue, as many theorists do, that the essence of sonata-allegro form lies in the interplay of related keys or tonalities on a framework of time, then it is clear that we are describing the form as it existed for the Classic and Romantic composer.

However, as we have seen, most musical formal patterns take on specific style conventions of their chronological period; the essence of their form lies not in any specific characteristic but in a much broader concept which applies equally to all works organized in this fashion. Thus, for example, the conventions of key relationships which were typical of an early phase of sonata-allegro form were already beginning to undergo expansion and eventual replacement in the early nineteenth century.

Stripped of these "nonessentials" the sonata pattern emerges as a starkly simple design of *exposition-development-recapitulation*. And as such, it can be shown that composers of the twentieth century have likewise found it an effective framework for their musical ideas.

Two compositions will be cited in the following discussion: Paul Hindemith's Piano Sonata No. 2, the first movement, and the final movement of Béla Bartók's Concerto for Orchestra. Both works should be studied from the score and represent the contemporary composer's reaction to both the basic underlying principle and the details of sonata-allegro form.

Hindemith's movement corresponds so closely to traditional sonata design that its link with earlier examples will be readily apparent. The sequence of musical events is as follows:

Exposition:

1. Statement of a theme in a clear, stable tonality (G is the tonal center).
2. Transition, unstable tonally.
3. A second theme, stable and in the tonality of F (minor is implied).

Development:

4. A development based upon a rhythmic ostinato, the transition material, and short scraps of the second theme; the tonality remains unstable throughout.

Recapitulation:

5. A restatement of the first theme in the original tonality, the ostinato continuing.
6. A short canonic passage replacing the original bridge passage (which was thoroughly explored in the development).
7. A restatement of the second theme—beginning in a new tonality but shortly returning to G.

Coda:

8. A short coda based upon the first theme, concluding in G.

The tonal organization of this movement warrants a closer look. It should first be observed that the relationship between tonalities is described in terms of the relationship between their *tonics*—a looser relationship than the interlocking web of related tones that we imply when we describe relationships between *keys*. Thus when we note that the first and second formal sections of Hindemith's exposition are in the tonalities of G and F respectively, we have still failed to relate their scales. However the basic point is clear: they establish the basic tonal contrast that is the hallmark of the sonata-allegro.

Secondly, tonal instability can now be realized through the *absence* of any tonality: passages that are (or seem to be) *atonal* can be used effectively to contrast with clearly tonal passages. In short, to the contemporary composer, tonal/atonal can take on a meaning similar to stable/unstable for his predecessors.

Examining the tonal structure of the entire movement, we can diagram its tonal plan as follows:

EXPOSITION   *DEVELOPMENT*   *RECAPITULATION*

G—unstable—f minor—unstable (F, B-flat, F-sharp, D, B, A)— G—unstable—c minor—G

These are obviously not the conventional tonal relationships of the eighteenth century or even of the late nineteenth century. The relationship of a second between first and second themes is perhaps the most apparent departure from the traditional mold. Despite this, however, the return to and emphasis of the main tonality in the recapitulation, the alternation of points of tonal activity and repose, as well as the thematic organization, reveal this movement's close allegiance to the bedrock of sonata-allegro form.

The examination of this movement provides us with some clues to the kinds of deviations we might expect to find in the twentieth-century sonata-allegro form. We should not expect to find tonality defined as in past centuries, nor should we expect to find the same near-related tonality schemes outlining main sections. We can expect to find, however, the relationships between thematic statements and their development, transition passages, alternation of tonal stability and instability, and the eventual return to the opening tonality that constitute the permanent features of this form.

A movement that displays a much freer approach to this pattern is the final movement of Béla Bartók's Concerto for Orchestra. In his program notes for this work, Bartók admitted that he structured it with the sonata-allegro design in mind. In many ways, however, it differs from the general outlines we have discussed thus far.

1. The recapitulation is much shorter than the exposition.
2. The second theme undergoes a significant transformation within the exposition and appears only in this latter form in the recapitulation.
3. Both the second and closing themes appear as *fugati* first in the exposition.
4. The closing material of the exposition is omitted in the recapitulation (although it figures prominently in the coda).

5. The movement begins and ends in *F*, yet *C-sharp/D-flat* appears to be the basic tonic of the exposition, while *F-sharp* is the tonic in the recapitulation.
6. The exposition contains much more contrast of tonality than would be present in classical examples of the form.
7. The development displays somewhat *less* contrast of tonal centers and tonal instability than one might expect.

Naturally one should not assume that all composers of the present day have discarded the exterior trappings of the sonata-allegro form they inherited. Composers who remained closer to the traditions of eighteenth- and nineteenth-century practice, such as Prokofiev, Shostakovitch, Sibelius, Vaughan Williams, and others, found in this form a source of formal strength and an appropriate vehicle for their thematic material. If there are any lessons to be learned from the past history of formal organization in music, one is that effective formal patterns do not die out but continue to coexist along with newer approaches. A subsequent chapter on twentieth-century formal procedures will explore the variety of experiments with formal structure in the music of this century.

Exercises

Additional materials and more detailed assignments are contained in *Materials and Structure of Music II, Workbook*, Chapter 12.

1. Analyze Ex. 12-2 for motive structure: identify the source of each motive used and the devices used to combine them (repetition, sequence, inversion, etc.).
2. Make a similar analysis of Ex. 12-3.
   a. Point out the source of each melodic idea in the transition.
   b. Analyze the modulation for type and exact location.
   c. Identify the various cadences occurring within this section.
   d. In what way is chromaticism a significant feature of this modulatory excerpt?
3. With recordings listen to the two movements outlined on page 286 and follow aurally the tonal plan of each development section. Does your aural experience substantiate the conclusions in the text?
4. Analyze the segments of Ex. 12-7 for key and identify each chromatic chord. Describe the texture at the beginning of each section in precise musical terms.
5. Name the various possible keys established in Ex. 12-6. Locate the areas of greatest tonal instability. Where does the retransition begin? Where does the recapitulation begin?
6. Listen to a recording of the first movement of Mozart's Symphony in *G* Minor, K. 550 and sketch out the main formal divisions. On repeated hearings determine the various developmental techniques used and as many of the key relationships as possible.
7. Listen to the following symphonic movements, noting in particular internal formal divisions and the means employed to mark the beginnings of main sections:
   a. Mozart: *Symphony in E-flat*, K. 543, I.
   b. Beethoven: *Symphony No. 2*, I.
   c. Brahms: *Symphony No. 3 in F*, I.
   d. Prokofiev: *Symphony No. 5 in B-flat*, I.

8. Contrast the introductions of the Mozart and Beethoven movements cited in 7a and 7b, noting key stability and changes of key, texture, and length of the sections.

9. Relate the thematic materials of Brahms' development section (7c) to the exposition.

10. Listen to the Piano Concerto in A Major (K. 488) by Mozart. Make a diagram of the main sections of the movement and compare to the structure of the E-flat Symphony, K. 543.

11. Listen to the opening movement of Bartók's Third Piano Concerto and determine the extent of its adherence to sonata-allegro design.

13

ENRICHED TONAL RESOURCES

In this chapter we shall deal with several bases for the expansion of harmonic resources and general weakening of tonality that occurred in the latter stages of the nineteenth century. Viewed from the standpoint of a contemporary musician, the breakdown of the major-minor system represents an important link in the chain of development of Western music.

Extended Tertian Chords;
Eleventh and Thirteenth Chords

When dealing with chords containing as many as five or six different pitches one must recognize the possibility of root ambiguity. It is possible to view chords such as (a) in different ways.

Ex. 13-1.

(a)

One possible interpretation of (a) would be as a tertian eleventh chord on *c* (ninth omitted), as it occurs in (b).

(b)

A second way of viewing this chord would be to regard it as a *nontertian* chord built in superposed fourths, as in (c). Our concern *here* is with chords that *clearly* exhibit a *tertian basis*.

(c)

The possibilities for constructing different types of tertian eleventh chords so exceed their use in actual practice that any comprehensive grouping of these chords would be unwarranted. Thirds of any size may be added to any of the numerous kinds of ninth chords we have seen, thereby producing eleventh chords of great variety. Play the chords in Ex. 13-2 on the piano and experiment with different spacings of each. All of these chords contain perfect elevenths. As we shall see, other elevenths, particularly augmented, outline the sonority.

Ex. 13-2. Eleventh chords.

As in the case of ninth chords, the seventh is generally present in four- (or more) voice arrangements of eleventh chords, whereas either the third, fifth, or ninth or any combination of two of these chord members may be absent. Eleventh chords generally occur in root position, and, as a little experimentation will show, they quickly lose their identity as tertian chords when the root occurs *above* the bass. These chords are more effective and also more frequent in five- or six-voice textures. *Major* thirds above the bass are most predictably omitted from the chord.[1] The root is the most frequently doubled tone.

A common feature of the voicing of these chords is that the eleventh is generally placed *above* the third of the chord when the latter is present. When the third is present in an eleventh chord containing a perfect eleventh, it will usually be a *minor* third. The most common and clearest arrangement of the chord has the chord members distributed as a series of superposed thirds, although other possibilities for arranging the chord with the root in the bass certainly exist.

Ex. 13-3. Ravel: *Le Tombeau de Couperin,* Rigaudon. Permission for reprint granted by Durand et Cie, Paris, copyright owners, and Elkan-Vogel Co., Inc., Philadelphia, agents.

$$C: \quad ii^9 \qquad ii^{11} \qquad V^{13} \qquad I$$

---

[1]This is probably due to the grating dissonance formed by the third with the eleventh of the chord.

The passage shown above consists of a ii_{11}—V_{13}—I cadence in C major, and the effect of the cadence, supported by root relations in fifths, is strong and direct. The supertonic eleventh on the second beat of measure 1 is a mmMp eleventh chord (consisting of a minor third, perfect fifth, minor seventh, major ninth, and perfect eleventh). The penultimate dominant chord contains both a perfect eleventh and major thirteenth above the root, and characteristically avoids the leading tone (major third of the chord). Chords such as these, and those in Ex. 13-4, may be regarded as combinations of two simpler chords combined through superposition, such as $\dfrac{ii}{V_7}$ or $\dfrac{IV}{V}$.

Ex. 13-4. Stravinsky: Octet for Winds. Copyright 1924 by Edition Russe de Musique; Renewed 1952. Copyright & Renewal assigned to Boosey & Hawkes, Inc. Revised Edition copyright 1952 by Boosey & Hawkes, Inc. Reprinted by permission.

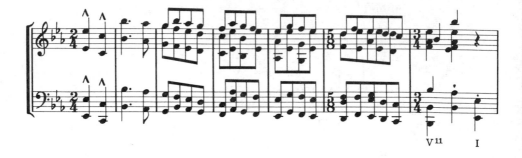

V^{11} I

We have seen that the distinction between chord tones and non-chord tones is often arbitrary. Eleventh chords frequently can be explained as much simpler chords embellished by prolonged or accented decorative pitches, usually in the form of 4-3 (11-10) suspensions or appoggiature. The pitches that occur on the second beat of measure 2 in Ex. 13-5 momentarily create a V_{11} chord in f minor. However, the eleventh (f) is nothing more than a rearticulated suspension (4-3), and the basic harmony is V_7.

Ex. 13-5. Hugo Wolf: Spanish Songbook, No. 26.

(V_{11})

Examples such as this suggest a basic question that is related to our aural experience of chords and melodic activity: At what point are decorative tones, because of prolonged duration, perceived as members of unstable chords? Although the answer to the question must always be based on a consideration of specific context, our decision can often be made on the basis of the prevailing harmonic rhythm. First, the *f'* in Ex. 13-5 that is recognized as a 4-3 suspension is heard as a decorative pitch for several reasons. The most obvious reason is its short duration, coupled with the fact that *e'* is heard as a point of relaxation. Second, a rate of two chord changes per measure has been established as the prevailing harmonic rhythm, and the acceptance of *f'* as a chord member would suggest a change that breaks the established pattern. Third, no change of root occurs with the movement from *f'* to *e'*, which further minimizes the effect of harmonic change.

Contrasting Ex. 13-5 with the revision shown in Ex. 13-6, one can see how *f'* might have been treated as the seventh of an eleventh chord on *g* (ii$_{11}$) through a change of root and an alteration of the prevailing harmonic rhythm.

Ex. 13-6. Ex. 13-5 rewritten.

In measure 3 of Ex. 13-7, *f* both creates an eleventh of a V$_{11}$ chord in *f* minor and acts as a leaning-tone embellishment of a V$_7$ chord. The entire passage prolongs dominant harmony; the function of the eleventh of the chord is essentially *melodic*. As anticipated, the resolution of the eleventh is by a step descent to *e* (4-3).

Ex. 13-7. Wolf: *Spanish Songbook,* No. 26.

Pitches of essentially melodic importance that have sufficient duration to be heard as chord members may be shown in analysis by placing parentheses around the numerical representative of the particular pitch, e.g., V ($^{11}_{7}$).

In the continuation of the same song by Wolf (shown in Ex. 13-8), other uses of embellishing eleventh chords may be found.

Ex. 13-8. Ibid.

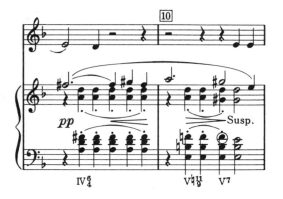

In Ex. 13-9, an eleventh above *F-sharp*, is heard for most of measure 3, and despite its treatment as a 4-3 suspension, *b* is established by its duration as a structural member of the prevailing harmony, V_{11} in *E*. The pitch of resolution of the eleventh, *a-sharp*, assumes the role of a passing tone in this context. In contrast to the preceding illustrations of embellishing elevenths, this chord (ii_{11}) represents an unusual use of the eleventh in that it is doubled and left by leap.

Ex. 13-9. Wagner: *Tristan und Isolde,* Prelude to Act I.

(E:) vii°$^{4}_{3}$ — I^6 vi^7 ii$^{11}_{7}$ — V^7

Augmented Eleventh Chords (+11)

The *augmented eleventh chord* is almost entirely a product of the current century, and it is associated chiefly with Impressionism and jazz. Like the diminished seventh and the Fr $^{+6}_{3}$ it contains two tritones (root—+11th and 3rd—7th). The effect of the chord is similar to the Fr $^{+6}_{3}$, but its tonal function differs from the Fr $^{+6}_{3}$. which is essentially a dominant embellishment. Contrast the two chords in Ex. 13-10.

Ex. 13-10. Fr $^{+6}_{3}$ and V^{+11}.

Fr^{+6} V^7 I   Fr^{+6} V$^{+11}_{7}$ I

The first chord, the Fr$^{+6}_{3}$, contains an augmented eleventh above the bass, as does the second, the V^{+11}, and both chords occur here in *G* major. However, the Fr $^{+6}_{3}$ precedes (or embellishes) the dominant and is built on *e-flat,* a half-step above its root. The second chord, the V^{+11}, *is* a dominant chord, and thus is more structural. A notational contrast between the two chords also exists, since the Fr $^{+6}_{3}$ contains an augmented sixth above the bass, whereas the other employs a minor seventh.

The similarity between the two chord types of different tonal function is more apparent in Ex. 13-10 than it would be if all members of the augmented eleventh chord were present, since the Fr $^{+6}_{3}$ is a four-note chord and the +11th (complete) is actually a six-note chord. Compare the two sonorities in Ex. 13-11.

Ex. 13-11. Fr$^{+4}_{3}$ and complete +11 chord (V^{+11}).

Fr $^{4}_{3}$ Complete V^{+11}
      $^{+}$ii Chord

The complete augmented eleventh chord consists of a major third (usually present), a perfect fifth, a minor seventh, a major ninth, and an augmented eleventh. The fifth and the ninth of the chord are frequently omitted.

One further point of contrast between the two chords should be noted: Whereas the +11 is obviously a tertian structure, the Fr^{+4}_{3} in its most characteristic arrangement (shown in Ex. 13-11) is less tertian because of the intervals present above the bass—M3, +4, and +6.

Augmented eleventh chords can be built on any scale degree. Their most common function, however, is that of dominant. Augmented eleventh chords are frequently built on the lowered (Neapolitan) second degree, functioning as embellishments of tonic. This latter function can be expressed in analysis as $^{\flat}II^{+11}$. Study Ex. 13-12 and note the tonal functions of the different augmented eleventh chords.

Ex. 13-12. Augmented eleventh chords embellishing diatonic chords in *C* major.

Augmented eleventh chords on *a* and *d*, the elevenths resolving as delayed appoggiature, are found in Ex. 13-13. The entire passage is tonally unstable, characteristic of the fact that these chords frequently occur in transitional sections, heralding a change of tonality or a new formal section. The tonal instability of such passages serves to heighten the expectancy of a clarification of tonality, while affording an excellent opportunity for the exploitation of chord color.

Ex. 13-13. Brahms: Symphony No. 3, II.

Mutations of the chord are common. These usually occur as a raised (major) seventh, raised (augmented) fifth, or an occasional raised or lowered ninth. In Ex. 13-14 two augmented eleventh chords built on the subdominant of *e* minor appear between articulations of the tonic triad.

Ex. 13-14. Ravel: *Le Tombeau de Couperin*, Forlane. Permission for reprint granted by Durand et Cie, Paris, copyright owners, and Elkan-Vogel Co., Inc., Philadelphia, agents.

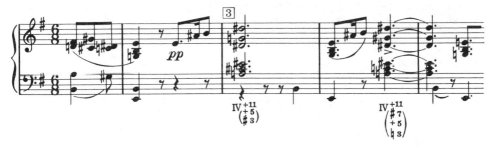

The chord in measure 3 contains a M3, +5, m7, and +11, while the syncopated restatement contains a m3, +5, M7, and +11. In both cases the augmented eleventh has been doubled, heightening the instability of the chord.

An idea of the variety of sonority obtainable through alterations of +11 chords can be gained by playing over the chords in Ex. 13-15, all of which contain the augmented eleventh interval.

Ex. 13-15. Alterations of the augmented eleventh chord.

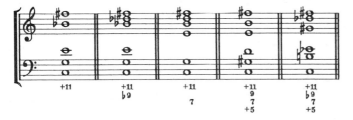

The augmented eleventh chord is similar in sound to a dominant seventh or ninth chord with *lowered* fifth. In contrast to the +11, whose eleventh generally resolves by step up or by remaining stationary, the lowered fifth of $V_{\flat 5}^{7}$ or $V_{\flat 5}^{9}$ invariably resolves by step down (to tonic). Compare the two chords and their resolutions in Ex. 13-16.

Ex. 13-16. Resolutions of $V_{\flat 5}^{7}$, $V_{\flat 5}^{9}$, and +11.

As shown in the last measure of Ex. 13-17, the ninth of the chord is sometimes notated enharmonically to emphasize the direction of its resolution. Parallel consecutive fifths normally occur in the resolution of complete augmented eleventh chords built on the half-step above the root of the chord of resolution. Locate the eleventh chords that occur in Ex. 13-17 and determine their tonal functions.

Ex. 13-17. Wolf: *Spanish Songbook*, No. 26.

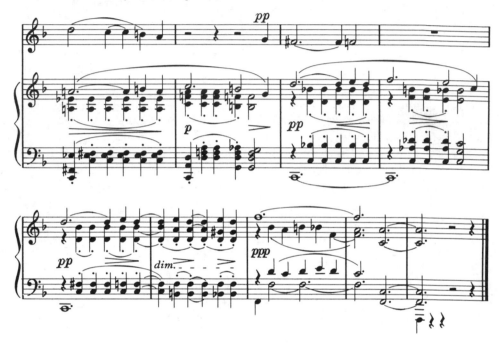

The Dominant Thirteenth Chord

Like seventh, ninth, and eleventh chords, thirteenth chords generally function as dominants, although they may be built on any scale degree. Dominant thirteenth chords (V^{13}) in *G* major and *C* are shown resolving to their respective tonics in Ex. 13-18.

Ex. 13-18. Schumann: *Phantasiestücke*, Op. 12, Fabel.

The V^{13} chord generally contains a major third (the fifth is generally omitted), a minor seventh, a major or minor ninth (often omitted), and a major or minor thirteenth above the root, depending upon the prevailing mode. All of the principles of resolution of the V^7 apply to the resolution of the V^{13} to tonic. The thirteenth itself has two common resolutions: by descending step to the fifth of the V^7, or by the descending leap of a major or minor third to the tonic.

Ex. 13-19. Resolutions of dominant thirteenth chords.

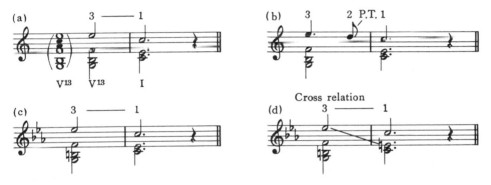

A typical V^{13} I cadential pattern is shown in Ex. 13-20. The thirteenth is resolved by a descending leap of a major third to tonic.

Ex. 13-20. Gounod: *Faust*, Act I.

This pattern, which appears in many nineteenth-century compositions, has become part of the stock in trade of contemporary American "pop tunes."

The V^{13} chord members are usually arranged so they clearly delineate the thirteenth. When the fifth is present it is spaced at least a ninth below the thirteenth, as in Ex. 13-21. No chord third occurs in this example.

Ex. 13-21. Kodaly: Cello Sonata, Op. 4, III. Copyright by Universal Editions. Reprinted with their permission.

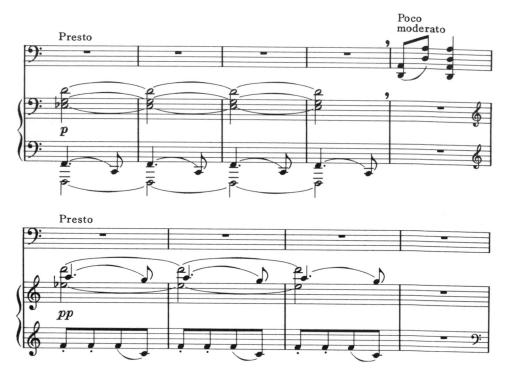

The resolution expectation created by the V^{13} is a product of two main factors: (1) the tritone usually found between the chord third and seventh (as in any V^7 chord), and (2) the two (interlocking) sevenths formed between the root and seventh and the seventh and thirteenth (above), as shown below:

It is the relationship of two interlocking sevenths, along with the tritone, that is consistently found in uses of the V^{13} chord. In Ex. 13-22 Schubert has used the 3-1 melodic pattern previously discussed. However, it is treated harmonically as part of the iii^6—i progression, and the interlocking sevenths are not present, nor is the tritone.

Ex. 13-22. Schubert: *Frühlingstraum*.

Contrast the harmonic treatment of 3-1 melodic patterns in Ex. 13-22 with Ex. 13-23. Note the interlocking sevenths in measure 1: *a—g* and *g—f*. The tritone occurs between *g* and *c-sharp*. The resultant chord is V^{13} in *d* minor. The *f* that occurs as the thirteenth of V^{13} in Ex. 13-22 is a pitch of essentially melodic importance. This is confirmed by the fact that it is not doubled in the piano accompaniment. The chord of the first measure might logically be indicated in analysis as a V$^{(13)}_7$, with the parentheses used to show an essentially *melodic* chord member.

Ex. 13-23. Schubert: *Ständchen*.

Ex. 13-24 is from the first of a series of eighteen piano pieces known as the *Davidsbundler*. This work contains considerable use of ninth, eleventh, and thirteenths in various keys.

Ex. 13-24. Schumann: *Davidsbundler*, No. 1.

Ex. 13-24 continued.

The chord that appears in Ex. 13-24 on the second beat of measure 14 is V^{13} in *a* minor. The different members of the chord, with the exception of the thirteenth itself, are spun out in an arpeggiated figuration. The chord is shown below in its fundamental position:

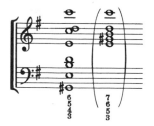

Since the third of the chord is actually the lowest note, as it occurs in the music, it must be described as a first inversion chord: $V^{6}_{4\ 3}$. Inversions of thirteenth chords, like those of ninth and eleventh chords, are infrequent, and rarely *heard* as inversions. Granting the possibility of *theoretical* inversions of thirteenth chords, we shall consider them as essentially root position sonorities.

Contrast earlier examples of V^{13} with those in Ex. 13-25.

Ex. 13-25. Dominant and secondary dominant thirteenths.

Implicit in the illustration of dominant thirteenth chords of Ex. 13-25 is the fact that the thirteenth chord affords numerous possibilities for mutation, some of which are shown in Ex. 13-26.

Ex. 13-26. Alterations of V^{13} in F.

Although virtually any chord member except the root may be mutated, the major third and minor seventh (which create a tritone) must be retained if the chord is to retain its dominant effect in a key.

Study and play through Ex. 13-27 in which the composer has merged interesting counterpoint and a full complement of seventh, ninth, eleventh, and thirteenth chords. Take into account the various melodic patterns that unify the excerpt.

Ex. 13-27. Rachmaninoff: Piano Prelude in E-flat.

Ex. 13-27 continued.

Nondominant Thirteenth Chords

Throughout much recent Western music different types of tertian chords occur which suggest the exploitation of harmonic color as an end in itself, or as a means of creating changing degrees of tension without reference to major-minor key relations. In Ex. 13-28 chords of the ninth and thirteenth in particular succeed each other, producing a stream of sonorities which are related more by identical quality and voice leading than by their function in a key.

Ex. 13-28. Ravel: *Le Gibet*. Permission for reprint granted by Durand et Cie., Paris, copyright owners, and Elkan-Vogel Co., Inc., Philadelphia, agents.

Uses of thirteenth chords such as those found in Ex. 13-28, where each chord corresponds to a dominant thirteenth in a key by reason of its notation but shows no relation to that key in its resolution, are common in some twentieth-century compositions. Nondominant thirteenth chords, such as those shown in Ex. 13-29, are virtually unused, as structural chords *in a key*, in music preceding the current era. They will be discussed in the closing chapters of this book.

Ex. 13-29. Nondominant thirteenth chords.

Chords such as these, all of which can be understood as tertian thirteenths, are often described as bichords or polychords (superpositions of simpler chords). They exist in great variety and have enjoyed quite a vogue in recent jazz.

Thirteenth chords of nondominant function, often called chords containing "added sixths," are frequently found built on tonic in contemporary works. Stravinsky's *Symphony in Three Movements* closes with the chord in Ex. 13-30, a tonic thirteenth chord (or tonic ninth with added sixth). The chord sounds quite stable in context, and the ninth and thirteenth (added sixth), spaced as they are, add a rich hue to the underlying triadic structure.

Ex. 13-30. Stravinsky: *Symphony in Three Movements*, III. Copyright 1946 by
          Schott & Co., Ltd., London. Reprinted by permission.

Incomplete eleventh and thirteenth chords on *B-flat* and *G* are found on the third and fourth beats of measure 1 in Ex. 13-31. Both chords produce a heightening of tension in the unfolding contrapuntal phrase in *A-flat*.

Ex. 13-31. Hindemith: *Ludus Tonalis*, Interludium. Copyright 1943 by Schott & Co.,
          Ltd., London. Reprinted by permission.

Variable Tonal Relations and Harmonic Ambiguity

Tonic, *A*, is almost entirely avoided as a melodically prominent pitch or chordroot throughout the first nineteen measures of the Chopin Mazurka seen in Ex. 13-32.

Ex. 13-32. Chopin: Mazurka, Op. 17, No. 4.

Some metric and intervallic prominence is given *A* in the bass at measure 13, but our anticipation of a tonic (*A* minor) triad here is thwarted by the incorporation of an appogiatura (*b*) and a progression of V_7 to iv_4^6. Strong confirmation of tonic is withheld until the terminal cadence at measure 20. We might conclude that the interaction between harmony and melody has achieved at least two important effects in the excerpt: (1) tonality has remained obscured for eighteen measures by avoiding assertions of the tonic chord, and (2) the tonality has been clarified (after eighteen measures) through an assertion of the tonic triad (preceded by its dominant) in a strong metric position.

Tonality is asserted through a traditional interplay of prominent tonic and dominant pitches in Ex. 13-33. However, Brahms has accompanied prominent assertions of the tonic note with chords other than tonic, or with inversions of the tonic triad. Not a single tonic chord in root position occurs after the first beat of measure 1; nor can we find a dominant-tonic progression after measure 2. The entire passage, however, operates within the broad tonal outlines of tonic-dominant. (Note the first and last chords of the excerpt.)

Ex. 13-33. Brahms: Symphony No. 1, II.

Brahms has extended the tonality-establishing pattern of tonic-dominant by using it as a tonal framework for a considerable span of music, rather than as a simple harmonic progression. Every occurrence of the dominant chord is lightened rhythmically by avoiding root position or strong beat placement.

Clear and emphatic assertions of tonic, dramatically reinforced by powerful rhythmic-dynamic force, occur in the opening of Beethoven's Third Symphony.

Ex. 13-34. Beethoven: Symphony No. 3, I.

After such a beginning it is improbable that any pitch other than *e-flat* will be perceived as tonic. Compare the Beethoven example with the Wagner excerpt of Ex. 13-35, and note the remarkably different expressions of tonic (*E-flat*) in the two works.

Ex. 13-35. Wagner: *Tristan und Isolde*, Act I.

One difference between the two is the fact that *e-flat* is never heard in a strong metric position accompanied by tonic harmony in Ex. 13-35. Wagner consistently evaded satisfying our "tonic expectations" by accompanying strong *melodic* assertions of tonic with *nontonic chords*; rhythm, melody, and harmony never really converge to confirm *E-flat*. This is particularly evident in measures 5, 10, and 15. At measure 15 the voice reaches a climactic strong beat on *e²-flat;* our expectation of the tonic triad is very strong, especially in view of the previous dominant emphasis. Tonic harmony, however, is withheld in favor of °7/V.

The point to remember from the preceding illustration is that a tonic may be implied melodically *even though the supporting chords fail to confirm it.*

Summing up the rhythmic considerations cited thus far we should note that:

1. Tonic and dominant chords in prominent positions, particularly terminal cadences, are important to the perception of tonality, even though they may be separated in time by considerable musical development.
2. The tonal weight of the tonic chord is lessened when it occurs in weak metric positions, especially when it is lightened by inversion.
3. Structural (basic) melodic pitches may affirm tonic even though the tonic chord itself is avoided in the accompanying chords.
4. Tonality is most clearly established by the agreement and coordinate activity of melody and rhythmically-stressed tonic chords.

Deceptive Harmonic Action

The deceptive cadence is one of the most significant manifestations of harmonic action leading to an expansion of the phrase. By avoiding the tonic chord, deceptive resolutions broaden the tonal scope of a phrase or section by postponing the harmonic confirmation of an expected tonic. For V—vi to be deceptive requires that tonic be previously established. In the progression of Ex. 13-36, *E-flat* rather than *G* might easily be perceived as tonic, for there has been no previous clear indication of tonic.

Ex. 13-36. Deceptive progression.

By way of contrast, *G* evolves as tonic in measures 1 and 2 of Ex. 13-37, and it is therefore easily understood as an evaded chord root at the close of the example. The result is a deceptive cadence.

Ex. 13-37. Deceptive cadence.

Reviewing various resolutions of a V^7 in G, we can see that the resolutions shown in Ex. 13-38 are typified by *step* root relations and voice-leading.

Ex. 13-38. Various resolutions of V^7 in G.

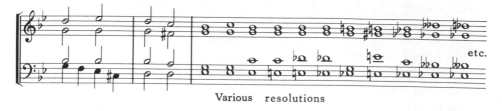

Various   resolutions

Three step resolutions appear in Ex. 13-39, each characterized by step motion in the bass.

Ex. 13-39. Franck: Prelude, Aria, and Finale.

In measure 5 of Ex. 13-40a, Wagner avoided the finality of a tonic resolution of $\dfrac{V_{9-(8)}}{A^\flat \text{ (pedal)}}$ — I through a deceptive resolution to an *f-flat* major triad.

Ex. 13-40a. Wagner: *Tristan und Isolde*.

Ex. 13-40a continued.

The *f-flat* chord at measure 5, then, acts as the launching point for sixteen measures of music which shift tonality continuously before *A-flat* is reaffirmed in measure 21. The same *f-flat* chord, so effectively used to evade tonic, is employed again at measure 20 as the Neapolitan of the dominant (N/V), and it is from this *f-flat* chord that Wagner moves to a reassertion of tonic. The entire excerpt might be reduced harmonically to the progression: I—V$_7$—^{b}VI—I—V$_7$ in *A-flat*. Since it is these chords which underline the tonality of the passage, the excerpt can be viewed tonally as an expansion of them. This will be more apparent from a study of the harmonic reduction in Ex. 13-40b.

Ex. 13-40b. Reduction of Ex. 13-40a.

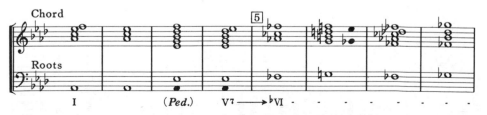

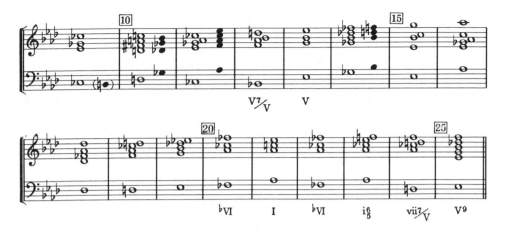

The structural importance of a deceptive resolution as a critical point in the form of the example above cannot be overstressed. We can summarize by pointing out that tonality has been virtually suspended for some fourteen measures (5-19) on the heels of a remarkably simple harmonic event.

Harmonic Sequences

Harmonic sequence is effected by the repetition of a chord pattern at different pitch levels. Harmonic sequence is perhaps most easily understood as a sequence of root relations, as seen in Ex. 13-41a and Ex. 13-41b.

Ex. 13-41a. Harmonic sequence.

Ex. 13-41b. Resulting root pattern.

Sequence has often been used to elaborate an essentially diatonic key scheme, acting as a vehicle for rich and varied chord patterns and sonorities, and frequently weakening or obscuring tonality altogether.

Any chord pattern may be the basis for a sequence, although root relations by fifths are most often found in music before the close of the nineteenth century. Triads, seventh chords, and more complex nontertian chords may be found in sequence, as well as patterns involving an alternation between stable and unstable sonorities.

Harmonic sequences, like melodic, represent one of the most common developmental techniques in music. Three statements of a sequence "at the third" (repetitions of an initial pattern at successive levels of a third below) constitute the opening of Ex. 13-42. The root pattern (lower stave) is changed at measure 4 with the reassertion of tonic. The *b-flat*, *g*, and *e-flat* chords (I, vi, and IV), form the harmonic centers of each unit of the sequence.

Ex. 13-42. Beethoven: Piano Sonata, Op. 106, Scherzo.

Sequential repetition commonly involves pitch relations that exceed those of the prevailing key, as can be seen in the preceding Beethoven excerpt. The *f-sharp*, introduced as the leading tone on a V/vi in *B-flat*, creates a momentary diversion from the main level of *B-flat*, reaffirmed at the phrase ending.

A considerably more unstable pattern of tonal digression may be found in the example that follows.

Ex. 13-43. Schubert: Sonata for Piano, Op. 53, Scherzo (Trio)

In this innovative passage the composer has juxtaposed four measure phrases in a sequence of third relations moving from *C* to *E-flat* to *G-flat* and returning via *B* minor and V of *C* to *C*. Passages such as this clearly reveal some of the means by which nineteenth-century composers such as Schubert enriched the harmonic spectrum of tonal music.

Compare the previous sequence with the one by Chopin that follows; the sequential units marked on the music consist entirely of root relations by *semitone*, almost completely wiping out, temporarily, any feeling for key. The tonic, *A-flat*, the point of departure of the sequence, is reinstituted at the close of the excerpt.

Ex. 13-44. Chopin: Impromptu in A-flat, Op. 29.

The first two measures of Ex. 13-45a form a *real* sequence, that is, a sequence produced by the exact duplication of a harmonic-melodic pattern on a different pitch level. An analysis of the root relations of the passage shows how the music unfolds in a drive to the cadence on *A* at measure 5.

Ex. 13-45a. Hindemith: Sonata for Flute and Piano, I. Copyright 1937 by
        B. Schott's Soehne, Mainz. Reprinted by permission.

Ex. 13-45b. Root analysis of Ex. 13-45a.

As in the preceding illustrations by Beethoven, Mozart, and Wagner, the composer has balanced the instability of a sequence with a reassertion of tonality, here achieved through a dominant-tonic cadence.

Sequences are often altered rhythmically or intervallically to avoid literal repetition and create variety. This generalization is more consistently applicable to twentieth-century works such as the one in Ex. 13-45a. It is not through any single process that the major-minor key system has been virtually superseded, but through the interaction of many tonal and formal processes.

Expanded Key Relations

Two related processes which constitute important bases for the enrichment and variability of tonality in nineteenth-century music are: (1) the use and exploration of very flexible key (or regional) relations, which in effect include all possibilities of key succession, and (2) a minimizing of the role of a principal tonic, or main key, by beginning and ending movements or large sections in different keys (open tonality), employing continuously changing keys, or avoiding prolonged emphasis on any one key.

Ex. 13-46 illustrates (1) above. The main key of the movement, which is actually an introductory adagio to the finale of a piano sonata, is *F*. However, a reading of the opening four measures shows that the movement clearly begins by centering pitch focus on *E* (the leading tone of *F*), rather than by affirming *F* major. Heard as part of the opening phrase, the beginning *F* major chord is treated as an +6 approach (note the "added" *d-sharp*) to an *E* major triad. And *E* (mutated to *e* minor) is confirmed as a temporary region by its dominant, *B*, in measure 4. This opening is clearly a departure from more traditional tonal schemes.

Ex. 13-46. Beethoven: Piano Sonata, Op. 53, Adagio.

A somewhat different process can be seen in Ex. 13-47. Like Ex. 13-46, the excerpt is part of an introduction to a finale, but its effect is far more than just an introduction.

Ex. 13-47. Beethoven: Piano Sonata, Op. 81a.

The main key is *c* minor, affirmed cadentially in measure 8. As in Ex. 13 46, the opening chord, *c* minor, is heard as part of a key (or region) other than tonic, in this case *g* minor. The second phrase, which is entirely in *c* minor, forms a sequence with the first. Following this brief establishment of *c*, eleven measures occur which prolong *g* minor, briefly touching *c* minor again in measure 20. The tonal-structural "meaning" of the tonic key in this movement has been so minimized that it is less than a predominant point of focus.

Key and Chord Relationships by Seconds and Thirds

Musicians often cite the late works of Beethoven as precedents for many of the tonal and formal events found in later music.

The unusual tonal successions found in Ex. 13-48 occur in the introduction of a Beethoven sonata movement, which is built out of three characteristic Baroque forms, *recitative, arioso,* and *fugue*. It seems paradoxical to find a merging of tonal and harmonic relationships which *forecast* the eventual dissolution of the major-minor key system in a composition based on forms which stem from an *earlier* historical period. An analysis of some of the most significant key relations of the work is shown below. The principal key is *A-flat*. (A more detailed study of the music is strongly recommended.)

Beethoven: Piano Sonata, Op. 110.
Principal Key Relations

1st Section (quasi recitative)	*2nd Section* (arioso dolente)
b-flat, E (a-flat implied)	a-flat
3rd Section (fugue)	*4th Section* (arioso dolente)
A-flat, c, D-flat, A-flat	g (closes in G major)
5th Section (fugue)	
G, g, trans-A-flat	

Ex. 13-48. Beethoven: Piano Sonata, Op. 110, Introduction.

Several pertinent observations can be made about the movement: (1) The eventual tonic, *A-flat,* is avoided at the outset of the work, which begins in *b-flat* minor. (Beethoven assigned the signature of five, not four, flats at the opening of the piece.) (2) The dominant *key* of *E-flat* is almost completely absent throughout the movement, and tonic-dominant key relations are consistently skirted in favor of more distant ones. (3) The keys of *A-flat* major and *a-flat* minor are placed in juxtaposition with keys a second removed, *g* minor, *G* major, and *b-flat* minor. Although both the subdominant and mediant keys are confirmed in the movement, the characteristic key relationship is that of a minor second, *A-flat—g.*

The overall effect of the Introduction (Ex. 13-48) is that of tonal elusiveness, because no key is stressed for an extended time. Furthermore, those chords which have the longest durations are unstable (Mm7th chords), while chords that create tonic feeling are of only one beat's duration or less. The duration of the tonic chord (X at measure 4) is equal to the briefest chord in the example. Again we find that tonal instability often corresponds to the duration and placement of tonality-establishing chords.

A subtle shift from *f-sharp* minor to *f* minor is followed by a solid assertion of *f* minor in measures 10–11 of Ex. 13-49.

Ex. 13-49. Schubert: *Schwanengesang.*

[V⁷

Ex. 13-49 continued.

This shift of a minor second is begun by chromatic inflections in measure 1(*c-natural* and *f-natural*) and later accomplished through an unusual chromatic third relation, *a* minor to *f* minor, in measures 4–5. Tonal instability prevails through measures 6 (last beat) and 7, in which there is a brief return to the level of *G-flat* (*F-sharp* enharmonic), which forms a Neapolitan relation with *f*. All voices resolve the conflict between *f* and *f-sharp* with the parallel descent to *f* in measure 8 and the subsequent V—i close.

Chords containing tritones, related by root movement in seconds and thirds, unfold all twelve tones of the chromatic scale in Ex. 13-49. Tonic is *a*. The chord succession at measure 3 consists of Mm7th chords on *b-flat, b*, and *a* and °7ths on *b-flat*. It would be hard to imagine a clearer illustration of tonal material including every chromatic pitch in a passage clearly oriented to *one* principal tonic. It is significant that the characteristic harmonic relationship of the *second* finds its precedent in the melodic semitone *a—b-flat* of measure 1. Dominant-tonic chord movement, as well as the dominant chord itself, is absent from the example.

Ex. 13-50a. Debussy: Prelude No. 4, Book I. Permission for reprint granted by
        Durand et Cie., Paris, copyright owners, and Elkan-Vogel Co., Inc.,
        Philadelphia, agents.

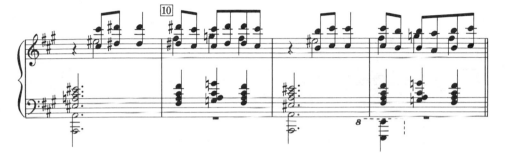

Ex. 13-50b. Root progression of Ex. 13-50a.

The importance of such an illustration is that tonal feeling has been established primarily through melodic repetition of *a* as a *pedal*, rather than through key-defining chord relations. One may conclude then that a feeling of tonality can persist despite the use of melodic and harmonic materials which are not aligned with any diatonic key. The use of such materials, however, sometimes weakens tonic perception, and factors which are essentially coloristic, e.g., sonority, spacing, and contrasts of dynamics, loom as important unifying elements. The structural importance of the semitone as a characteristic relation between tonic (*a*) and *b-flat* can be seen in the root pattern shown as Ex. 13-50b.

The overall movement of the passage is framed by motion from *a* to *f-sharp*. The tonic (*a*) is embellished by root movement up a second to *b-flat* while *f-sharp* is approached and embellished by movement up a third to *a*. A capsule reduction of the example is shown:

Ex. 13-50c. Reduction of Ex. 13-50a.

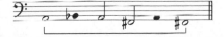

Chords Containing Tritones

We are familiar with many of the chord types which contain one or more tritones:

I. *One Tritone*
° triad
Mm 7th chord
ø 7th chord

II. *Two Tritones*
° 7th chord
Mmm 9th chord
Fr $^{+6}_{4\ 3}$ chord (and other +6ths)
+11th chord
V^{13}_{+11}

Ex. 13-51. Chords containing tritones.

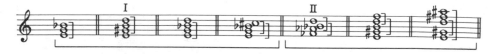

The use of many of these chords involves chromatic alteration. Chords containing tritones create harmonic tension and are frequently aligned with chromatic pitch relations, both harmonic and melodic. It is through a study of the juxtaposition of these chords that we can easily trace the enrichment of tonality and the increased harmonic color of much music of the nineteenth and twentieth centuries.

In Ex. 13-52, all but two of the twenty chords contain tritones (see measures 3 and 11), and the entire excerpt lacks strong key confirmation, despite references to *d* minor in measure 3 and a deceptive reference to *c-sharp* minor in measure 11. Sequence, motive repetition, and contrasts of register are important in the organization of this orchestral texture, but the continuously sustained harmonic tension of the music is the most obvious cause of its continuity.

Ex. 13-52. Wagner: *Tristan und Isolde*.

In contrast to the smoothly connected tritone chords in Ex. 13-52, the sonorities in Ex. 13-53, both juxtaposed and superposed, show very little contrapuntal relationship and involve a use of the tritone that is virtually "keyless" and essentially coloristic. Here the tritone's ambiguity is exploited both vertically and horizontally, as can be seen from the root relationship of the Mm7th on *a-flat* in measure 3 and the Mm seventh chord on *d* in measure 4. Tonality is achieved primarily through accented melodic repetitions of the tone *c*.

Ex. 13-53. Moussorgsky: *Boris Godunov*, Coronation Scene.

The instability of chords containing tritones is often accompanied by *melodic* tritones as well. Contrasted with the cadential tritone leaps that are supported by dominant seventh chords (which usually resolve to tonic in works of the Classical period), the tritones found in the group of melodic fragments under Ex. 13-54 reveal a more structural use of that melodic interval.

Ex. 13-54a. Debussy: *Afternoon of a Faun*.

Ex. 13-54b. Strauss: *Thus Spake Zarathustra*.

Ex. 13-54c. Sibelius: Third Symphony, I.

Ex. 13-54d. Schoenberg: *Moses and Aaron*, Act I, Scene 2. Reprinted by
        permission of Mrs. Gertrud Schoenberg, copyright owner.

The degree to which the tritone pervaded Western music toward the close of the nineteenth century as an element of harmonic color is unsurpassed in all previous music. The exposed tritone (between the outer voices) in measure 2 of Ex. 13-55, so strikingly set off by its metric placement and duration, occurs as an isolated, tension-producing interval, completely devoid of any particular diatonic harmonic function.

Ex. 13-55. Wolf (Romantic period): Italian Songbook Song.

The tritone is used as a characteristic interval in the four chords which accompany *c-sharp* in the cello in Ex. 13-55. Here it both prolongs tension and unifies the harmonic materials of the passage. The tritones of this excerpt deny allegiance to any key.

Ex. 13-56. Webern (twentieth century): Five Pieces for String Quartet, Op. 5.
ⓒ by Universal Editions. Used by their permission.

Contrapuntal Factors

As performers and listeners, we are often so diverted by the rich palette of chords with which composers such as Wagner and Strauss have assailed us that we overlook or minimize the importance of melodic relations in their music. Although contrapuntal forms such as the fugue and passacaglia occur rarely amid the abundant homophonic forms and textures typical of nineteenth-century composition, contrapuntal procedures are important to the organization of that music.

The passage in Ex. 13-57a is unfolded around movement from the dominant of *b-flat* minor to *b* (*-natural*) minor. Syncopated chords, broken by statements of the motive in the right hand, are accompanied by octave repetitions of a series of chords in the left hand which form an ascending chromatic line from *F* in measure 1 to *f* in measure 7. Although the effect is essentially chordal, the two textural levels can be seen as a simple two-voice frame.

Ex. 13-57a. Brahms: Rhapsody, Op. 79, No. 1.

Ex. 13-57a continued.

[V in B♭min]

Ex. 13-57b. Two-voice reduction of Ex. 13-57a.

[V B♭min]

[V B♭min]

Several contrapuntal factors contribute to the organization of the passage. The dissonances that occur in the second part of measure 1 (in the bass) and in the first part of measure 2 are passing tones. Further contrapuntal variety is created through a mixture of similar, parallel, oblique, and contrary motion, with contrary motion used to highlight the tonal and contoural climax of the excerpt in measures 7 and 8. A rhythmic intensification is reached in measure 8 with the introduction of stretto. Rhythmic independence between the two textural levels (as seen in the right- and left-hand parts) is consistently maintained through displacements of the right-hand chords in contrast with the on-the-beat sonorities of the left-hand part.

The organization of two chromatic lines which frame successions of unstable chords is often in contrary motion. The possibilities for "filling in" two outer parts, related by contrary motion, are numerous. In Ex. 13-58 two lines, both of which move consistently by step in contrary motion, have been filled in with a complement of chords, most of which contain tritones.

Ex. 13-58. Contrapuntally organized chord succession.

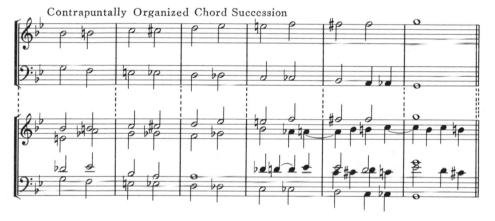

A linear harmonic design, similar to the one of Ex. 13-58, is the basis of measures 4–8 of Ex. 13-59.

Ex. 13-59. Wagner: *Tristan und Isolde*, II.

Ex. 13-59 continued.

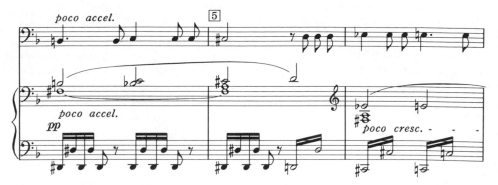

Out of context the chords in measures 4–8 of the Wagner excerpt would be virtually keyless. In other words, measures 4–8 are ambiguous tonally, and they prolong harmonic tension which has no real release in the passage. The excerpt is terminated by a progressive melodic cadence that suggests *d* minor.

Linear chords, underlined by an essentially diatonic chord pattern in *A-flat* major, result in the continuous tonal instability of Ex. 13-60. Play the reduction and the complete excerpt and compare the two.

Ex. 13-60a. Wagner: *Tristan und Isolde*, II.

Ex. 13-60a continued.

Ex. 13-60b. Harmonic reduction of Ex. 13-60a.

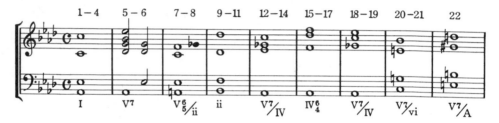

The role of the underlying harmonic movement (as exemplified in the reduction) is one of providing a solid foundation for the web of counterpoint and decorative chords that constitute the foreground of the passage.

In measures 2–4 of the same example continuous eighth-note motion is unfolded in the upper voice of the orchestral accompaniment. All of this activity, shown in Ex. 13-61, can be regarded as melodic elaboration of an *A-flat* triad, the tonic chord, resulting in an acknowledgement of the basic (melodic) pitches shown in the example.

Ex. 13-61. Wagner: *Tristan und Isolde*, II.

However, when this same voice is heard in relation to the three (upper) moving parts, we are aware of a tension and rhythm, established by the resulting linear chords, that produce the root pattern shown in Ex. 13-61 above the *A-flat* pedal in the bass.

Ex. 13-62a. Ibid., upper voices.

Ex. 13-62b. Ibid., root pattern of linear chords.

By isolating different levels of activity, as discussed above, we can better understand a complex musical foreground made up of counterpoint and chords, supported by a stable substructure.

Two opposite trends, one involving extended use of chromaticism, the other the use of modes other than major and minor, contributed to the ultimate dissolution of the major-minor system.

We should note, however, that just as the development of chromaticism can be observed in the music of particular composers such as Wagner and Franck, so the use of modality is a matter of a specific composer's style or is even characteristic of individual works, rather than a widespread trend. It is not until the twentieth century that the full weight of either of these two contradictory trends, the former of which is of more telling impact, is felt.

Modality

Few late nineteenth-century works are organized entirely on a modal basis. On the contrary, modality is limited mainly to thematic construction and cadence patterns. These allusions to modes involve the use of materials which imply certain modes rather than rigidly adhering to them. Compositions organized entirely within the scope of a single mode are practically nonexistent, with the exception of some chant melodies and folksongs.

The introduction of the late nineteenth-century song shown in Ex. 13-63 could be interpreted as Aeolian on *e*, closing with a Picardy third.

Ex. 13-63. Wolf: *Mörike*—Lied, No. 23.

The same pattern is repeated throughout the song on different tonal levels. It is shown in Ex. 13-64 as a Phrygian reference.

Ex. 13-64. Ibid.

Even in these basically diatonic modal references, some chromaticism is evident in the form of mutations of the mediant degree, such as the *g-sharp* in measure 2 of Ex. 13-64.

An allusion to the Phrygian mode is found in the unaccompanied first statement of the principal theme of the finale of Brahms' Third Symphony. The movement as a whole is clearly in *f* minor, (which can be seen from a study of the score) even though the theme itself apparently unfolds on *c* (the dominant of *f*). See Ex. 13-65.

Ex. 13-65. Brahms: Symphony No. 3, IV (first theme).

This same movement incorporates frequent Phrygian references, particularly in the form of Phrygian cadences on the dominant. Ex. 13-66 contains one of many Phrygian cadences from the movement.

Ex. 13-66. Ibid.

The characteristic scalar relationship of the Phrygian mode—the minor second that occurs above both tonic and dominant—is asserted several ways in the passage shown in Ex. 13-67 from the coda of the same movement.

Ex. 13-67. Ibid. (coda).

Minor seconds are an important organizing feature of the motive (♩ ♫ ♩) in this passage. They are heard in the bass in measures 2 and 4, and between the movement from *g* to *f-sharp* in measures 5 and 6. The horn line of measures 4–7 (augmentation of the initial motive) is comprised mainly of minor seconds, as is the bassoon passage in measures 6–8. A more subtle Phrygian relationship is found in the tonal relationship of *b-flat* and *b-natural* which frames the excerpt. The modulation to *b* minor is brought about through a Phrygian cadence, measures 5–6.

The inscription "In der Lydischen Tonart" ("In the Lydian Mode") appears as part of the title of the third movement of a string quartet by Beethoven. The closing section of this movement, which recapitulates the opening, ends on an *F* major triad. Not a single *b-flat* appears throughout the close of the movement. As shown in Ex. 13-68, this passage is tonally ambiguous. The first part of the excerpt hangs between the tonics of *C* and *F* (*C* major and *F* Lydian). *F* is stated cadentially.

Ex. 13-68. Beethoven: String Quartet, Op. 132, III (close).

The Lydian inflections of the Beethoven Quartet result from melodic and harmonic centering on *F* as the point of focus of a section whose scale consists of *f g a b c d e*. Beethoven has, in effect, created an ambiguous tonality, which unfolds by a series of shifts between an apparent tonic *C* and its subdominant, *f*. It is precisely this ambiguity that is heightened by the cadence on *f*.

As pointed out earlier in this chapter, entire movements or sections that adhere to a single diatonic scale without some use of chromatic inflection, mutation, or modulation are rare. A comparison of the Beethoven excerpt with Ex. 13-69 will illustrate this.

Ex. 13-69. Mussorgsky: *Boris Godunov*, III.

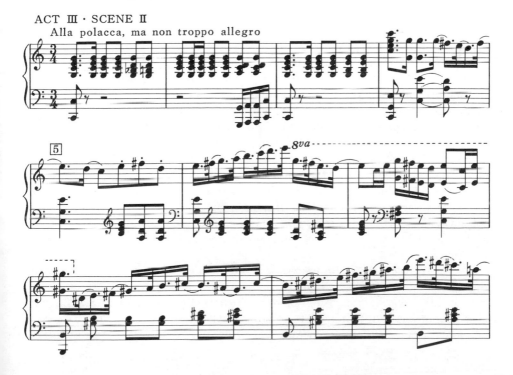

Ex. 13-69 continued.

The opening pitch material of the example comprises a Lydian mode on *C* (*c d e f-sharp g a b*). This Lydian mode is characterized by the repeated use of *f-sharp* melodically and harmonically, as seen in measures 4–7. Dominant-tonic root relations are nonexistent in the excerpt except for measures 1 and 13 (the close of the example). The composer has used a chord pattern that embodies the most characteristic element of the Lydian mode, the tritone. This chord pattern is heard for four measures, and it strongly establishes the tritone as a fundamental melodic component.

A change of tonality by third relationship is introduced at measure 8. The mode of this section employs a mutation between *a-sharp* (creating a Lydian inflection in *E*) and *a-natural* (which implies *E* major). The excerpt closes with a third-related shift to the principal tonality of *C*, which is confirmed by a V-I cadence. A clearer illustration of the use of modal references would be hard to find.

Tonal Regions

As we have seen in previous examples, we are often confronted with passages involving sudden departures from the principal key, which both weaken our perception of the principal tonic and imply a new tonic or key, without establishing a full-fledged modulation. The use of a secondary dominant similarly creates a momentary emphasis on a degree other than tonic without bringing about a modulation. In contrast to brief areas supported by secondary dominants, *tonal regions* are short passages, usually contained *within* a phrase or short section, which clearly imply a change of tonic, but which lack the confirmation identified with a modulation. Many of the brief shifts of tonic discussed earlier as transitory modulations can be described as tonal regions. In other words, *tonal region* denotes a short passage that both weakens the polarity of a previous tonic and creates an expectation of the affirmation of a new one, without sufficient subsequent emphasis to confirm our expectation. As we shall see, tonal regions vary in length, and their variability in this sense is often related to both tempo and harmonic rhythm.

The use of the term *region* implies that the "tonic" of the region is related to the *main* key somewhat as a secondary dominant is related to its "tonic." However, the secondary dominant is a single chord, which usually has a specific and predictable relationship to the chord that it precedes, whereas *tonal region* denotes a group of chords *of any function* that generally constitute more than a simple embellishing relationship to a single chord of resolution. For example, the region of V (in a given key) is a short passage which centers tonally on the dominant degree of the main key. Any scale degree or non-scale degree can act as "tonic" of a tonal region.

A series of brief regions succeed each other in Ex. 13-70. *D-flat, d, c,* and *g* occur within a section whose principal key is *B-flat* major. Each region employs two different chords, usually tonic and dominant. Passages such as this are susceptible to more than one analysis or interpretation. Looking at the passage as a whole, we may well regard the polarity of *B-flat* as strong enough to perceive the "tonic" of each region as a member of the *B-flat* tonality, embellished by a secondary dominant, or, as in measures 9–10, by a German augmented sixth chord. On the other hand, it is also possible to hear each two-measure unit, beginning with measure 7, in a different region of *B-flat* (as shown in the example). Either analysis should be based on the listener's *aural* experience of the passage, considering both possibilities.

Ex. 13-70. Schubert: *Sei mir gegrüsst.*

Ex. 13-70 continued.

In making an analysis, the point at which a tonal region begins is shown by: (1) indicating the "tonic" of the region; (2) showing the relation of "tonic" of the region to the principal key by a bracketed roman numeral; (3) indicating the function of those chords that occur in the region by roman numerals; and (4) indicating the return to the initial key.

In Ex. 13-71, a *c* minor triad, heard for four measures, is treated as a N/V in *e*. The striking relation of this chord to the prevailing key (*e*) weakens the "pull" of *e*, and *c* minor is heard as a point of focus for four measures, creating a tonal region of its own (vi$^{(b3)}$ in *e* minor). As examples such as this suggest, the "tonic" chords of regions are often *not* contained within the diatonic framework of the principal key. If the chord that occurs in measures 8–11 were a *C* major triad (VI in *e*), the relationship would not be as striking.

Ex. 13-71. Schubert: *Schwanengesang*, No. 5.

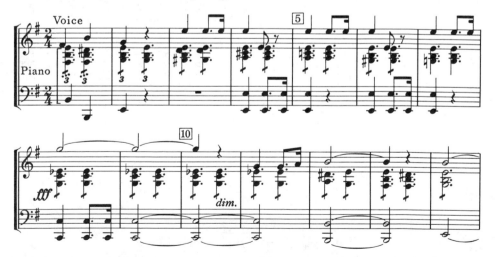

The *tonal region* often involves an excursion into a new key, emphasized cadentially. The subsequent phrase, however, reaffirms the *principal* key or begins in a new region; since the subsequent phrase does not reaffirm the key of the region, no modulation occurs.

In Ex. 13-72 the principal key of *C* major is established in measures 1–6. The next four measures involve movement to the region of *A* (both *a* minor and *A* major), with a rhythmically weak cadence in *A* in measure 12. The next phrase, however, returns directly to *C* major and thus does not confirm a modulation to *A*. Measures 8–12 are in the submediant region (VI) of *C* and, as can be seen from a study of the example, create considerable emphasis on a new tonal level.

Ex. 13-72. Brahms: Op. 119, No. 3.

In Ex. 13-72 the movement to *A* can be explained through a pivot[2] chord that is common to both *C* major and *a* minor. The *d* minor triad heard on the first beat of measure 8 operates as the pivot. The return to *C*, however, involves a *common tone e*, that is sustained through a change of harmony from vi$^6_5$ in *a* to I in *C*. The

---

[2]Where pivot chords occur between regions, or between regions and principal keys, they are indicated the same as in modulations.

change of key to *C* (actually reaffirmation of *C*) is less subtle than the previous shift to *a*, since no real pivot chord is heard.

A striking use of the *Neopolitan* region can be seen in Ex. 13-73.

Ex. 13-73. Beethoven: Piano Sonata, Op. 106, III.

In Ex. 13-74 only two chords are used to establish the region of ii (*f* minor) in *E-flat* major. However, *f* minor, set apart by cadences from the preceding and following phrases and lasting as long as the previous phrase (eight measures), is undoubtedly heard as an important key area. It would be possible to regard measures 9–16 as a self-contained modulation to *f* minor, but the reassertion of *E-flat* in the subsequent phrases minimizes its importance as a new key (*f* minor). Its role in the example as a whole is best explained as a tonal region. In a different tempo, however (the tempo here is fast), it might easily be explained as a modulation that occupies an entire phrase without confirmation in the next passage.

Ex. 13-74. Haydn: Piano Sonata in E-flat.

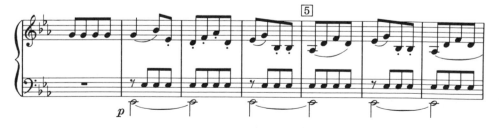

The reader may recall from earlier study of the invention and fugue that an interplay between the tonic key and the region of the dominant typifies many contrapuntal expositions. In Ex. 13-75, *b* minor, the dominant region of *e* minor, forms the tonal basis for the second statement of the subject.

Ex. 13-75. Bach: Three-part Invention in E Minor.

Some compositions consist almost entirely of successions of regions, with little use of prolonged tonalities. Regions are most easily perceived when they occur as brief departures from a clearly established tonic key that is immediately re-asserted on the heels of the region. Ex. 13-76 illustrates two successive regions, *C* major and *F-flat* major, interpolated between assertions of the main key of *A-flat*.

Ex. 13-76. Wolf: *Spanish Songbook II*, No. 2.

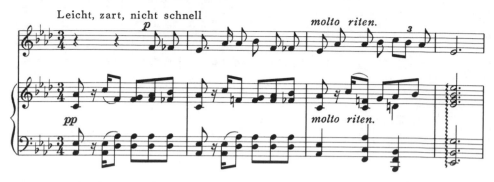

Ex. 13-77 contains several examples of melodic and harmonic activity which deny traditional tonal relationships. Unstable chords are used in such a way that key feeling is almost completely avoided, and melodic patterns and figurations weave a trail of melody which avoids clear tonality-defining cadences in favor of formal continuity.

Ex. 13-77. Debussy: *Afternoon of a Faun*, Prelude.

Exercises

Additional materials are contained in *Materials and Structure of Music II, Workbook*, Chapter 13.

1. Use examples from development sections of eighteenth- and nineteenth-century compositions for analysis and recognition of tonal regions.
2. Plan a short composition for piano around a series of regions, interpolated between clear assertions of a principal major or minor key.
3. Listen to a recording of the prelude to *The Afternoon of a Faun* by Debussy, and study the use of tonal regions as well as extended tertian chords therein.
4. Use examples from the works of the Russian nationalistic composers of the close of the nineteenth century for continued study of modality and modal reference.
5. Compose a vocalise which illustrates modality in the form of thematic construction, cadences, and mutation. Then add a suitable piano accompaniment.
6. Listen to the Prelude to Act I of *Tristan und Isolde*, by Wagner. Follow the music with a score, then answer the following questions:
   a. Describe the overall form of the movement in terms of large sections.
   b. What repetitive-developmental techniques constitute the melodic organization of the main voice(s)?
   c. Cite several contrapuntal techniques in the example.
   d. What are some of the most characteristic kinds of chords that occur?
   e. What expression would best describe cadence types in the movement?
   f. Make a harmonic reduction of a section of the movement.
   g. Cite several ways in which this movement represents an expansion of the tonal materials commonly found in composers such as Haydn and Mozart.
   h. In what way(s) are major and minor keys evident in this composition?

14

MELODY IN
TWENTIETH-CENTURY MUSIC

Twentieth-century music reflects new attitudes about sound resources and many new approaches to the organization of musical materials. Some of the changes in attitude appear to be radical departures from those of previous eras, particularly when dimensions other than pitch and rhythm are primary, rather than secondary, musical materials. It is not unusual to hear musical compositions in which sound properties such as loudness, color (timbre), and different types of articulation shape the musical substance. This inclusive attitude is also characterized by greater use of the sound potentials of traditional instruments, for example, the use of extremes of instrumental and vocal range, and percussive sounds produced by tapping, or other means, the body of the instrument. In addition there are electronic means of sound production available today that were not in existence before. The tape recorder makes it possible to manipulate traditional sounds through variability of speed: the result is new types of sounds. Further, electronic sound generators of various kinds make it possible to create sounds never heard before.

Along with the multiplicity of sound resources now available there are resultant changes in the organization of these materials. In this chapter we shall examine some of the materials and organizational features that distinguish twentieth-century melodies from their predecessors. We shall also point out organizational patterns that are clearly derivative.

Rhythmic Structure

The rhythmic structure of many melodies of this century represents a distinct departure from the preceding century. Generally speaking, rhythm is less closely aligned with meter now than in earlier periods. Even though meter signatures are usually retained, the notation frequently indicates only the rhythmic accents that shape a phrase or section.

Ex. 14-1 illustrates rhythmic patterns that do not consistently confirm the meter signature. In this melody a beam designates rhythmic grouping; the result is a change from predominant duple patterns to a grouping by three in measure 8. This hemiola is immediately apparent, as is the relation of the triple grouping to the closing of the phrase.

Ex. 14-1. Bartók: *Mikrokosmos*, Vol. VI, No. 146. Copyright 1940 by Hawkes & Son (London) Ltd. Renewed 1967. Reprinted by permission of Boosey & Hawkes, Inc.

Ties may be used within conventional meters to create asymmetrical structures. In Ex. 14-2 agogic accents are produced by ties. Because the first note is tied, a four-unit rhythmic group results, whereas the next rhythmic group contains three units. The stressed a^1-*flat* in measure 3 resembles a downbeat, as do both the e^2-*flat* in measure 5 and the *b-flat* in measure 7. Such aperiodic stresses lead to asymmetric rhythmic structures, traditionally not associated with compound meters.

Ex. 14-2. Carter: Piano Sonata, II. Copyright 1948, by Music Press, Inc.

Furthermore, the meter signatures of some works seem completely divorced from the rhythmic accents of passages within the compositions. When this is the case, the meter as indicated is merely a *notational* framework that has been retained, even though it may have little to do with the organization of the actual durations, as in Ex. 14-3.

Ex. 14-3. Schoenberg: Op. 10, IV. Reprinted with permission of Universal Edition (London and Vienna).

In some recent music successions of patterns consistently vary in length. In Ex. 14-4 the bar lines designate rhythmic accents. The 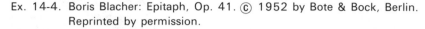 is constant throughout; therefore, the duration of each rhythmic unit and the time that elapses between each dynamic accent is variable except for the last four measures of the example.

Ex. 14-4. Boris Blacher: Epitaph, Op. 41. © 1952 by Bote & Bock, Berlin.
    Reprinted by permission.

The ♪ ♩ motive in Ex. 14-4 begins the structural groupings. Each of these groups elides with the next. The entire melody, then, consists of eight groupings, each of which has a different rhythmic structure. Since there is no clearly defined rhythmic cadence until the end of the excerpt, the rhythmic motive marks off each group by serving as its beginning. To cadence, periodic placement of accents, measures 22–25, and immediate repetition of the motive, measures 24–25, are brought into play.

Each of the rhythmic groupings in this example might have been designated by a different meter signature, $\frac{2}{4}$, $\frac{3}{8}$, $\frac{2}{4}$, $\frac{3}{8}$, $\frac{5}{8}$, etc. Such notational practice can be seen in Ex. 14-5. However, even with the use of changing meters, the composer also uses beaming to indicate rhythmic grouping. The rhythmic structure of both phrases is asymmetrical, as is the formal unit resulting from the combination of the two phrases.

Ex. 14-5. Stravinsky: Octet, I. Copyright 1924 by Edition Russe de Musique;
    Renewed 1952. Copyright & Renewal assigned to Boosey & Hawkes, Inc.
    Revised Edition copyright 1952 by Boosey & Hawkes, Inc. Reprinted
    by permission.

Certain successions of different meters have the effect of lengthening or shortening the metric pattern that has been established. The first two measures of Ex. 14-6 lead us to expect a continuation of the $\frac{3}{8}$ meter; suddenly, however, the truncated measure destroys this metric regularity.

Ex. 14-6. Bartók: Concerto for Orchestra, I. Copyright 1946 by Hawkes & Son (London) Ltd. Reprinted by permission of Boosey & Hawkes, Inc.

Complex (asymmetric) meters[1] also are common in recent music. Since they contain recurring accents, they are often similar to more simple meters. Ex. 14-7 has two meters; one is composite ($\frac{5}{8}$), the other is simple.

Ex. 14-7. Ravel: Quartet in F Major, IV.

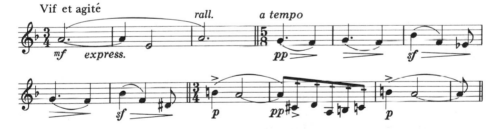

The rhythmic structure of each phrase becomes clear in retrospect, and is signaled by the departure from the $3+2$ patterning established at the beginning.

In Ex. 14-8 the composite meter is grouped in two ways, $4+3$ and $3+4$. In measures 1–2 and 3–4 the grouping is alternated so that the phrase structure is $4+3+3+4$, producing a type of rhythmic symmetry. Measures 5 and 6 contain the same arrangement, indicating that $4+3$ followed by $3+4$ can be regarded as symmetrical.

---

[1] Meters with groupings other than the simpler groupings of two, three, and four beats; e.g., groupings of 5, 7, or 11. Numerically, they are symmetric, but their interior arrangement reveals uneven groupings such as $2+3$, $3+2$, or $4+3$, etc. Any such measure grouping adheres to a *constant duration* at the sub-pulse level.

Ex. 14-8. Henri Dutilleux: Sonatine for Flute and Piano. By permission of
Alphonse Leduc & Co., 175 rue Saint-Honoré, Paris, Owners and
Publishers. Copyright 1946. Reprinted by permission.

Unequal divisions of a common meter are another possibility. For example,
$\frac{9}{8}$ meter is usually divided 3 + 3 + 3; it may also be divided 4 + 2 + 3. Even though
both types of divisions contain nine eighth notes in a measure, the latter is no
longer a compound meter; it is asymmetric.

Ex. 14-9. Bartók: *Mikrokosmos*, Vol. VI, No. 148. Copyright 1940 by Hawkes & Son
(London) Ltd. Renewed 1967. Reprinted by permission of Boosey &
Hawkes, Inc.

Rhythmic complexities multiply when there is a constant changing of sub-basic
durations, as in Ex. 14-10. Although the composer designates common meter
signatures, only in measures 3 and 5 are the beat patterns those ordinarily associated with these simple meters. Measures 1 and 3 illustrate a type of proportional

notation. Measure 1 contains seven ♪ rather than the customary six of a $\frac{3}{8}$ meter.
Measure 3 with its meter signature of $4/\frac{3}{2}$ illustrates a subtle proportional scheme;
the meter signature designates that the measure is to be performed as if four triplets
are occupying the time allotted to three triplets.

Ex. 14-10. Boulez: *Le marteau sans maître*, III.

Proportional rhythmic patterning may be notated in various fashions; another solution is shown in Ex. 14-11. The notes above the staff designate the duration of events (an event may contain only one element or several); thus, the first event has the duration of a quarter note and the second event is to occupy the amount of time equivalent to a double whole note plus an eighth (𝄼 ♪). The beams connecting the elements of the total event indicate relative velocity, as ⌊⌊⌊ = very fast; ⌊⟍⌋ = accelerando; and ⟍⌊⌋ = ritardando. In compositions of this type *chance* is an important musical factor.

Ex. 14-11. Stockhausen: *Klavierstück* X.

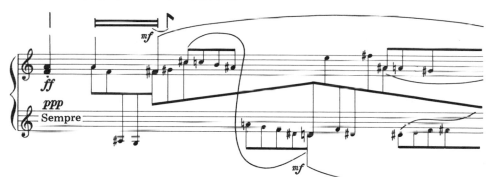

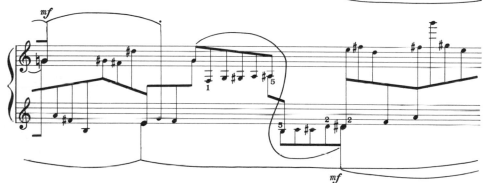

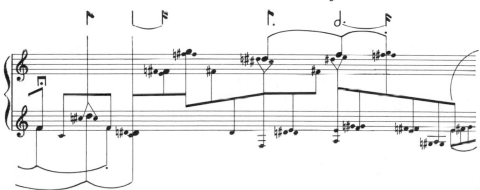

dicke Noten betont(pp, p oder mf)

Proportional organization may be notated by designating the duration of a passage in clock time. In Ex. 14-12 the passage is to last from 40 to 45 seconds. None of the note values (stemless note-heads with horizontal line and "eighth notes") has an "absolute" length. The duration of each note is approximated by the length of the horizontal line used, e.g., + ▬ as compared to + ▬▬▬.

Ex. 14-12. Ligeti: *Aventures*. Copyright © 1964 by Henry Litolff's Verlag. Reprint permission granted by C. F. Peters Corporation, 373 Park Avenue South, New York, N. Y. 10016

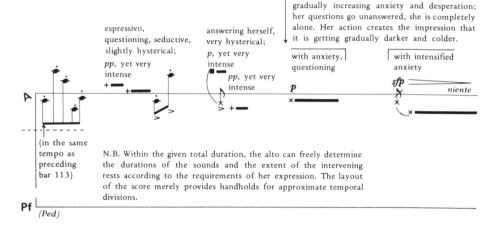

This brief survey of rhythmic practice in twentieth-century music is only indicative of some procedures. Never before in the history of music, except for some isolated experiments (latter part of fourteenth century), has so much interest been expended on the rhythm-duration dimension.

Pitch Organization

Until recently, the pitch materials of Western music consisted of simple diatonic patterns, or at the most, chromatically embellished patterns. While such patterns still form the basis of many recent melodies, other ways of organizing pitches, including sounds of indefinite pitch, also have been developed. In some compositions the pitch resources drawn upon are greater than in the past; in others, the pitch materials are fewer. In this section we shall discuss various types of organization representative of twentieth-century melody.

The natural minor scale basis of the melody of Ex. 14-13 does not distinguish it from many other melodies; however, the way the notes of the scale are used is distinctive. For example, the successive skips by fourths in measures 2 and 3 form a nontertian chordal outline rather than the major and minor triads that we associate with the natural minor. In addition, the subtonic degree is assigned considerable importance, as in measures 6, 7, and 8.

Ex. 14-13. Vaughan Williams: Symphony No. 5 in D Major, III. © 1946 by Oxford University Press, London. Reprinted by permission.

Sometimes melodic structure is even more closely aligned with pre-twentieth-century diatonic melodies than the Vaughan Williams excerpt. The scale basis of Ex. 14-14 is *G* Mixolydian. One chromatic tone, f^1-*sharp*, is used to embellish tonic in the final cadence. The subtonic only appears twice, and in each case it is also used as an embellishing tone. Limited range and a simple tonality frame also add to the illusion of something ancient.

Ex. 14-14. Henry Cowell: *Persian Set*, III. Copyright © 1957 by C. F. Peters Corporation, 373 Park Avenue South, New York, N. Y. 10016. Reprinted with permission of the copyright owner.

In part, the use of modal pitch resources in the present century is a reaction to the expectations associated with the leading tone in major and minor melodies. Modes which do not contain the leading tone create a contrast with this traditional melodic factor. The use of modal patterns in contemporary melody represents an awareness of the potentials of all types of diatonic pitch patterns.

In Ex. 14-15 segments of more than one scale are implied. The opening measures (1–6) indicate a pentatonic scale basis because only five notes appear. However, in measure 7 other tones are introduced that counteract the implication of a pentatonic scale.

Ex. 14-15. Bartók: String Quartet No. 3, Prima Parte. Copyright 1929 by Universal Edition; Renewed 1956. Copyright and Renewal assigned to Boosey & Hawkes, Inc., for the U.S.A. and to Universal Edition for all other countries of the world. Reprinted by permission.

By scanning the notes of this example we can find a twelve-note scale. However, an examination of the melody's tonality frame (Ex. 14-16) reveals that the chromatically notated tones do not have a consistent secondary or embellishing function as is found in some melodies of earlier periods. In melodies like that of Ex. 14-15, tonic is an important organizational factor, but the tonal significance of the tones other than tonic is not as easily determined.

Ex. 14-16. Tonality frame of Ex. 14-15.

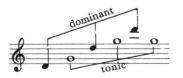

Various pitch configurations that have been used in the past point to the expansion of tonality. In many instances the tonic effect is created almost solely by duration or contextual position as a prominent pitch. In Ex. 14-17 the outlined augmented triads create tonal instability, as well as presenting each of the twelve notes without repeating any one. Consequently, any note could be used to create a tonic effect, provided that emphasis be given it by some means (such as duration).

Ex. 14-17. Liszt: *Faust* Symphony.

A similar situation prevails in Ex. 14-18. Here each four-measure phrase is clearly punctuated by an octave skip and a silent beat. Each of the cadence tones is a potential tonic. The patterns within the phrases do not point conclusively to a particular tone, nor is there a repetition of any cadence pitch. When the cadence pitches are reached, however, there is no doubt that they are momentary points of focus and repose. Melodic form is created by the similar intervallic relationships (the recurrent octaves) and the durational accents produced by a beat's rest after each cadence tone.

Ex. 14-18. Bartók: Suite, Op. 14, II. Copyright 1918 by Universal Edition; Renewed 1945. Copyright & Renewal assigned to Boosey & Hawkes, Inc., for the U.S.A. and to Universal Edition for all other countries of the world. Reprinted by permission.

Tonic (*C*) receives little emphasis in Ex. 14-19. Tonal unity results mainly from the repetition of simple chordal and rhythmic patterns rather than from continued affirmation of a tonic.

Ex. 14-19. Hindemith: *Philharmonic* Concerto. ⓒ 1932 by B. Schott's Soehne, Mainz. Renewed 1960. Reprinted by permission.

Ex. 14-20 illustrates tonality expanded through chromaticism. Here duration gives importance to some pitches, as, b^2, a^2, d^3, f^2, etc. Ultimately, f^1 is most important because of its location at the end of the excerpt, because f^2 appeared as an important pitch, and because it completes the overall descending pitch motion.

Ex. 14-20. Bartók: Sonata for Two Pianos and Percussion, II. Copyright 1942 by Hawkes & Son (London) Ltd. Renewed 1969. Reprinted by permission of Boosey & Hawkes, Inc.

Confirmation of a tonic and its consequent role as a unifying factor is a prominent feature in many compositions of this century. As we have seen, the tonic effect is produced mainly by contextual and durational factors, which in reality link it to earlier practices.

Atonal and Serial Melody

Tonality is not always a factor in music. Other means of organizing pitched sounds dominate a great amount of music composed since the turn of the century.

A basic premise for any atonal melody is that no single pitch or interval is more important tonally than any other pitch or interval. Such a premise presupposes that a hierarchy of tonal relations is to be avoided. It is apparent, then, that other means for organizing the available pitches are used.

The melodic line shown in Ex. 14-21 has a simple motivic structure, but its pitch and interval organization does not set up a focal point. It is intervallic constancy (plus rhythmic repetition) that provides melodic unity. This group of three notes is a reference set, and although this set performs an important unifying role, it does not take on the function of a tonic.

Ex. 14-21. Webern: Movements for String Quartet, Op. 5, I.

In Ex. 14-21 the referential set occurs at three different pitch levels: measure 1, ; measure 3, ; and measure 5,

. As important as this unifying set is the recurrence of rhythmic figures and the step progression, by half-steps, from a^2 to f^2 in measures 4–6.

Repetition of note groups also is a prominent organizational factor in the next excerpt, but this repetition does not lead to the creation of a tonic or a hierarchy of pitch relations. The overall pitch motion initially is to move in a gradual, additive process from f^1 to f^2-sharp, followed by three statements of a motive having f^2-sharp as its beginning pitch. Even though the third motivic idea ends with the same pitch, enharmonically, as the second motive, pitch focus is not created.

Ex. 14-22. Lutoslawski: *Paroles Tisseés*. Reprinted by permission of J & W Chester Limited. © Copyright, 1967, Edition Wilhelm Hansen, London, E.C.I.

Ex. 14-22 continued.

un chat qui s'é - mer - veil - le   le cri   du ba - te - leur   le

cri   du ba - te - leur   le   cri du ba - te - leur.

Atonal melodies as the two illustrated above may have referential collections of pitches. These referential sets are generally unordered, i.e., the elements of the set may appear in any order during the course of a composition. Thus, if *0 3 4* represents the elements of a set, successive statements may occur as *0 4 3, 3 4 0, 4 3 0, 3 0 4,* or *4 0 3.*

In serialized compositions the elements of a set are ordered precompositionally. These elements may be pitches, durations, types of attack, degrees of loudness, etc. Very often only one dimension is serialized. If a composer elects to serialize the pitch dimension, he orders the pitches in any succession that does not repeat any note. In spinning out the composition, the set or row can be repeated, broken into segments, transposed, turned upside down, stated backwards, and upside down and backwards simultaneously. A melody having as its pitch basis a tone row is known as a *serialized melody.*

A tone row or set may contain the twelve notes of the chromatic scale or less than twelve notes. The melodic excerpt of Ex. 14-23 is based on the twelve-tone arrangement shown above it. This row establishes the order in which the tones are presented. In many works the total horizontal and simultaneous pitch relationships are predetermined by the tone row. A row is an abstract set of relationships to which durations and registers are applied, thereby producing melodic patterns. The set is *abstract*, for it represents only note names or pitch classes[2] without consideration for octave register or, as we shall see, enharmonic spelling.

Ex. 14-23. Schoenberg: String Quartet, Op. 37, I. Reprinted by permission of the copyright owner, G. Schirmer, Inc.

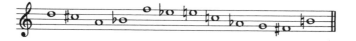

Allegro molto; energico

---

[2] Pitch class designates all pitches having the same name; thus, C, c^1, c^2, c^3, etc. all belong to the pitch class (P.C. or p.c.) C.

Another twelve-note series is given in Ex. 14-24, together with a melody derived from it. As in the Schoenberg excerpt, the predetermined arrangement specifies note succession. The coherence of the melodic pattern that results is produced from the limited variety of durations, the symmetrical contour, and the constant motion by wide leaps.

Ex. 14-24. Webern: Symphony, Op. 21, II. ©️ by Universal Edition; Reprinted with their permission.

Various sets of pitches derived from a pitch row can be used to achieve different orders of relationships. The original series can be *inverted, reversed,* or this reversed form can be inverted. Furthermore, each form of the series may be transposed to begin on any note name.

The illustration of Ex. 14-25 gives the *inversion* (I), the *retrograde* (R), and the *retrograde inversion* (RI) of the series in Ex. 14-23. Together with transpositions of each, these arrangements, or other arrangements of the twelve notes, can form the basis of a *serial composition,* all successions and combinations of pitches directly or indirectly derived from the original matrix, the "O" ($=original$) or P ($=prime$)[3] form of the row.

Ex. 14-25. I, R, and RI forms of Ex. 14-23.

Inversion (I_0)

Retrograde (R_0)

Retrograde Inversion (RI_0)

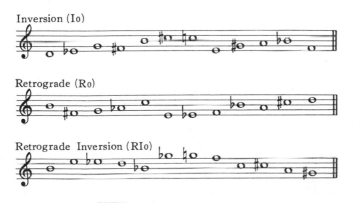

[3]The *prime* (untransposed) form of the row is often designated with the integer, zero (0); thus I_0 is the inverted form of the row beginning on the prime note. I_1 would be I transposed up one half-step.

The second phrase of Ex. 14-26 is based on a transposed *inversion* of the pitch series of the first. This brings into play a pitch order that would not be possible if a transposition were not used. For example, if only the original form of the row appeared, *g-flat* would be preceded only by *d-sharp* and followed by *f*; in the transposed inverted form *f-sharp/g-flat* occupies a different point in the series: it is preceded by *b*, and succeeded by *b-flat*. Note the preservation, however, of the interval successions of the original row.

Ex. 14-26. Dallapiccola: *Cinque Canti*, "Aspettiamo la stella mattutina." ©️ 1957
    by Edizioni Suvini Zerboni, Milan.

A melodic line based on a row of less than twelve pitches is vividly demonstrated by Ex. 14-27. In this instance the various forms of a five-tone row provide the pitch and intervallic basis. Since the canonic subject and the five-tone row are the same, the row has a motivic (structural) function.

Ex. 14-27. Stravinsky: *In Memoriam Dylan Thomas*, Dirge-Canon. Copyright 1954 by
    Boosey & Hawkes, Inc., New York. Reprinted by permission.

The three derived forms of the row offset any possibility of the original becoming well established as a recognizable melodic pattern. Duration and high-low positions of a tone may make it temporarily more significant. As a result, duration, register, and interval succession become the principal guideposts of delineation, rather than relationship to a tonal center.

In Ex. 14-23, Ex. 14-24, and Ex. 14-26 each tone has potentially equal significance as an abstract entity; however, significance of individual tones can be determined only in context, not by the abstraction that is represented by a serial order. Since there are numerous ways in which twelve different notes can be arranged, and since the tones can have equal tonal significance, the chromatic scale as such has no innate structural meaning for serially organized melodies.

Other Organizational Factors

Many contemporary melodic contours are remarkable because of their wide range, contrasting with the large body of earlier melodies that rarely exceed the range of an octave or a twelfth. The use of a wide range gives added prominence to high and low points, accentuating contour patterns that are, generally speaking, variations of common shapes. The extended arch of Ex. 14-28 distinguishes this line from similarly contoured melodies by separating widely the high and low points.

Ex. 14-28. Carter: Piano Sonata, I. Used with the permission of the copyright owner, Mercury Music Corporation.

In sharp contrast to this is the contour that results from a limited number of tones moving in a tightly restricted range. The pitch activity in such melodies often consists of motion by seconds, as in Ex. 14-29. Here the outer pitch limit is a perfect fifth filled in with combinations of only three intervals, the minor second, major third, and minor third. The resulting contour is a series of miniature arches, each of which is a variant of the one preceding it.

Ex. 14-29. Bartók: Music for Strings, Percussion and Celeste, I. Copyright 1937 by Universal Edition; Renewed 1964. Copyright & Renewal assigned to Boosey & Hawkes, Inc., for U.S.A. and to Universal Edition for all other countries of the world. Reprinted by permission.

Some melodic contours of the twentieth century are distinctive because the high and low points are punctuated by disjunct pitch activity producing a "jagged" design. High and low pitch relationships between phrases may form an extended arch; in a single phrase or parts of a phrase, however, "jaggedness" may be the primary contour factor.

Ex. 14-30. Schoenberg: Serenade, Op. 24, IV. ©️ Copyright 1924 & 1952 by Wilhelm Hansen, Copenhagen. By permission of the Publishers.

Ex. 14-28, Ex. 14-29, and Ex. 14-30 are samples of the kinds of contours encountered in contemporary melodies. As is evident, this aspect of melody is a variant of earlier melodic designs.

Chordal outlining also is an organizational factor in many twentieth-century melodies. Many chords used in contemporary music are multi-note structures such as ninth chords, eleventh chords, and quartal chords.

Various chord types are outlined in the melody of Ex. 14-31. The prolonged ascending line suggests seventh and ninth chords as well as a minor and a diminished triad. Beginning in measure 11 the characteristic intervals, sixths and sevenths, are used sequentially. In measures 14–26 the outlining of quartal chords is an important factor.

Ex. 14-31. Barber: Concerto for Violin, I. Reprinted by permission of the copyright owner, G. Schirmer, Inc.

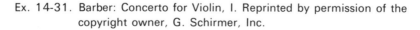

The second phrase of Ex. 14-32 illustrates melodic outlining of a quintal chord. Throughout this example the fifth and its inversion (the fourth) constitute the characteristic intervallic content.

Ex. 14-32. Hindemith: Second Sonata for Piano, III. © 1936 by B. Schott's Soehne, Mainz. Renewed 1963. Used by permission.

The pitch materials of contemporary melody are more diverse than those used in previous periods. General principles of pitch organization—contour, durational emphasis, metric position, relation to tonic, etc.—still form the basis of coherent melodies. Because of the changing role of tonality, however, structural unity often results from factors other than pitch resources.

Exercises

For more detailed assignments see *Materials and Structure of Music II*, *Workbook*, Chapter 14.

1. Write several melodies using a modal scale basis, but in which nontertian chord outlining plays a predominant role.

2. Create several motives that will become the primary unifying factor of one or more melodies that you write. Organize your melodies so that little or no implication of major or minor keys is present.

3. Devise a tone row and use it as the basis for an instrumental melody.

4. Analyze several contemporary melodies assigned by your teacher. Follow the analytic procedures that he outlines. Select the melodic lines from such works as:

   Bartók: *Concerto for Orchestra; Second String Quartet*
   Boulez: *Structures*
   Copland: *Piano Variations*
   Dallapiccola: *Notebook for Anna Libera*
   Hindemith: *String Quartet* No. 2
   Kagel: *Sonant*
   Ligeti: *Aventures*
   Penderecki: *Anaklasis*
   Webern: *Cantata No. 2*, Op. 31.

5. Write a melody in which new tonics appear in close succession, but that ends and begins with the same tonic. Use an uneven grouping of a compound meter such as $\frac{9}{8}$ as the metric basis.

6. Make a plan for an extended melody for oboe (approximately thirty measures long). Sketch in cadences, tonal centers, unifying rhythmic patterns, unifying pitch patterns, etc.

15

HARMONY IN
TWENTIETH-CENTURY MUSIC

The harmonic material of contemporary music includes all sonorities of the past, as well as some which have come into use primarily in the twentieth century. The most apparent link with the past in some music is the incorporation of simple triads and seventh chords. Other tertian chords, such as ninths, elevenths, and thirteenths, also are part of the available harmonic fabric of twentieth-century music.

We first shall discuss chords in stacked thirds, turning then to chords that depart from the harmonic norm of the past.

Tertian Chords

Tertian triads provide the harmonic material for Ex. 15-1. These triads appear in simple, paired sequential relations.

Ex. 15-1. Prokofiev: Piano Sonata No. 2, Op. 14, I. © Copyright MCMLVII by
Leeds Music Corporation, New York, N. Y. Used by permission.
All rights reserved.

Major and minor triads are not always associated with familiar relationships, however. In Ex. 15-2 major and minor triads that share the same root are alternated. The juxtaposition takes place in different registers, so that the minor triads are always higher than the major. The result is a fascinating parallelism of inverted triads separated in register. (In measures 57 and 58 the triadic spelling is enharmonic. The pattern continues, even though notation suggests a change.)

Ex. 15-2. Bartók: *Contrasts,* III, ''Sebes.'' Copyright 1942 by Hawkes & Son (London) Ltd. Renewed 1969. Reprinted by permission of Boosey & Hawkes, Inc.

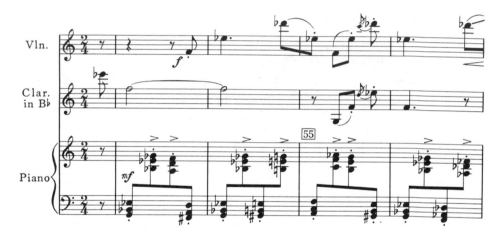

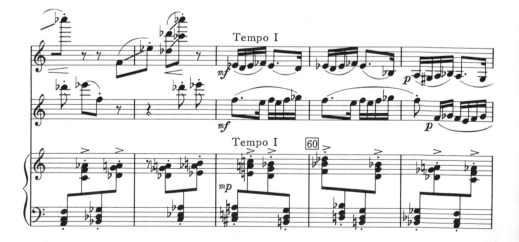

Both of the preceding examples illustrate two possible uses of simple triads. In music of the twentieth century extended passages containing only major and minor triads generally occur as a contrast to surrounding sections dominated by more complex structures. In still other instances major and minor triads appear in their traditional functions as points of departure and repose.

The *e-flat* minor triad in Ex. 15-3 is succeeded by chords having *b-flat* for their lowest note. Each of the structures on the first beats of measures 1–3 is of a different type. Only the mm$_7$ of beat 1 in the first measure is clearly tertian.

Ex. 15-3. Hindemith: Sonata for Organ, No. 1, II. © 1937 by B. Schott's Soehne, Mainz. Reprinted by permission.

Tertian chords may constitute the principal harmonic material of a section. Parallel sevenths are used exclusively over the double pedal in Ex. 15-4. As such, the stream of seventh chords continues the coloristic use of chords begun by Wagner and Debussy.

Ex. 15-4. Paul Creston: Symphony No. 2, I. Reprinted by permission of the copyright owner, G. Schirmer, Inc.

Both chords in measures 1 and 2 of Ex. 15-5 contain major sevenths as their delimiting intervals. The first chord contains intervals other than thirds; it contains the tritone *d-flat—g* that moves to *c—g* in the augmented major seventh chord that follows. Note that this "resolution" chord is more stable than the preceding chord. Each of the chords in this excerpt is connected with the common tone *g*. As a whole, the progression involves motion from two relatively dissonant chords to a more consonant chord.

Ex. 15-5. Barber: Piano Sonata, I. Reprinted by permission of the copyright owner, G. Schirmer, Inc.

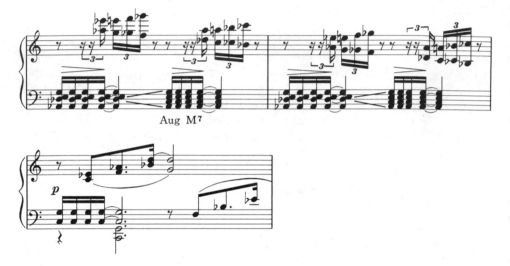

In Ex. 15-6, Mm_7 chords are the simplest harmonic element. The first two sonorities are composite chords of both tertian and nontertian elements. Harmonic motion is created by the succession of different sonority types. Because of its greater complexity and spacing, the first chord of the excerpt produces a textural accent. Its repetition at regular intervals actually creates a $\frac{5}{4}$ meter, in spite of the measuring in $\frac{4}{4}$.

Ex. 15-6. Honegger: Symphony No. 1, I. © 1942 by Editions Salabert, Paris, by permission of Franco Colombo, Inc., New York.

Basically tertian structures may acquire a completely new character by the addition of "added tones." The chords in Ex. 15-7 can be interpreted as seventh chords; however, the seventh is consistently placed below the root of the chord. As a result, a second interpretation is possible: The passage consists of major and minor triads with "added tones," all of which form seconds with simple chord members.

Ex. 15-7. Stravinsky: *Firebird* Suite, Finale.

The preceding discussion indicates some of the possibilities involving various types of tertian chords. Since seventh, ninth, and eleventh chords do not represent new sonority types, their continued use is significant only because they occur so frequently at points of structural importance. Even though major and minor triads still occupy these important roles, more complex chords may perform the same function if they occur at important locations, such as at a cadence.

Nontertian Chords

Chords containing only perfect fourths are important in some recent music. They consist of stacked perfect fourths, such as *c—f—b-flat*. Chords containing both perfect and augmented fourths, such as *c—f—b*, also are called "quartal." Although the latter is a mixture of two different types of fourths, we shall use the term *quartal chord* to apply to those sonorities in which the *perfect fourth* is the characteristic interval.

Quartal chords containing only perfect fourths are illustrated in Ex. 15-8, as on the second beat of measure 1 and the first beat of measure 2. The dyad appearing at the beginning of this passage joins smoothly with the quartal chords because its basic intervals are an octave, fifth, and fourth. This passage is dominated (both melodically and harmonically) by perfect fourths.

Ex. 15-8. Hindemith: *Nobilissima Visione*, III. Used by permission of the copyright owner, B. Schott's Soehne, Mainz.

Because the quartal chords in Ex. 15-9 are the principal harmonic material their use is comparable to that of major and minor triads in earlier music.

Ex. 15-9. Copland: Piano Fantasy. Copyright 1957 by Aaron Copland. Reprinted by permission of Aaron Copland, Copyright Owner, and Boosey & Hawkes, Inc., Sole Licensees.

Each of the four- or five-note chords in Ex. 15-10 contains the fourth as a prominent interval; some of the chords also contain the interval of a third. Chords such as those on the first beat of measures 1 and 3 might be considered seventh chords, but in this context they probably are not heard as third inversion seventh chords but as two fourths joined by a minor third. In either case, it is clear that the section is based on harmonic combinations of fourths.

Ex. 15-10. Berg: *Wozzeck*. ⓒ by Universal Editions. Used by permission.

Chords of superposed fifths (*quintal chords*) are another harmonic possibility. In Ex. 15-11 a quintal chord is used cadentially; because of its spacing, this sonority illustrates another chord that is bounded by a perfect fifth. Since the last chord of this example contains doubled pitches, it takes on the character of a quartal chord, with which it has much in common because of the fourth-fifth inversion relationship.

Ex. 15-11. Bartók: Sonata for Piano, III. Copyright 1927 by Universal Edition; Renewed 1954. Copyright & Renewal assigned to Boosey & Hawkes, Inc., for U.S.A. and to Universal Edition for all other countries of the world. Reprinted by permission.

Since seconds and sevenths occur as structural intervals in many contemporary compositions, chords containing a predominance of these intervals are two more basic sonority types. Spacing is a vital factor when stacked seconds or sevenths are used; otherwise, the unique sonority might be lost.

The *secondal chords* in Ex. 15-12 are associated with a two-voice frame that consists of parallel sevenths. Two tones are doubled in each of the chords. Since the doubling is altered in relation to the lowest second, variety is created within the framework of the sevenths.

Ex. 15-12. Copland: Sonata for Piano. Copyright 1942 by Aaron Copland. Renewed 1969. Reprinted by permission of Aaron Copland, Copyright Owner, and Boosey & Hawkes, Inc., Sole Licensees.

Sometimes secondal chords are used to accompany simple melodic lines. The accompanimental pattern shown in Ex. 15-13 continues for approximately twelve measures, creating a static harmonic rhythm in which the dynamic accents form a metric clash with the notated $\frac{2}{4}$.

Ex. 15-13. Villa-Lobos: String Quartet No. 3, IV. © 1929 by B. Schott's
    Soehne, Mainz. Reprinted by permission.

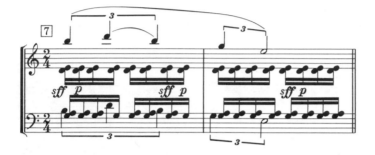

Three seconds are superposed in Ex. 15-14. This type of construction by seconds is called a *tone cluster*. Normal usage of this term indicates that a combination of three or more consecutive seconds qualifies as a tone cluster.

Ex. 15-14. Bartók: Sonata for Piano, III. Copyright 1927 by Universal Edition;
    Renewed 1954. Copyright & Renewal assigned to Boosey & Hawkes,
    Inc., for U.S.A. and to Universal Edition for all other countries of the
    world. Reprinted by permission.

In comparison to Ex. 15-13, the secondal chords here are unstable. In the former excerpt, e^1 and d^1 of the accompaniment are a perfect fifth above g and a, while the most stable interval in Ex. 15-14 is the major third (except in measures 2–4 with the fifth between the melody and one of the accompanying voices).

A tone cluster is used as a pedal to set into relief the simple melodic line in Ex. 15-15. In contrast to Ex. 15-14, the conglomeration in the left-hand part produces a sonorous effect that is overshadowed by the simpler relations formed in voice and right hand.

Ex. 15-15. Ives: "Majority." From *Nineteen Songs*, copyright 1935, Merion Music, Inc. Used by permission.

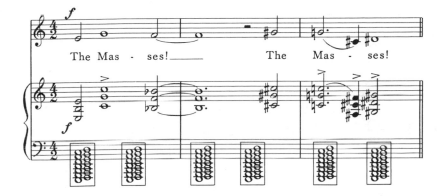

Stacked Chords

Contemporary compositions also contain sonorities created by stacking chords, commonly called *bichords* or *polychords*. This means that two or more simple units that can be recognized as separate entities are combined to form one complex chord.

Spacing is an important factor in the effectiveness of bichords. If the individual members of the chordal units involved are rearranged so that the separate basic structures are no longer distinguishable, the bichord identity is not discernible. Both chords in Ex. 15-16 contain the same notes; however, the first consists of stacked chords (*g-sharp* major over *a* major), while the second implies a harmonic piling of several different intervals.

Ex. 15-16. Chords of identical notes but different structures.

The bichords in Ex. 15-17 are created by combining either major or minor triads, or both. Variety is maintained by varying the combinations of simple triads. Here the two lowest notes always form a fifth, which contributes to the unity of the excerpt, as does the planing in contrary motion.

Ex. 15-17. Honegger: Symphony No. 5 ©️ 1951 by Editions Salabert, Paris, by permission of Franco Colombo, Inc., New York.

Bichords also form the harmonic basis of Ex. 15-18. In contrast to the Honegger excerpt, the stable fifth does not appear as the lowest interval, and the two strata of voices do not move in contrary motion. Notice that each of the bichords forms a second inversion MM9th chord in measures 1 and 2.

Ex. 15-18. Wm. Schuman: *A Free Song*. Reprinted by permission of the copyright owner, G. Schirmer, Inc.

The accompaniment in Ex. 15-19 consists entirely of arpeggiated bichords. Even though the roots of the combined chords are consistently a half-step apart, the arpeggiated patterns form sixths throughout the passage and suggest two simultaneous tonalities, or *bitonality*.

Ex. 15-19. Stravinsky: *Rake's Progress*. Copyright 1949, 1950, 1951 by Boosey & Hawkes, Inc. Reprinted by permission.

Since bichords are complex structures, they frequently support climactic points of a phrase. In Ex. 15-20 the phrase begins and ends with a *D* major triad. As the climax is reached, bichords are introduced, emphasizing the peak of the melodic arch. The first chord in measure 2 suggests a combination of two chords, a *C-sharp* mm_7 over a *C-sharp* major triad. The chord on the third beat in measure 2 begins as the combination of a *d sharp*$^o_7$ chord over an *F* Mm_7.

Ex. 15-20. Hindemith: Second Sonata for Piano, III. © 1936 by B. Schott's Soehne, Mainz. Reprinted by permission.

Combining thirds that do not share the same root creates another type of bichord that is similar to those already illustrated. The first chord of measure 1 (accompaniment) in Ex. 15-21 could be spelled *a c-sharp e g-sharp*. However, the spacing separates the two thirds and gives the effect of harmony produced by joining two different harmonic units of the same type (major thirds).

Ex. 15-21. Bartók: Sonata for Violin No. 2, I. Copyright 1923 by Universal Edition; Renewed 1950. Copyright & Renewal assigned to Boosey & Hawkes, Inc., for U.S.A. and to Universal Edition for all other countries of the world. Reprinted by permission.

Frequently, great independence exists between the parts as in Ex. 15-22. In such cases, the simultaneous sounding of the parts produces the chordal effects, rather than some systematic chordal ordering.

Ex. 15-22. Carter: Sonata for Flute, Oboe, Cello, and Harpsichord, II. Used by permission of Associated Music Publishers, Inc., New York.

Other Chord Types

Most of the chords discussed in previous sections of this chapter consist of combinations that *could* be reduced to a tertian basis. For example, all of the chords in Ex. 15-23 could be reduced to the tertian structure shown at the end. Because of such factors as spacing, however, some of the chords bear little resemblance to this hypothetical reduction. It thus seems tenuous to relate them as such.

Ex. 15-23. Chords containing identical tones but of different structures.

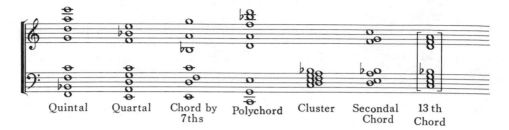

Quintal   Quartal   Chord by   Polychord   Cluster   Secondal   13th
                     7ths   Chord   Chord

Each of the chords in Ex. 15-23 has individual characteristics that distinguish it from the notational reduction; therefore each is heard as a particular chord type. Since one factor dominates each chord, we can identify it by this singular characteristic; i.e., *secondal* chords (built of seconds), *quartal* chords (built of fourths).

The chords discussed in the following paragraphs do not always contain such common factors, although a certain interval type may be more prominent because it appears more than once, or because of spacing.

Various means for describing sonority types have been evolving gradually. In general, spacing and register are discounted for the purposes of classification; two means for describing sonority types and for determining harmonic similarities are (1) calculating the total interval content and (2) showing the pitch content in relation to a prime.

To calculate the total interval content each of the intervals is accounted for as belonging to one of six interval classes (I.C. or i.c.).[1]

Ex. 15-24. Interval content analysis.

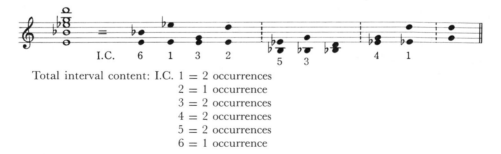

I.C.   6   1   3   2   5   3   4   1

Total interval content: I.C. 1 = 2 occurrences
                             2 = 1 occurrence
                             3 = 2 occurrences
                             4 = 2 occurrences
                             5 = 2 occurrences
                             6 = 1 occurrence

A second procedure is to determine the pitch content of a collection of notes in relation to a prime, which is shown in terms of half-steps above it.[2] Any of

---

[1] The six interval classes are: 1 = m2, M7
                                 2 = M2, m7
                                 3 = m3, M6
                                 4 = M3, m6
                                 5 = P4, P5
                                 6 = tritone

[2] This method of classification has much to recommend it. For example, a single number identifies an interval; thus *4* = major third; *7* = perfect fifth.

the notes of a group can be selected to represent the prime, provided the arrangement expresses the pitch content in the most primary fashion possible.

Ex. 15-25. Pitch content analysis.

As Ex. 15-25 demonstrates, the five-note collection in its simplest form spans either a major or minor sixth. Since the half-step is the measuring unit, version 17-25a can be said to be primary.

In Ex. 15-26 chords containing various combinations of major and minor thirds, perfect fourths, augmented fourths (diminished fifths), and sixths occur over a stable lower part. The interval content analysis shows that each of the chords has certain intervals in common; each of the chords contains the same number of first and second class intervals, whereas the number of class three intervals alternates between two and three. Most notable is the absence of a class six interval in the last chord. Such an interval content analysis assists in describing similarities and dissimilarities between chords in a composition, as well as providing one means for establishing relations between chords based on similar interval content.

Ex. 15-26. Webern: Five Pieces for String Quartet, Op. 5, No. 5. ⓒ by Universal Editions. Used by permission.

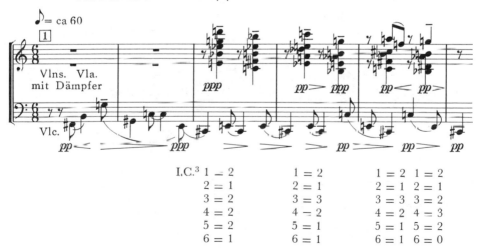

The chords in Ex. 15-27 are less complex than those illustrated in Ex. 15-26 as the chords on the first beats of measures 3 and 4 are quartal chords. However,

---

[3]This analysis applies only to the notes in the treble clef of this excerpt.

the combination of both perfect and augmented fourths creates a different sonority type than is represented by a four-note quartal chord of perfect fourths. An analysis of the intervals above the bass clearly shows the different chord types present.

Ex. 15-27. Schoenberg: Song No. 12, from *Das Buch der hängenden Gärten*.
Reprinted with the permission of Mrs. Gertrud Schoenberg.

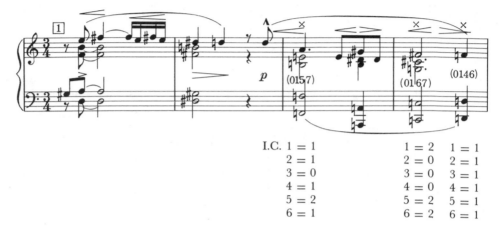

	I.C.	1 = 1		1 = 2	1 = 1
		2 = 1		2 = 0	2 = 1
		3 = 0		3 = 0	3 = 1
		4 = 1		4 = 0	4 = 1
		5 = 2		5 = 2	5 = 1
		6 = 1		6 = 2	6 = 1

In Ex. 15-28 the cadence chord contains twelve different notes. These notes are arranged so that seconds are concentrated in the middle register, and sixths, fifths, fourths, and thirds in the outer registers.

Ex. 15-28. Helm: Concerto for Five Solo Instruments, Percussion and Strings, II. © 1954 by Schott & Co., Ltd., London. Used by permission.

Since twelve different notes can form the pitch materials of a single chord, it is possible to arrange them to form twelve-note quintal chords, twelve-note quartal chords, or in any other systematic arrangement of twelve separate notes. However, the tones would have to be spaced over a wide range to make evident the two types just mentioned.

Harmonic Succession

Harmonic predictability for twentieth-century music has not yet been formulated because the patterns of harmonic succession vary from one composition to another. In other words, norms cannot be clearly identified for all contemporary music as though it were all cut from the same cloth. For the present, then, we are limited to generalized descriptions of chord types and generalized observations about chord succession.

Some general principles of harmonic succession are still discernible. For example, common-tone relations, connection by contrary motion or similar motion, and familiar root or bass progressions still are basic to much music. Harmonic succession also may be predicated on serialized organization or any other system, as is discussed later in this chapter. If simple major and minor triads form the principal harmonic material, composers often connect the chords in ways that obscure or expand tonality. Thus certain relationships, such as root movement by a tritone, occur more frequently than in earlier music.

Root movement of a tritone and of a second are illustrated in Ex. 15-29. Here major and minor triads form the principal harmonic material. The root movement by major seconds connects the parallel harmonic construction and leads to a section containing tritone root relationships.

Ex. 15-29. Bartók: Suite, Op. 14, I. Copyright 1918 by Universal Edition; Renewed 1945. Copyright & Renewal assigned to Boosey & Hawkes, Inc., for U.S.A. and to Universal Edition for all other countries of the world. Reprinted by permission.

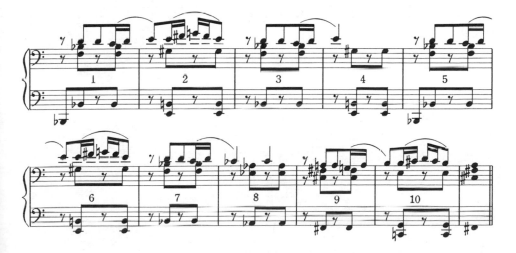

Major and minor triads also are the basic harmonies in Ex. 15-30. Although longer relative duration gives emphasis to the *G-flat* chord in measure 2 and the *A-flat* chord in measure 5, the prevailing activity does not necessarily enable us to predict the appearance of these chords as harmonic goals. Even so, the succession of chords is smooth, a result of the contrary motion between the parts. Note that the most frequent root relation is by thirds.

Ex. 15-30. Wm. Schuman: Symphony No. 4, II. Reprinted by permission of the
        copyright owner, G. Schirmer, Inc.

In measures 5 and 6 of the excerpt shown as Ex. 15-31, the basic quintal chords are smoothly connected by the contrary motion of the voice pairs. A similar procedure occurs in measures 3–4 and 8–9. Note that in measure 4 quartal chords are joined by this same procedure. The linear chords that fill in the span between the two *A*-major chords in measures 1–2 are all joined together by the common tone *A*.

Ex. 15-31. Hindemith: Piano Sonata No. 1, I. Used by permission of the copyright
        owner, B. Schott's Soehne, Mainz.

In Ex. 15-32, three-note clusters (measures 1–4) accompany a simple tertian melody. Here harmonic succession is the result of parallel step motion except for the progression to the chord in measure 5.

Ex. 15-32. Cowell: String Quartet No. 5, II. Copyright 1962 by C. F. Peters Corporation, 373 Park Avenue South, New York, N. Y. 10016. Reprinted with permission of the publisher.

Common-tone relationships help to unify Ex. 15-33. Each of the chords in measures 7–10 has at least one tone in common. The presence of this melodic link produces smooth succession between different chord types.

Ex. 15-33. Copland: Sonata for Piano. Copyright 1942 by Aaron Copland.
Renewed 1969. Reprinted by permission of Aaron Copland,
Copyright Owner, and Boosey & Hawkes, Inc., Sole Licensees.

Serialized Harmony

Harmonic materials can be derived systematically from serialized note combinations. The chords that result from this procedure may be of diverse or similar types. For instance, if twelve notes are arranged as in the series shown in Ex. 15-30, the chords noted in Ex. 15-34 are potential harmonic structures through a simple partitioning of the row into four parts of three notes.

Ex. 15-34. Partitioning of a row into chords.

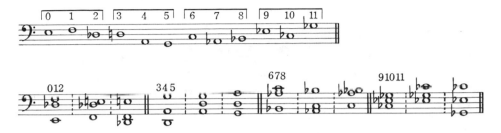

The resulting chords are the product of the combination of three successive notes, and the sonorities created are dependent upon the relative positions assigned these three notes. Consequently, the members of individual chords are determined by the order in which they appear in the tone row.

A passage consisting of serially derived chords is shown as Ex. 15-35. Chords containing successive groups of three notes occur at the outset and proceed in that manner until all twelve notes of the row have been exhausted. In measure 2 a six-note chord is produced by combining the first six notes of the row, followed by a chord (measure 3) that contains the last six notes.[4] The seventh through twelfth notes of the row are rearranged in measure 4, creating a new chord.

Ex. 15-35. George Rochberg: Bagatelle No. 5. © by Theodore Presser
         Company. Reprinted by permission.

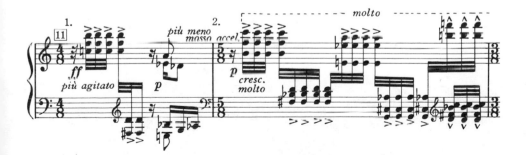

_____

[4]This division of a twelve-note row into two units of six is commonly referred to as *hexachordal*, i.e., a hexa (or six-part) set division.

Ex. 15-35 continued.

As can be seen, notes 0 1 2 and 9 10 11 combine to form the same chord type; whereas 3 4 5 create an augmented triad, and 6 7 8 create still a different type.

A composer who uses serial technique frequently chooses certain note combinations of serial order to the exclusion of others because they contribute to continuity. In other words, a composer may select certain serially derived chords for the harmonic successions of a work or a section. On the other hand, sonorities consisting of the same notes or containing similar intervals may become prominent because they are present in the different forms of the tone row.

Each of the three bracketed notes in Ex. 15-36 represents a potential chord. Some of the segments contain identical notes, and some segments contain identical interval relations.

Ex. 15-36. Schoenberg: String Quartet No. 4, Op. 37, tone row. Reprinted by permission of the copyright owner, G. Schirmer, Inc.

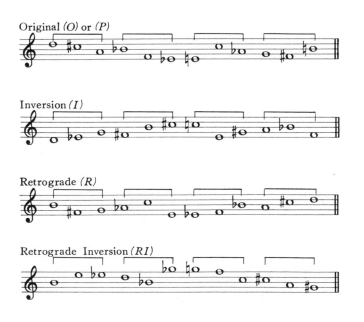

In Ex. 15-37 the first five measures of the melody are based on the *P* form of the row cited in Ex. 15-36, as are most of the accompanying chords. Considering only the chords in measure 1, each is the result of combinations of the segments 3 4 5, 6 7 8, and 9 10 11. The chord appearing on the fourth beat of measure 2 is derived from the set 8 9 10 of the *RI* form.

Ex. 15-37. Schoenberg: String Quartet No. 4, Op. 37, I. Reprinted by permission of the copyright owner, G. Schirmer, Inc.

Chords derived from tone rows, then, are based on the original and its derivative forms. Consequently, the resultant sonorities are related to segments of the series, but not necessarily related to any central tone. If a tone row contains combinations that can yield chords of a similar sonority type, then that type might be heard as an important organizational factor. Furthermore, such harmonic successions are a by-product of the note organization of the original row (or its segments) that serve as its pitch basis; they are not usually related to a key system in the conventional sense.

Although the procedures and examples cited in our discussion are typical of serial techniques in general, they are based specifically on rows of twelve tones. It should be clear that rows of less than twelve tones could also serve as the raw material for the same techniques.

Melodic and Harmonic Interaction

It remains now to examine how melody and harmony, the horizontal and vertical dimensions of music, interact. Since composers are less dependent upon traditional functional relations and draw upon a much larger body of potential musical resources, it is logical to assume that a multiplicity of relations exists. In this discussion we shall explore some of these interrelations by examining several representative examples.

Initially, the melodic and harmonic elements may seem to be operating independently in Ex. 15-38 and that any resulting relations are arbitrary. That such is not the case becomes clear through an examination of the processes at work.

Ex. 15-38. Berg: *Schlafend trägt man,* Op. 2, No. 2.

The apparent independence of the voice and piano in measures 1–4 is part of the expository character of this opening statement. Several germinal figures are presented in the voice part and each is essential to the linear processes. To clarify, the opening figure of the voice part is a 0 3 4 group. It is duplicated, transposed and in a different order, in the piano (both are designated "0" in Ex. 15-38).

The half-step figure (0 1 2) designated "2" of measures 3 and 4 also appears, transposed a tritone, in the piano. This vertical joining by a tritone relates to the total harmonic palette: each chord of measures 1–4 contains two tritones as an essential component. Another aspect of interaction relates to the three-note melodic figure designated "1." This whole-step component is an important vertical factor, since each of the chords of measures 1–4 is relatable to some symmetrical whole-tone segment. The structure of the first chord serves as a model for the other chords in the phrase

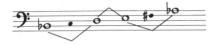

Vertical and linear relations in serial compositions are directly determined by the manner in which a composer derives his harmonic structures. The excerpt shown in Ex. 15-39 illustrates a serialized melody and accompaniment in which both dimensions are based on four-note segments of the row.

Ex. 15-39. Webern: Variations for Orchestra, Op. 30.

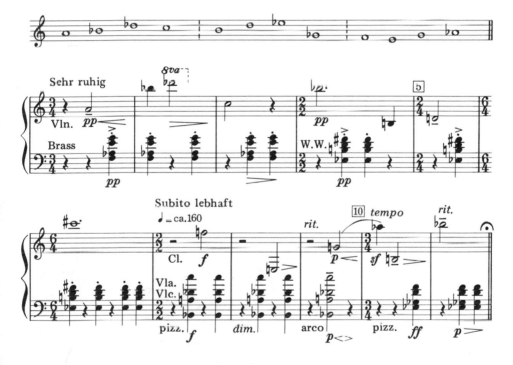

The four-note chords in measures 1–10 are derived from R_0; the melodic line is derived from both P_0 (measures 1–3 and measures 7–10) and P_1 (measures 4–6). It is evident that in measures 1–3 and 7–10 there are no pitch class duplications in the melody and accompaniment; the interval content, however, of both the melody and accompaniment in these measures is the same. In measures 4–6 there is pitch class duplication; namely, B and D, which occur in the same register in both melody and accompaniment. This plan of duplication and non-duplication of pitch classes helps to shape this section of the movement. Considering only chords, it is evident that the four notes are spaced so as to produce spatial expansion (measures 1–9) and contraction (measure 10).

Sometimes melody and harmony are not as distinctly separated texturally; Ex. 15-40 illustrates one such instance. The lines designated with a ★ contain the principal melodic material but in each instance these starred lines are coupled to produce a "color line"; for example, the three clarinets, *petite* trumpet, and French horns are coupled to produce a melodic stratum, and the piano and *cencerros* another. Counterpointed against these two melodies are trumpets and trombones, and xylophone, xylorima, and marimba. Although there is *much* harmony in this excerpt, it is the color combinations that draw our attention. Such emphasis on color is a logical extension of coloristic uses of harmony by the Impressionistic composers. The total effect is one of color strands weaving through a multicolored fabric.

Ex. 15-40. Messiaen: *Couleurs de la Cité Céleste.* By permission of Alphonse Leduc & Cie, 175 rue Saint-Honoré, Paris Ier, Owners and Publishers. Copyright 1966.

A totally different concept of horizontal-vertical interaction is illustrated by Ex. 15-41. Both the vertical and the horizontal are made out of the same stuff, with the horizontal starts and stops articulating moments of the total sonorous event rather than delineating separable parts of a texture, such as melody and harmony. Harmonic progression in a conventional sense is absent; changes in vertical density together with the horizontal starts and stops, however, do provide motion toward a musical goal.

Ex. 15-41. Penderecki: *Anaklasis*.

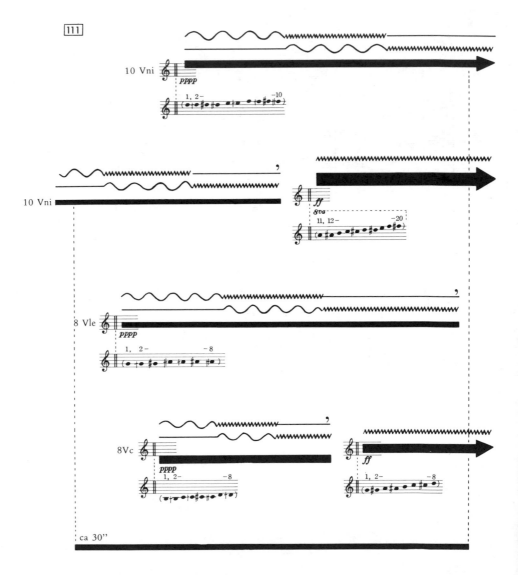

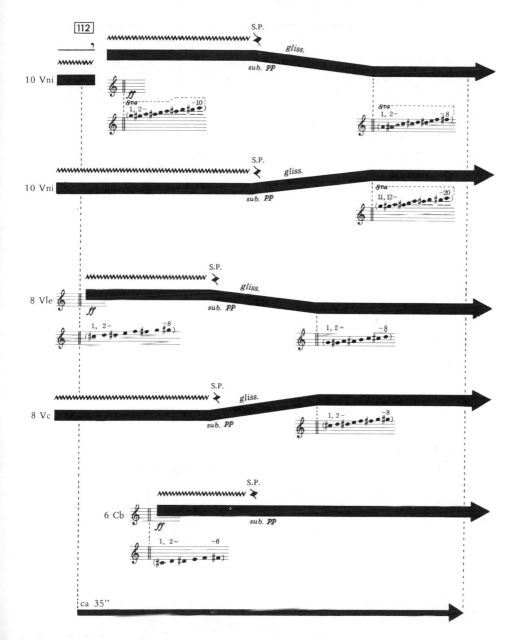

Each of the preceding examples uses traditional instruments as its sound sources. In our day electronically produced pitched and non-pitched sounds are used as the basis for extended compositions. Ex. 15-42 is a graphic representation (a score) providing instructions for re-creating an electronic composition on tape.

The duration of each pitch is designated in terms of centimeters of tape (76.2 centimeters = 1 second); pitches and pitch mixtures are obtained from a frequency

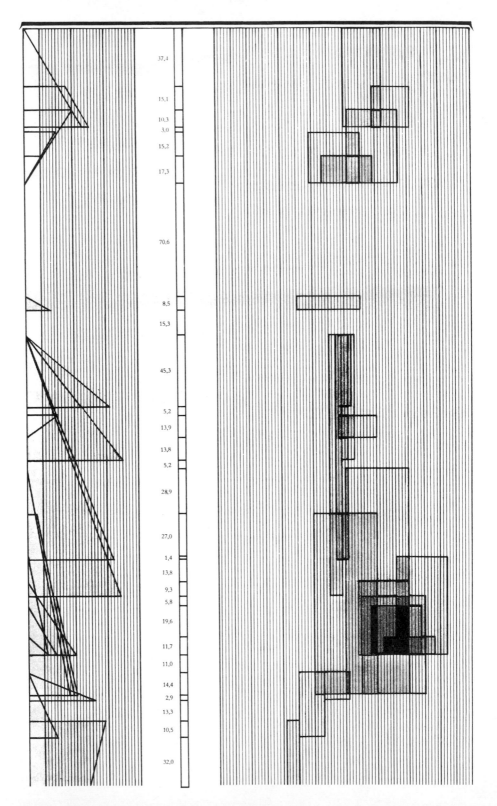

scale of 81 steps selected from 100 to 17,200 cycles per second; and dynamics (envelope) of any event is selected from an intensity scale of 31 steps between 0 to 30 decibels.

As the graphic score vividly illustrates, the harmonic component is one of varying degrees of lesser or greater vertical density; similarly, the linear component is produced by proximity of attack or frequency of attacks.

Exercises

For more detailed assignments see *Materials and Structure of Music II, Workbook*, Chapter 15.

1. Write a composition for flute and piano (approximately 16 measures) in which the harmonic material of the accompaniment consists only of successive and superposed major and minor triads. The scale basis of the flute part might be pentatonic.
2. Make a harmonic plan for a three-part composition in which sonorities are the foremost factor in delineating the form; for example, Section I might contain only tertial chords; Section II might contain quartal, quintal, or superposed chords; Section III might be similar to Section I or different.
3. Devise a row of twelve different tones; then use this row and its derivative forms as the basis of a short composition for clarinet, violin, and piano.
4. Analyze each of the examples in this chapter to determine the factors that govern harmonic succession. In addition, analyze and listen to works by Shostakovitch, Bartók, Stravinsky, and Hindemith for more study relating to harmonic succession.
5. Find examples from literature that contain quartal, quintal, and secondal chords.
6. Listen to and analyze in detail the sonorities of compositions such as those found in Volume VI of Bartók's *Mikrokosmos*. Identify chord types and describe the principles of harmonic succession found in each of the examples studied.
7. Make a sketch of an experimental composition in which some sections are based on serial techniques and in which other sections are not. Include in your sketch ways in which the materials of each section might be commonly related because of similar sonority types, or by some other means.
8. Listen to and analyze horizontal-vertical relations in works such as those listed below.
   Berio: *Rounds* (both piano and harpsichord versions)
   Boulez: *Le marteau sans mâitre*
   Dallapiccola: *Quaderno Musicale di Annalibera*
   Davidovsky: *Study No. 2.*
   Erb: *In no strange land*
   Gaburo: *Antiphony IV*
   Kagel: *Sonant*
   Ligeti: *Atmospheres*
   Partch: *And on the Seventh Day Petals Fell in Petaluma*
   Penderecki: *Stabat Mater*
   Stockhausen: *Klavierstücke* I–IV
   Varèse: *Déserts*

16

TONALITY AND ATONALITY
IN TWENTIETH-CENTURY MUSIC

Many of the factors that contributed to a broadening of the tonal spectrum pave the way for relationships that are present in contemporary music. In this chapter we shall examine some of the common relational patterns that occur in music of this century.

Tonal Relations

Tonality implies pitch focus, as well as relationships of pitch ingredients to a focal point. Although they may be considerably disguised or transformed, these relationships frequently occur in music of the twentieth century.

Ex. 16-1 illustrates one type of modification of earlier relational patterns. *F* is the tonal center—it is the first melodic and harmonic root and the last pitch heard, as well as the first note of the phrase beginning in measure 7. However, it is the final occurrence of *f* that confirms its tonal significance. Several other factors corroborate *f* as a focal point: (1) the radical change of texture in measure 16; (2) the bass movement from *C* to *f* in measures 15–16; and (3) the descending melodic contour in measures 13–16.

Ex. 16-1. Bartók: Concerto for Orchestra, I. Copyright 1946 by Hawkes & Son (London) Ltd. Reprinted by permission of Boosey & Hawkes, Inc.

416

Another type of relational modification is illustrated in Ex. 16-2. Here the final cadence succinctly confirms *E-flat*. With the exception of the opening measures, *E-flat* is not a predictable convergence point until the tonic is established by this final progression. The tonal relationships of this excerpt resemble those of the past. For example, the emphasis given to the *e-flat—b-flat* fifth early in the accompaniment, the simple chords, and the modified plagal cadence at the end are reminiscent of earlier procedures. What is different is the avoidances of *E-flat* as a structural pitch within the interior of the passage.

Ex. 16-2. Vincent Persichetti: Fourth Piano Sonata, II. Permission for reprint granted by Elkan-Vogel Co., Inc., Philadelphia, copyright owners.

Modification of stereotyped harmonic patterns is only one of many techniques that establish a tonal center in contemporary music. In the Persichetti example the effect of tonic results from the terminal position of the *e-flat* chord, as well as from its prominence in the first three measures.

Sometimes durational emphasis, as with a pedal, is the primary factor in creating a tonic. In Ex. 16-3 tonic is immediately established by the pedal in the first four measures. By the end of the excerpt a temporary change to *C* occurs, a result of the motion of the individual lines and the duration and position assigned to *c*.

Ex. 16-3. Hindemith: *Mathis der Maler*, I. © 1934 by B. Schott's Soehne, Mainz. Renewed 1961.

Tonal stability is often achieved by an ostinato, as in Ex. 16-4. The persistent bass pattern establishes *F* as tonic, even though the melodic activity does not point conclusively to that pitch. Tonic, then, is the product of repetition rather than melodic convergence.

Ex. 16-4. Hindemith: Second Sonata for Piano, I. © 1936 by B. Schott's Soehne, Mainz. Renewed 1963.

Recurrence of a fragmentary harmonic pattern also has a stabilizing effect, even if the constituent chords are complex. In Ex. 16-5 the recurrent bichord with *E* as lowest note has a tonic function: It is consistently preceded by a *D-sharp* major chord, forming a leading-tone relation. The tonal digressions beginning at the end of measure 5 are transpositions of the opening figure. The return of the opening progression reaffirms *E* as the tonal center.

Ex. 16-5. Copland: *Music for the Theatre*, Prologue. Copyright 1932 by Cos Cob Press, Inc.; Renewed 1960 by Aaron Copland. Reprinted by permission of Aaron Copland, Copyright Owner, and Boosey & Hawkes, Inc., Sole Licensees.

Ex. 16-5 continued.

Bitonality and Polytonality

The simultaneous presentation of two or more tonalities is symptomatic of the desire to expand tonal relationships. In this practice there is a striking contrast between what music *looks like* on the printed page and what it *sounds like*. Although the potential exists for hearing two or more tonics simultaneously, the listener probably can perceive only one tonic at a time. In so-called bitonal passages, then, we have the option of focusing on one or the other tonic successively. In any event, the desired effect generally depends upon clearly established patterns that are separated by register and texture.

Two keys, *C* and *G-flat*, occur together in Ex. 16-6, illustrating *bitonality*. Both the right- and left-hand parts have their own tonal identity because the upper part contains the melodic material, the lower the accompaniment. The two tonalities are created by the outlined major triads. Registral and rhythmic separation also are vital tonality establishing factors.

Ex. 16-6. Milhaud: *Saudades do Brazil,* "Ipanema." © 1925 by Editions
Max Eschig, Paris. Renewed 1953.

Sometimes the parts of a bitonal passage are entwined within identical registers. In such instances separation of the parts is generally established by making one or the other prominent as melody, the other an accompaniment. This type of separation can be seen in Ex. 16-7.

Ex. 16-7. Honegger: Symphony for Strings, III. ⓒ 1942 by Editions Salabert, Paris, by permission of Franco Colombo, Inc., New York.

Perception of a tonal center becomes even more difficult when three potential tonics exist. In such *polytonal* sections textural spread is even more essential than in bitonal passages. Ex. 16-8 contains three possible tonics, *B-flat, E,* and *C-sharp.* Separation is effected by the *B-flat* pedal, the parallel thirds with octave doubling in the left hand, and the parallel fifths with octave doubling in the right hand. The individuality of the upper two strands is further intensified by contrary motion.

Ex. 16-8. Bartók: Sonata for Piano, I. Copyright 1927 by Universal Edition. Renewed 1954. Copyright & Renewal assigned to Boosey & Hawkes, Inc., for U.S.A. and to Universal Edition for all other countries of the world. Reprinted by permission.

An effect similar to bitonality, or polytonality, may occur when one or more of the parts is not in an obvious key, as in Ex. 16-9. Here separation is established by the arpeggiated minor chord in the lowest part and the conjunct motion of coupled upper parts. Although the coupled upper parts do not clearly establish any tonality, in combination with the lower part the effect of bitonality is apparent. Note, however, that the upper and lower parts here converge at cadential points to a simple *B* major triad (enharmonically).

Ex. 16-9. Stravinsky: *Symphony of Wind Instruments.* Copyright 1926 by
Edition Russe de Musique. Copyright assigned to Boosey & Hawkes,
Inc. Revised Version Copyright 1952 by Boosey & Hawkes, Inc.
Reprinted by permission.

Atonality

In contrast to tonality, *atonality* refers to the absence of a tonal center. In this sense atonality is a negation of tonality.

Atonality very often is associated only with serially organized music. This association is not necessarily justified, because a serialized composition might well manifest a tonic, and a nonserial work can be atonal. In passages such as Ex. 16-10, the descriptive term *atonality* is appropriate.

Ex. 16-10. Webern: Symphony, Op. 21, II. Copyright by Universal Editions.
Reprinted by permission.

Tonality may be minimized by avoiding simple harmonic and melodic relations so that no one tone or interval stands out as a focal point. Such a process can be seen in Ex. 16-11; *b*, *g-sharp*, and *g* form an important three-note contour motive. This contour motive provides the primary material for the basic melodic shape of the movement. The three notes also occur as a simultaneous component in measures 2, 4, 6, and 8.

Ex. 16-11. Schoenberg: Piano Piece, Op. 11, No. 1. Copyright by Universal Editions. Reprinted by permission.

In this context the contour motive functions as a referent rather than as a focal point—other tones have equal significance. The relationships, then, are more "tone to tone" than "tones to a tonic."

Another characteristic of many atonal compositions is the persistent appearance of successive complex chords that do not produce dissonance-resolution effects.

Since a high degree of harmonic tension is maintained, resolution to a central point is eliminated. In Ex. 16-12 successive complex sonorities prevail. There is a decided change in rhythmic events, producing musical tension as well as release of tension, but such activity does not lead to establishing pitch focus.

Ex. 16-12. Ernst Krenek: Toccata. Used with the permission of the copyright owner, Mercury Music Corporation.

Pandiatonicism

The basic pitch material of *pandiatonic* music is the diatonic scale, usually the major scale. Pandiatonicism is not a return to the functional tonal relations of pre-twentieth-century music. On the contrary, it incorporates a very free use of the diatonic scale resulting in harmonic successions having no apparent calculated order.

Ex. 16-13 illustrates a pandiatonic passage. Although the excerpt is in *C* major the harmonic relationships here are not those of clear tonic and dominant interplay which we associate with earlier music.

Ex. 16-13. Richard Donovan: *Adventure*. Copyright 1957, Merion Music, Inc. Used by permission.

In Ex. 16-14 a harmonic ostinato in the upper staff establishes the tonality framework. Three additional lines, two of which are in canon, form a pandiatonic texture that includes only pitches which are diatonic to *G-flat* major.

Ex. 16-14. Copland: *Appalachian Spring*. Copyright 1945 by Aaron Copland, Renewed 1972. Reprinted by permission of Aaron Copland, Copyright Owner, and Boosey & Hawkes, Inc., Sole Licensees.

Like many atonal compositions, most pandiatonic passages are contrapuntal, as is Ex. 16-15. Here the parts for the two pianos are partially differentiated by their contrapuntal association, contrary motion, register, and rhythmic structure (beginning in measure 2).

Ex. 16-15. Stravinsky: Sonata for Two Pianos, I. © 1945 by Associated Music Publishers, Inc., New York. Reprinted by permission.

Tonality Schemes

Since tonality still is an important facet of musical organization and structure, tonality changes also are a vital factor. In contrast to earlier relationships, much current music that is tonal incorporates relations that are, for the most part, remote. Furthermore, temporary tonal centers, such as tonal regions, frequently appear in close succession. If such succession is followed by recurrence of the initial tonality, tonic becomes more prominent as a basic factor of organization.

The scheme of relationships in Ex. 16-16 is often referred to as "free," because the tonal centers are in distant relationships to tonic and are so brief. This example begins in *C*, cadences on *G-sharp* in measure 4, returns to *C* in measure 6, and then moves to *C-sharp* in measure 10.

Ex. 16-16. Hindemith: *Mathis der Maler*, II. © 1934 by B. Schott's Soehne, Mainz. Renewed 1961. Reprinted by permission.

Two principal tonal centers, *D* and *E*, occur in Ex. 16-17. The change to *E* is accomplished through a common-chord modulation. In contrast to Ex. 16-16 the common-chord relation smooths out the tonal digression. Again, the antecedents of this technique lie in earlier music.

Ex. 16-17. Copland: Third Symphony, I. Copyright 1947 by Aaron Copland.
Reprinted by permission of Aaron Copland, Copyright Owner,
and Boosey & Hawkes, Inc., Sole Licensees.

The old trick of shifting abruptly to a new tonal center occurs in many passages.
Such shifts often involve a common-tone relation between keys. Ex. 16-18 begins
in *F*, followed by a shift to *A-flat* in measure 7.

Ex. 16-18. Shostakovitch: Symphony No. 5, Op. 47, I. ⓒ Copyright MCMXLV
by Leeds Music Corporation, New York, N. Y. Used by permission.
All Rights Reserved.

Ex. 16-19 contains two successive tonal centers, *E* and *G*. In this example,
however, the new tonic is reached by a modulatory sequence.

Ex. 16-19. Bartók: *Mikrokosmos*, Vol. VI, No. 150. Copyright 1940 by Hawkes & Son (London) Ltd. Renewed 1967. Reprinted by permission of Boosey & Hawkes, Inc.

Tonality changes have always had a direct bearing on musical form. In general, such changes occur more frequently and in closer proximity in contemporary music than in most compositions of the eighteenth and nineteenth centuries. The types of tonal relationships that occur cover the gamut of possibilities. Many such relationships may first appear to be uncommon or complex; in context, however, they occur as new solutions to old problems. In much contemporary music, however, the absence of tonality precludes its relevance to musical organization.

Exercises

For more detailed assignments see *Materials and Structure of Music II, Workbook*, Chapter 16.

1. Using Ex. 16-1 as your guide, write a sixteen-measure piano composition in *G*.
2. Write an experimental composition for a combination of four different instruments in which bitonality plays an important formal role.
3. Analyze portions of a composition such as Berg's *Piano Sonata* to determine the unifying factors that occur in lieu of tonal centers.
4. Compose two phrases for oboe and piano. Within these two phrases include at least three common-tone shifts to new tonal regions.
5. Plan a short composition for string quartet in which quartal chords are the most "consonant" sonorities. Avoid creating any tonic effect.
6. Make an aural and visual analysis of the tonality scheme of a work such as the first movement of Hindemith's *Mathis der Maler*.
7. Listen to and analyze bitonal passages in de Falla's *Harpsichord Concerto*, Milhaud's *String Quartet No. 5*, and other appropriate works.
8. Make an aural and visual analysis of atonal works of Schoenberg and Webern, e.g., Webern: *Movements for String Quartet*, Op. 5 or *Pieces for Orchestra*, Op. 6; or Schoenberg, *Piano Pieces*, Op. 11 or sections from *Pierrot Lunaire*.

17

FORMAL PROCESSES IN TWENTIETH-CENTURY MUSIC

Since many innovations of melody, harmony, rhythm, texture, etc., have taken place in twentieth-century music, we might expect far-reaching changes in formal processes; this is not the case, for repetition, contrast, and variation continue as principles basic to musical form.

Forms have been adapted to individual styles and practices, but they remain essentially the same as their earlier prototypes. These can be found particularly in works of composers such as Hindemith, Barber, and Bartók.

A second group of composers such as Honegger, Ives, and Stravinsky have used novel and often quite original means to organize compositions which still adhere nominally to the broad outlines of earlier forms.

A third group of composers have, in effect, renounced organizing principles such as melodic repetition and tonality in favor of a variety of procedures that take root in serialism. Composers such as Schoenberg, Webern, Berg, and many of the composers who deal with electronic sound sources have all dealt with serial techniques in one way or another, and the forms which their works achieve are in many instances departures from traditional stereotypes of formal design.

Another group of composers has elevated *chance*, either in composition or in performance, to heights never before attempted. In effect such compositions are "of the moment," with each performance, ideally, presenting a different aspect of the same composition. Composers such as Cage, Brown, Boulez, and Stockhausen have included chance operations in some of their works.

In an effort to achieve forward motion and yet minimize sectionalization, many contemporary composers use essentially contrapuntal textures. Procedures typical of counterpoint, such as fugato, canon, stretto, ostinato, and *cantus firmus* are common to many twentieth-century works.

Vocal music, opera, song, and choral works continue to thrive, but like other forms of contemporary music they are sometimes organized with techniques of sectionalization that would have seemed incompatible to their eighteenth- and nineteenth-century models.

The development of an entire movement from an initial "germ motive," such as Stravinsky's Symphony in C, or the division of a movement by contrasts of instrumental color, as in Bartók's *Concerto for Orchestra*, represent some processes that have been used to create form in the twentieth century.

429

Formal Punctuation

Cadences punctuate internal juncture, formal change, or the end of a composition. As long as decisive cadences are present, this functional role continues to be filled. In some contemporary works melodic, harmonic, and rhythmic forces sometimes do not converge to create a strong caesura. Consequently, the end of a formal unit is created by contrasts of musical elements such as texture, rhythm, sonority types, or tempo.

Nonetheless, the surge of interest in neo-classicism that occurred during the beginning of this century is typified by a reliance on the cadence as a formal delineator. In Ex. 17-1 the close of the introduction of a piano concerto is marked by a V—I cadence in C major (colored by a kind of unresolved double suspension in the middle voices). The subsequent section is further marked off from the previous by a change of tempo and the figurative pattern in sixteenth notes.

Ex. 17-1. Prokofiev: Concerto for Piano No. 3, I. Copyright by Edition Gutheil. Copyright assigned to Boosey & Hawkes, Inc., 1947. Reprinted by permission.

The beginning of the development section of a sonata-allegro movement occurs in measure 5 of Ex. 17-2; the composer's instructions (*molto rit.*), accompanied by two successive *fermati*, clearly set off the two sections. The cadential effect of such a passage is achieved by both a change of pace and a relative absence of activity. The change of texture from four voices to one helps to delineate the division, as does the introduction of a new motive in the cello, measure 6 (derived from the opening of the movement).[1]

---

[1] The beginning of this section also corresponds with the introduction of a transposed statement of the row.

Ex. 17-2. Schoenberg: Quartet No. 4. Reprinted by permission of the
copyright owner, G. Schirmer, Inc.

Several general observations about cadences in twentieth-century music will explain the structural role they may play in delineating form. For example, a cadence may occur as a short pause in only one of several voices. Second, harmonic tension may be relaxed suddenly, thereby implying arrival at a structural point. It should be understood that rhythmic and harmonic factors may be independent, the one by no means coinciding with the other at cadential points. Third, the harmonic relationships traditionally associated with cadences may be completely avoided.

The cadence in measure 2 of Ex. 17-3 gives to C no more duration than the eighth notes that dominate the preceding measure. Furthermore, it occurs in a weak position and is overlapped by the anacrustic f^1 in the first violin. C is nonetheless perceived as a cadential pitch: it creates a relaxation of the preceding harmonic-melodic tension, reasserts the tonic of the movement, and heralds a restatement of the first theme.

Ex. 17-3. Bartók: Quartet No. 4, I. Copyright 1929 by Universal Edition; Renewed
1956. Copyright & Renewal assigned to Boosey & Hawkes, Inc.,
for the U.S.A. & to Universal Edition for all other countries. Reprinted
by permission.

Some compositions close with a pattern or sonority that sounds final only in
the sense that it is the last thing heard. This makes it logical to close a composition
with complex sonorities which do not necessarily represent a *harmonic resolution* of
preceding activity.

The chord that appears at the end of Ex. 17-4 closes a movement. By its very
nature, this chord bears no resemblance to traditional "final" chords. In the context
of the movement, however, both the melodic motion down a half-step and the
symmetric chord produce a logical close. They are both events that are structurally
significant throughout the movement; the descending half-step is the final interval
of the basic melodic shape and the symmetric chord is the initiator of activity
at the beginning. By bringing these aspects together, the close is a type of musical
synthesis.

Ex. 17-4. Schoenberg: Piano Piece, Op. 11, No. I. Copyright owned by
Universal Edition. Used by permission.

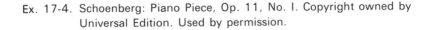

The structural delineation in Ex. 17-5 is accomplished through an interaction of several factors, the most prominent of which are clearly articulated cadences to tonic, *B-flat* (measures 5, 7, and 12). Tonic is supported by its dominant in measures 2, 6, and 8 as a prominent melodic pitch in the flute and as a chord root at beat 3 (measure 8). The tonal organization of the example and its divisions into phrases are remarkably clear.

Ex. 17-5. Hindemith: Sonata for Flute and Piano, I. © 1937 by B. Schott's
        Soehne, Mainz. Reprinted by permission.

Heiter bewegt

Ex. 17-5 continued.

Other Factors Which Delineate Phrases and Create Continuity

Clearly defined phrases or sectional cadences are largely absent from many contemporary works. When this is the case we can usually point to a variety of other factors which may contribute to phrase and sectional delineation. For example, phrases may be marked off through the simple expedient of a change of dynamics, or by a change of harmony, as at measure 7 of Ex. 17-6.

Ex. 17-6. Stravinsky: Symphony in Three Movements, I. © 1946 by Schott & Co., Ltd., London. Reprinted by permission.

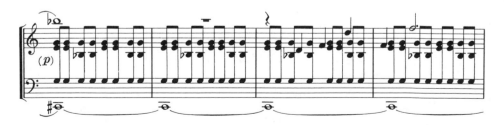

The change of chord that occurs at measure 7 (from a prolonged *c-sharp* $°_7$ to a $°_7$ on *a*) is set off by a *sforzando*. Several contrasting textural factors occur at the same point (with the thematic activity given to the bass and pizzicato chord in the upper strings).

Four pairs of like instruments (2 bassoons, 2 oboes, 2 clarinets, and 2 flutes) succeed each other in a series of short sections in Ex. 17-7. These contrasts of colors help to delineate the form of the movement. The successive appearances of the instrumental pairs are further contrasted by the consistent use of characteristic intervals, the sixth, the third, the seventh, and the fifth, respectively. In addition, each successive section is marked by a higher register, as the ranges of the different instruments suggest.

Ex. 17-7. Bartók: Concerto for Orchestra, II. Copyright 1946 by Hawkes & Son (London) Ltd. Reprinted by permission of Boosey & Hawkes, Inc.

Ex. 17-7 continued.

Overlapping entrances of a two-measure theme occur in the clarinet, horn, and trumpet in Ex. 17-8. Since the voices overlap, the cadential effect of each melodic statement is obscured. A repeated chord pattern comprised of only two different chord types accompanies the upper parts. Although the chords do not establish a tonic, they play a significant role in creating formal divisions. The introduction of a contrasting chord in measure 4 harmonically divides the melodic activity in half.

Ex. 17-8. Webern: Six Pieces for Orchestra, Op. 6, IV. © by Universal
       Editions. Used by permission.

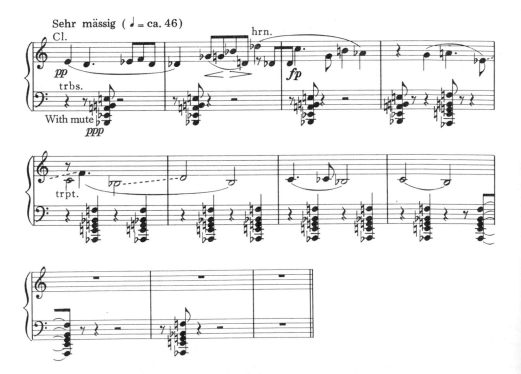

A persistent accompanimental figure tends to destroy the effect of repose, as in Ex. 17-9. Here the constant repetition in the accompaniment rules out a rhythmic caesura until a change in the rhythmic structure occurs. The repetitious pattern clouds the significance of the two melodic cadences shown. The rests in measure 7 do help to punctuate the upper part; since this is not confirmed by the accompaniment, however, it is apparent that a decisive cadence is not intended at this point.

Ex. 17-9. Stravinsky: *Soldier's Tale*, Part II By permission of the International Music Company, New York.

Ex. 17-10 contains a two-part canon at the octave. The contrapuntal texture of the excerpt contains no cadences in which both parts simultaneously abandon their melodic activity. However, we perceive clear melodic cadences in the separate voices at several points.

Ex. 17-10. Milhaud: Quartet No. 9, III. Reproduit avec l'autorisation des Editions "Le Chant du Monde," Paris.

Ex. 17-10 continued.

The two phrases of the upper voice are delineated by a relaxation of rhythm and the d^1—e^1-*flat* leading tone—tonic effect in measure 5, and by the melodic cadence to c^1 in measure 7. The lower voice imitates the upper with a cadence to e^1-*flat* in measure 5, and it cadences on b^1 at the close of the example.

The fact that these singular cadences do not coincide creates "breathing points" in textures that are essentially continuous unfoldings of independent lines. Without such periodic points of relaxation, the structure of the composition might be shapeless and monotonous. The overall rhythmic effect of the Milhaud example is one of continuous eighth-note flow.

It would be difficult to name any repetitive schemes found in twentieth-century music that are totally unprecedented. Literal, unmodified repetitions of motives, phrases, harmonic patterns, and other organizational factors are found less frequently today than, for example, in late eighteenth-century works. Repeated motives are likely to be rhythmically altered, as are harmonic patterns or sequences. But these basics of musical ordering, somewhat more subtly treated, are as prevalent in today's music as they were two hundred years ago.

In Ex. 17-11 a simple motive has been spun out for several measures by the process of adding and deleting pitches, so that in successive restatements different tones of the basic motive are stressed. The changing meters emphasize the regrouping of accented pitches that constitutes this type of motive variation.

Ex. 17-11. Stravinsky: *The Rite of Spring*, Part I.

Techniques of motive repetition such as this have largely replaced the literal restatement of motives prevalent in earlier music. Such repetitive schemes also typify the asymmetrical phrase divisions that are characteristic of much present-day music.

Motive repetition comprises the basis for an extended development in Ex. 17-12. A rhythmic representation of just one voice of the four-part texture has been indicated.

Ex. 17-12. Bartók: Quartet No. 4, I. Copyright 1929 by Universal Edition;
          Renewed 1956. Copyright & Renewal assigned to Boosey & Hawkes,
          Inc., for the U.S.A. and to Universal Edition for all other countries
          of the world. Reprinted by permission.

This line consists of two alternating motives. Motive (a) first appears in measure 2
of Ex. 17-12. It consists of the pattern ♩♫ ♫♩. The six derivative patterns
that occur in Ex. 17-12 consist of fragments of the initial form:

     (a¹)   (a²)   (a³)   (a⁴)   (a⁵)

as well as an extension of it.   ♫♩ (♫) ♫♩
                                     (a⁶)

    The continuity of the passage can be attributed primarily to the reshuffling of
both patterns and the successive variants of (a) that recur in different metric
positions.

    Sequential repetition in twentieth-century music most frequently appears in
modified forms, although instances of exact sequence may be found. In Ex. 17-13
outlined seventh chords comprise the basis for the melodic sequence. However,
the harmonic accompaniment is not sequential, although it is unified by an
ascending eighth-note figure (heard twice in the celli and once in the violins) which
outlines clear changes of harmony and creates the root pattern *B-flat, e-flat,* and
c¹-sharp.

Ex. 17-13. Berg: Violin Concerto, I. Copyrighted by Universal Editions. Used by permission.

The Variation Process

As discussed in earlier sections, the process of variation can be applied to both large and small formal units. For example, the technique of variation can apply to motives, phrases, or whole sections, to successive treatments of an initial theme, to a chord progression, and even to the return of a multi-thematic exposition. In a period during which *literal* repetition of both small and large formal units has been largely abandoned, variation has been exploited in a vast number of ways.

Successive repetitions of an important motive are treated imitatively in Ex. 17-14. The motive first heard in the first violin (measure 1) is restated an octave lower in the second violin two measures later, while a rhythmic variant of the same motive is heard in the viola in measure 4. The viola statement involves both a rhythmic extension of the first note and a duple grouping of the remaining pitches. Our perception of the latter version as a variant of the first is based on their similar contours; the variation is essentially rhythmic.

Ex. 17-14. Bartók: Quartet No. 6, I. Copyright 1941 by Hawkes & Son (London) Ltd. Renewed 1968. Reprinted by permission of Boosey & Hawkes, Inc.

A contrapuntal dialogue based on imitative entrances of several variants of a two-measure motive is shown in measures 24–40, Ex. 17-15.

The different variants occur in the form of intervallically expanded repetitions, repetitions in which both the duration and direction of the motive are varied, and restatements which contract the intervallic span of the motive. Every subsequent entry of the motive is a variant of the initial statement which fills in the dominant octave a^1 to a^2.

Ex. 17-15. Ibid.

Contrasting the preceding examples of modified restatements of motives with Ex. 17-16, we find a different, less obvious application of the principle of variation. Two phrases, each of which begins a different section of a movement in *ABA* form, are shown in the example. A comparison of them will show that (b) derives its material from the ascending melodic third of the first measure of (a). Both examples contrast texturally, tonally, and rhythmically, but the melodic relationship of (b) to (a) is quite clear.

Ex. 17-16. Hindemith: Chamber Music for Five Winds. ⓒ 1922 by Schott & Co., Ltd., London. Renewed 1949. Reprinted by permission.

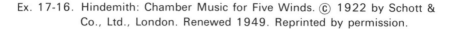

A process typical of both tonal and atonal music of the current era is shown in Ex. 17-17 and Ex. 17-18. Both passages involve a textural variation of essentially simple materials—a motive or a chord. In Ex. 17-17 a four-note fragment consisting of c^1, c^2-*sharp*, f^2, and e^3, distributed between two pairs of instruments, is asserted in measure 1. The same pitches are immediately transformed into a different textural arrangement and articulated as a chord, repeated three times.

Ex. 17-17. Webern: String Quartet, Op. 5, I. Copyright by Universal Editions. Reprinted by permission.

Later in the development of the same movement this basic process is reversed.

Ex. 17-18. Ibid.

Ex. 17-18 continued.

The end of measure 1 (Ex. 17-18) involves two statements of a chord which superposes sixths (or augmented fifths). Then the same interval and the same pitch classes are treated contrapuntally in a stretto. In a sense, the stretto consists of a projection of sixths in a completely contrasting texture, and because of the repetition of one characteristic interval, we perceive the second part of the example as a variation of the first.

Many large works of the twentieth century have been unified through the reintroduction (in successive sections or movements) of material which, while retaining some characteristic aspect of design, is consistently varied or transformed into new patterns.

Stravinsky's *Symphony of Psalms* does not contain a "variations" movement as such. However, the process of variation, along with other techniques of development, is partially responsible for the formal cohesiveness of this three-movement composition. A study of the score reveals many subtle transformations of material presented at the outset of the first movement. The entire work seems to be organized mainly through variation and contrast rather than repetition, although the latter does occur. Some of the most important materials of the first movement are described below.

The *e* minor chord (a) begins the work and recurs to delineate large sections of the movement. Stravinsky has voiced it so as to highlight the interval of a third (both major and minor).

(a)

Pattern (b) involves an arpeggiated figure that further emphasizes the third and joins arpeggiated thirds with seconds.

(b)

Item (c) juxtaposes the thirds of (a) and re-emphasizes the seconds of (b), while developing its rhythm.

(c)

The horn theme of (d) is a variant of (c), based entirely on the interval of the second.

(d)

Item (e) is an accompanimental ostinato based on the thirds of (a) and (b). This ostinato recurs, consistently varied, in all three movements, and might be described as the nucleus of the entire work. The first fugue subject of the second movement is a derivative or variation of this ostinato. (See Ex. 17-19.)

(e)

Ex. 17-19. Stravinsky: *Symphony of Psalms*, II. Copyright 1931 by Russischer Musikverlag; Renewed 1958. Copyright & Renewal assigned to Boosey & Hawkes, Inc. Revised Version Copyright 1948 by Boosey & Hawkes, Inc. Reprinted by permission.

Items (f) and (f') are clearly variants of the ostinato in (e), as is the theme in (g), while (h) is a soprano line that is obviously built of (a).

It is difficult, because of the "chain-development" established by these successive materials, to point to any one idea as basic. The movement expands and develops through the introduction of a seemingly inseparable chain of passages, each of which harks back to previous materials, and these materials are related through certain common melodic properties. The process is essentially variational, but it is a variation process that is more developmental than repetitive; the thread of continuity is more subtly woven into each variational segment than in most "traditional" variation movements.

More than any other group, serial composers have exploited different variation techniques in the twentieth century, often treating the tone row as a kind of *cantus firmus*. Webern's *Variations for Orchestra* exemplifies this trend and contains some unique treatments of the row.

The melodic theme of this work is presented in three groups of four tones, distributed among the string bass, oboe, and muted trombone, as shown in Ex. 17-20. An abstract note form of the row is shown following the excerpt.

Ex. 17-20. Webern: *Variations for Orchestra*, Op. 30. Copyright by Universal Editions. Reprinted by permission.

A study of this excerpt shows that another form of the row, transposed up a half-step, overlaps the first statement. It begins in the violas, in the third measure.

To grasp better the relationships of the succeeding variations to the principal theme (the original form of the row), it is important to notice certain properties of the row itself. A study of its three segments shows that the row clearly emphasizes certain intervals, as marked in Ex. 17-21.

Ex. 17-21. The three four-note segments of the row.

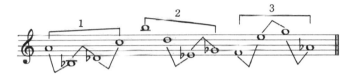

Segments 1 and 3 contain the pattern M7, m3, M7; and segment 3 is a melodic inversion of the first. Segment 2 contrasts with 1 and 3 since it contains the M6th, b^2 d^2. It also contains the M7 and m3. Both intervallic contrast and repetition are created by this arrangement of a tone row into two like and one unlike units. Lines have been drawn in Ex. 17-21 to connect those intervals which are common to all three segments. A great deal of the subsequent development of this work is based on the exploitation of these intervallic properties.

Two *sforzando* chords occur before the close of the exposition. Both are derived from simultaneous occurrences of members of the row. The chords shown in Ex. 17-22 obviously are derived from a verticalization of the pitches previously heard melodically. Chord (a) has the same pitch and interval content as the second four-note segment. Chord (b) has the interval and pitch content of the first segment.

Ex. 17-22. Ibid.

The first variation begins at measure 21, and contrasts with the exposition by its essentially chordal texture. A single strand of melody "floats" over repeated chords. All the chords, the first three of which are shown in Ex. 17-23, are derived from successive notes of the row and clearly unfold the same intervallic properties discussed above.

Ex. 17-23. Ibid. Variation I.

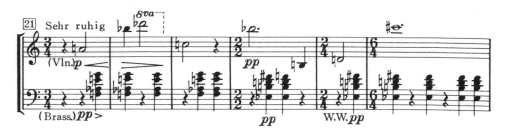

Variation II begins at measure 56, and is almost entirely chordal. The same basic intervals, reordered and contrasted by changes of orchestration and dynamics are found in this variation. Measures 56–59 are shown in the reduction in Ex. 17-24.

Ex. 17-24. Ibid. Variation II.

Variation III is monophonic and involves tiny snatches of melody derived from reorderings of the row, tossed back and forth between different isolated orchestral colors. Repeated rhythmic fragments, delineated by sudden changes of dynamics, comprise the contrasting effect of this section.

The tempo is twice as fast in Variation IV. The melodic fragments are couched in a contrapuntal texture, and the climax of the movement occurs toward the close of the variation. The reduction in Ex. 17-25 shows how the composer treats the different voices (all of which derive their material from segments of the row or its different possible permutations) so as to emphasize the intervallic properties (M6ths, M7ths, and m3rds) which were stated at the outset of the movement.

Ex. 17-25. Ibid. Variation IV.

The fifth variation is short and very quiet, and contains both chordal and contrapuntal writing, developing further the same properties of the row that we have seen. It is transitional in effect and leads quickly to the sixth variation, which is set off by a change of tempo and the muted statement of a chord progression which contains an interval not found in the chords heard thus far, the tritone, *b-flat* to *e*.

Ex. 17-26. Ibid. Variation VI.

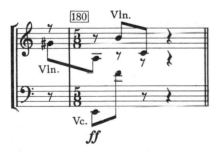

The coda (the sixth variation) recapitulates the different kinds of textures which have occurred in the movement, and the row is unfolded both melodically and chordally. The last melodic interval heard is a major seventh, the upper member of which forms a harmonic tritone with the f^1 in the cello:

The details and subtleties of this short work are almost unprecedented in earlier composition. In common with many earlier variations, it illustrates the development of material, in this case properties which are peculiar to its tone row. The materials (and their treatment) have been economically chosen. They represent a distillation or reduction to the barest minimum.

Organization and Structure of Three Contemporary Compositions

Now that some of the materials and organizational procedures of contemporary music have been discussed, a detailed study of representative compositions not only will reveal their elemental structure and organization, but also will portray analytic techniques that can be used to disclose similar musical processes in other works.

The work quoted in its entirety in Ex. 17-27 is a diminutive ternary design in which each section is of a different length, and in which the return is an abbreviated form of the opening section. Some of the most significant form-delineating factors present are: (1) the strong cadences that close the first section and end the composition (measures 10 and 24 respectively); (2) the change of melodic contour and rhythm in measure 11; and (3) the abrupt change of texture (measure 19) that coincides with the beginning of the abbreviated return of the first section.

In addition to these features, tonality also is an important delineating factor. The work is framed by a *G* tonality (*G* is the principal tonal center because it appears both at the beginning and at the end of the composition). Within this framework other tonalities are established, each associated with the beginning or end of a formal unit. For example, *C-sharp* is clearly heard as tonic at the midpoint of the first section (measure 5), and *D* is the tonic at the end of this section.

Ex. 17-27. Hindemith: *Ludus Tonalis*, Interludium in G. © 1943 by Schott & Co., Ltd., London. Reprinted by permission.

Tonality changes, together with sequential repetition, are characteristic of the contrasting middle section (measures 11–18). In this section, contrasts are a result of the juxtaposed tonal regions—D (measures 11–12), F-sharp (measures 13–14)—and the bitonal separation of B and D-flat (measures 16–18), whereas in the first section four measures elapse before a change of tonality occurs: G (measures 1–4), C-sharp (measures 5–8), and D (measures 9–10). In this sense, the middle section is less stable than the sections which precede and follow it, because tonality changes are more frequent. As a matter of fact, instability is still present in the return of measures 5–10 (in measure 19); instead of G the restatement begins in F-sharp and then moves abruptly to G at the close of the movement.

The tonality scheme of this work shows a characteristic feature of many contemporary compositions: frequent tonality changes framed by a principal tonal center.

	A			B			A′	
	G	*C-sharp*	*D*	*D*	*F-sharp*	*D-flat*	*F-sharp*	*G*
ms.	1	5	10	11-12	13-14	16-18	19	24

As can be seen, numerous different tonalities occur within the span of twenty-four measures. However, each of these tonics coincides with the beginning or end of a formal unit, clearly delineating formal sections as well as divisions within these sections.

While the foregoing discussion reveals some gross features, other factors of organization come to light when the movement is reduced to a two-voice framework. (Before proceeding, the piece should be performed again, keeping in mind the broad aspects discussed above.) As will be recalled, such a reduction contains only basic pitches, a skeletal version of the actual work.

Ex. 17-28. Two-voice reduction of Ex. 17-27.

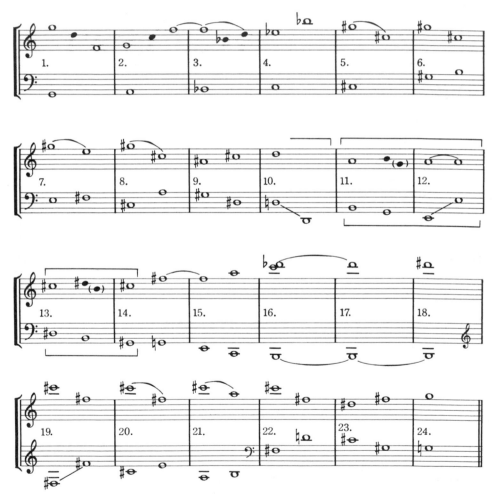

Octaves between the outer parts appear only three times, at the beginning, in measure 10, and at the end. In each instance they help to establish the most stable parts of the musical structure. In other words, the octaves at the beginning and end define the principal tonality, as well as the movement from and back to a point of repose. The octave in measure 10 creates the strongest secondary point of repose, a terminal cadence on *D*. A comparison with other cadential points, such as measures 12 and 14 (enclosed in brackets), clearly shows another factor that contributes to the contrast of the middle section—the cadential intervals here are fourths, which explains the effect of progressive cadences.

Another comparison can be made between the structural pitches that appear at the beginnings of formal units. For example, the phrases that begin in measures 5 and 19 have as structural intervals perfect fifths; in contrast, the phrases that begin in measures 11 and 13 have as structural pitches minor sevenths. The contrast created by the middle section thus becomes even clearer: its beginning and ending structural pitches are less stable than those in the first and last sections.

The two-voice reduction also reveals a basic difference between the succession of structural pitches in the outer parts. As the sketch shows, melodic fifths and sixths dominate the top line, whereas melodic thirds and seconds prevail in the lower. Note that perfect fifths occur only twice (measures 5–6 and 19–20) in the latter. Furthermore, each of the terminal cadences (measures 10 and 24) contains both a lower and an upper leading tone.

A musical synthesis made by restoring portions of the melodic overlay discloses other organizational factors which must be ignored in any reduction. Ex. 17-29 shows three instances of the elaboration of structural pitches.

Ex. 17-29. Melodic elaboration, measures 3–5 and 9–10.

In Ex. 17-29a both a 4-3 and a 6-5 suspension appear. The resolution of the latter is ornamented. In Ex. 17-29b the E is a leaning tone, the F-*sharp* is a basic associate.

If we continue the synthesis to include the harmonies associated with the structural framework, it is evident that tertian chords predominate. Here only a few instances will be cited. First, the opening four measures of the left-hand part consist entirely of parallel minor and major triads (note that the fifth of each chord is embellished by a leaning tone). The result is essentially the same if both parts are considered in combination.

Ex. 17-30. Triadic parallelism, first four measures.

Second, the harmonic motion that immediately precedes the cadence in measure 10 involves a three-note quintal chord and a three-note seventh chord, both moving to the cadential dyad of *d—a*.

Ex. 17-31. Cadential reduction, measure 10.

Ex. 17-32 shows the sonorities that appear in measures 14–16. The first chord is a perfect eleventh chord and the second a mM_7. The third chord can be described as a mmM_9 chord, or as the stacking of two different thirds. Similarly, the next sonority can be described as a thirteenth chord (with an augmented eleventh) or as a bichord. The last chord of the example contains two tritones (*b—f, d*-sharp—*a*) but no perfect fifths.

Ex. 17-32. Chords of measures 14–16.

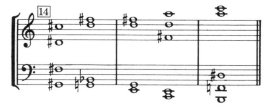

Although the preceding study does not account for every detail, it does indicate ways in which the principal organizational factors of a composition can be perceived through aural and visual analysis.

Many compositions of our day are formed (shaped) by successions of events. In such works successive events have the role commonly assigned to melodic-harmonic themes. Although melodic-harmonic factors may have less formal significance, the qualitative dimensions, such as the coloristic, may become more important. The sound sources are inclusive, from totally electronically produced sounds to traditional instruments, or combinations of the two, but as in all musical forms *sameness* and *change* are essential to the formal processes.

Penderecki's *Threnody: To the Victims of Hiroshima* is representative of works in which successive color events are basic formative elements. In this instance the composition contains events that have a "sustained" or a "nonsustained" quality.[2] Since the sustained sounds return, an arch-like design results; this design is made

---

[2] Sustained is used here to designate sounds that are continuously audible for at least several seconds; nonsustained designates the shortest durations to those of approximately three seconds in duration.

up of the statement, measures 1–25; the contrast, measures 26–61; and the return, measures 62–70.[3]

Loudness (dynamics) and silence are structural factors as well, particularly in the closing of the first section (measures 1–25). This section closes with a 50-second *decrescendo* from *fff* to a five-second silence. The cadencing activity is reinforced (measures 20–24) by a change from a *molto vibrato* to a very slow vibrato with a $\frac{1}{4}$ tone frequency difference to *senza vibrato*. Not only is there a change in the manner of performance, but also a reduction from 52 players to *solo* cello (at measure 23).

Such clear separation of sections does not recur when the sustained-sound idea returns. Rather, there is an overlapping of the contrasting section and the return, with different aspects of the return restated gradually (beginning in measure 62). The composition closes with the full ensemble in a 30-second decrescendo, *fff* ⟹ *ppp*.

Each of the sections is characterized by processes of gradual change. Ex. 17-33 shows measures 1–24[4] of the movement. As the notation indicates, groups of players are to enter at different moments in a pseudo-random fashion, playing the highest note of the instrument (indefinite pitch) at a *ff* level and *senza* vibrato. Measure 2 is signalled by the *subito f* and two types of vibrato in the violins and violas;[5] measures 3–5 continue *subito* dynamic changes and the two types of vibrato (by measure 4 all of the instruments play either ⌇⌇⌇⌇⌇ or ∿∿∿∿ ; in measure 5 violins are *senza* vibrato).

Ex. 17-33. Penderecki: *Threnody: To the Victims of Hiroshima.* Copyright © 1961 by Deshon Music, Inc. & PWM Editions, Used by permission.

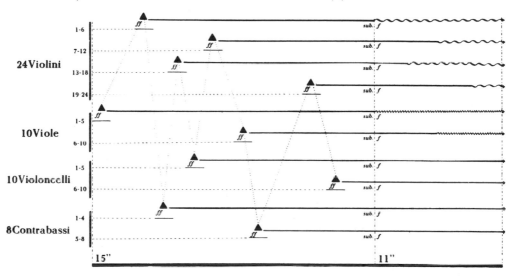

----

[3] All measure numbers refer to the published score.

[4] Each of the measures in this composition is designated in clock time: thus, during measure 1, 15 seconds are to elapse before measure 2 begins.

[5] ⌇⌇⌇⌇ = *molto* vibrato; ∿∿∿ = slow vibrato with a $\frac{1}{4}$ tone frequency difference.

Different articulations of the sustained tone, a rapid alternation of *pizzicato* and *arco*, played behind the bridge, are introduced in measure 6; the articulation changes are a variant of the vibrato-like quality in the preceding bars. Its effect is *change*, delineating a new musical phrase.

Ex. 17-34. Ibid., measures 6–7.

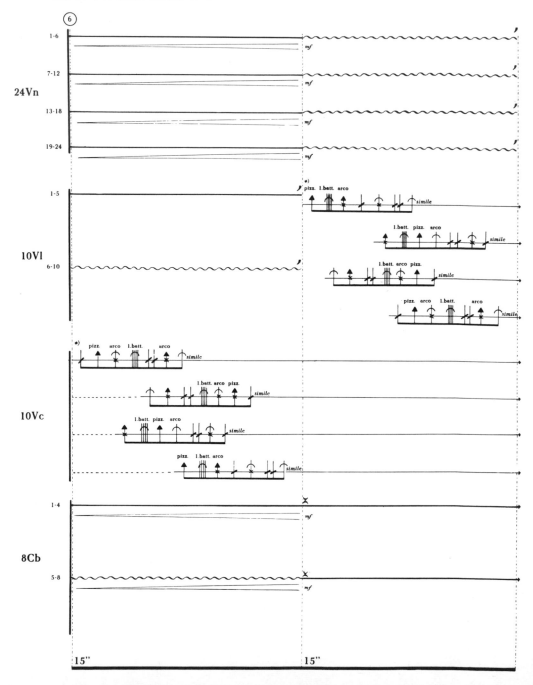

A distinctly new event is presented in measure 10. At this point the cello section is assigned notes at a lower pitch register. The phrase begins with a sustained unison that is gradually changed, in the manner of a sound wedge, to span a vertical perfect fourth; the phrase closes by gradually returning to a unison. A similar musical idea is present from measures 10–20, even though the width of wedge is of different vertical intervallic sizes (see measures 11 and 14).

Ex. 17-35. Ibid., measure 10.

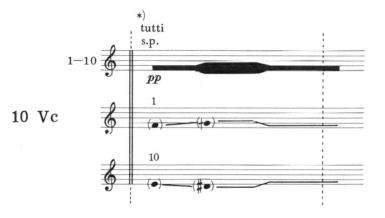

In measure 18 (shown in Ex. 17-36) overlapping wedges are created by the individual entries of each of the players. Each player sustains his assigned pitch, with a *crescendo* from *pp* to *f* (cellos) and to *ff* all other instruments; by measure 19 *fff* in the cellos and string basses. Measures 18–19 contain the dynamic climax of this portion of the movement. From measures 20 to 25 a decrease in dynamics and number of players closes the section.

Ex. 17-36. Ibid, measure 18.

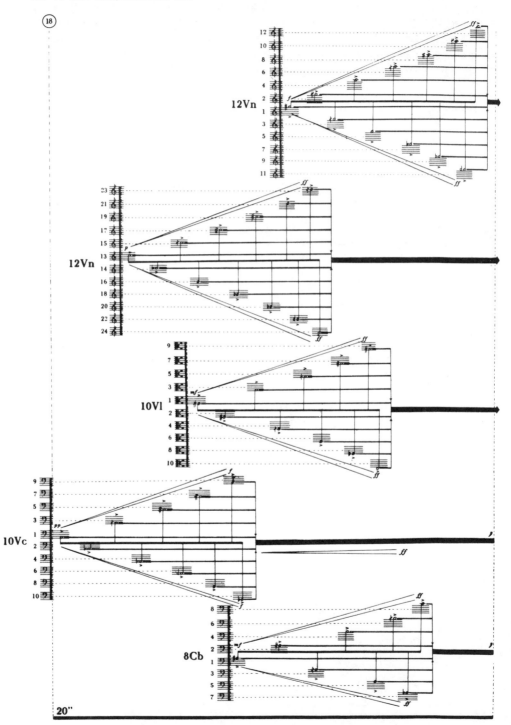

Measures 1–25 are shaped, then, by dynamics, articulation devices, and pitch. It is apparent that the process also involves gradual change from several instruments playing a similar sound or pitch to each instrument playing a different note with a subsequent return to a single sound (as at measure 23).

The section beginning at measure 26 does not introduce new materials; rather, a drastic change in attack density occurs. For example, in measures 26–34 very few attacks are designated to occur simultaneously. On the other hand, measures 35–37 call for simultaneous attacks and a tone sustained for a few seconds; even so, the section is characterized by the attack density change that begins in measure 26.[6]

Ex. 17-37. Ibid., measures 26–31.

As in the first section, there is a gradual increase in vertical density. This increase, in part, results from the change from twelve players (measures 26–37) to twenty-four players (measures 38–43) to thirty-six players (measures 44–61). By measure 65 all fifty-two players are performing, but by measure 65 each is performing a sustained note rather than individual attacks.

<hr/>

[6]Although precisely notated, measures 26–34 and 38–46 create the effect of randomness, as if unfolding by chance. The element of chance is present for the performer, as in measures 10–12, and as a musical effect, as in measures 26–34 and 38–46.

The form of this work is the result of the interaction of properties that often play subsidiary roles. The formal process is characterized by a multiplicity of changes that range from the subtle to the obvious,[7] and *vice versa*.

In some compositions form is produced as much by the actual act of performance as it is by the relations and interrelations preestablished by a composer. Thus, it is not surprising that chance comes to play an important compositional and performance role; similarly, it is not surprising that the concept of *open form*, in which the form of the piece depends entirely on a performance, arises. The score for one such work is shown in Ex. 17-38.

Ex. 17-38. Ashley: *in memoriam . . . ESTEBAN GOMEZ*. Reprinted by permission of Source: Music of the Avant Garde.

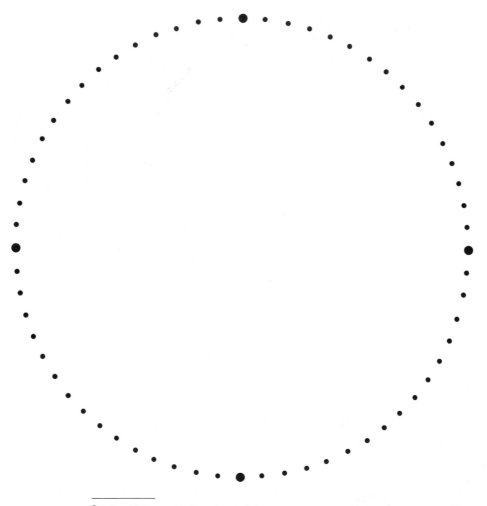

---

[7] It should be noted that many of the compositional techniques employed by Penderecki are similar to those employed by some electronic composers.

The circular graph is divided into quadrants; each quadrant is divided into sixteen equal units which represent a constant unit of time. Before a performance, each performer assigns one sound dimension to each quadrant, i.e., *pitch, intensity, timbre,*[8] and *density.*[9] These dimensions may be assigned to any quadrant, but when determined the pattern remains constant throughout the performance.

Each performance begins with a reference sonority that is prepared in advance. This sonority serves as a tonal reference for the sound play that makes up the performance:

> Whenever any performer first becomes aware of a deviant element (other than his own) in the reference sonority, his pattern of assigned sound elements (quadrants) shifts circularly so that the mode of deviation he recognizes is assigned to the quadrant opposite that in which he is playing or will play next. (As the pattern of quadrants remains constant, thus, all quadrants will be redesignated.) The pattern of quadrant designations remains in its changed position until the performer has played through the succeeding (newly designated) quadrant, after which it is subject again to transposition through the appearance of deviant elements in the sonority.[10]

Such a work evolves as it is performed and any discussion must by necessity refer to a specific performance. Form and structure are realized anew with each performance of the work; it is unlikely that any realization duplicates another.

Exercises

For more detailed assignments see *Materials and Structure of Music II, Workbook,* Chapter 17.

1. Make aural and visual analyses of the broad form of works such as the following:
   Bartók: *String Quartet* No. 4, III.
   Berio: *Circles*
   Brown: *Available Forms*
   Carter: *Piano Sonata,* II.
   Davidovsky: *Synchronisms* No. 1
   Erb: *Sonata for Harpsichord and String Quartet*
   Hindemith: *Organ Sonata in E-flat*
   Kagel: *Sonant*
   Lutoslawski: *Paroles Tisseés*
   Prokofiev: *Violin Concerto* No. 2, I
   Schoenberg: *Piano Pieces,* Op. 11
   Stockhausen: *Studie II*
   Stravinsky: *Symphony in C,* I
   Webern: *String Quartet,* Op. 28
   Xenakis: *Akrata*
   Consider how formal divisions are delineated, i.e., use of clear-cut cadences, change of texture, change of tonality, change of chord types, etc.

---

[8]The composer stipulates that *timbre* refers to changes of tone color produced by mutes, bow movements, etc.
[9]*Density* designates mixing of tonal ingredients, as flutter-tongue, double stops, etc.
[10]Source: *Music of the Avant Garde,* 1:41.

2. Using the partial analyses of Stravinsky's *Symphony of Psalms,* Webern's *Variations for Orchestra,* and the Hindemith "Interludium" as a starting point, make detailed analyses of sectional form, melodic, harmonic, and rhythmic structure, and decorative pitches.

3. Write a 28-measure three-section composition for oboe, horn, and piano. The tonality scheme of the Hindemith "Interludium" quoted in this chapter might form the tonality basis of your work. Or, make an elaboration of the two-voice reduction of the same work (given in Ex. 17-28) for the combination of instruments given above.

4. Devise a row of twelve different notes that will form the pitch materials of a composition for five winds. Plan a sectional composition in which the sections, in part, are delineated by exploiting characteristics of segments of the row.

5. Make a formal plan for an extended movement for piano. Sketch in the features that will be used to establish the large sections, such as dominating texture, chord types, etc. Write in some of the principal motivic, melodic, rhythmic, and harmonic material. Plan to include an ostinato in one of the sections.

GLOSSARY

Anticipation: A decorative pitch that preannounces the appearance of a basic pitch. In a harmonic context an anticipation may be either consonant or dissonant.

Appoggiatura: A decorative pitch that is approached by leap and resolved by step, generally by descending step.

Basic Consonances: Those consonant intervals that are frequently found as the beginning and cadential harmonic intervals, i.e., octaves, fifths, and thirds.

Basic Duration: The time-span between a pulse (or beat) and the beginning of the next pulse. Basic duration also designates notational representation; for example, $\quad \downarrow$ = basic duration in $\frac{2}{4}$

$\quad \downarrow.$ = basic duration in $\frac{6}{8}$

Basic Melody: The basic pitches of a melody. (See *Basic Pitch*).

Basic Pitch: Those individual pitches that make up a basic melody as determined by relative duration, accent, or any melodic means that would make one pitch more important than others which surround it.

Cadential Consonances: See *Basic Consonances*.

Close Spacing: Any arrangement in which the three upper members of a chord are in their closest possible position.

Contrasting Phrase Construction: Refers to successive phrases that do *not* have the same rhythmic structure.

Decorative Consonances: Those consonant intervals that are not frequently found as cadential intervals, i.e., sixths and perfect fourths.

Dissonant Intervals: Intervals other than basic or decorative consonances, i.e., major and minor seconds, major and minor sevenths, augmented fourths, and diminished fifths (and their compounds).

Escape Tone: A decorative pitch that is approached by step and moves to a structural pitch by skip. In a harmonic context, escape tones may be either consonant or dissonant.

Heterogeneous Spacing: Refers to any chord in which the members are spaced in gapped relations of unequal sized intervals.

Homogeneous Spacing: Applies to any texture, close or open, in which approximately equal-sized intervals occur between the adjacent voices.

---

*This glossary includes only terms that are used for the first time in *Materials and Structure of Music* or traditional terms whose meanings require some clarification.

Imperfect Terminal Cadence: See *Terminal Cadence*.

Meter: The grouping of patterns of weak and strong beats into regular units of time.

Mode: Scales consisting of different arrangements of five whole- and two half-steps. For example, Ionian (*C* major)

Modulation: The process of changing from one tonal center to another.

Mutation: Chromatic inflection of a scale step, producing a change of mode. For example, a change from *C* major to *C* minor is a *mutation;* an *A-flat* in *C* major would be a *mutated* 6th degree.

Neighbor Group: A figure of decorative tones that embellish a single basic pitch. One of these pitches is located a step above the basic pitch, the other a step below. In a harmonic context, either one or both of the decorative pitches may be either consonant or dissonant.

Neighbor Tone: A decorative pitch moving by step away from a basic pitch and returning to it; in a harmonic context neighbor tones may be either consonant or dissonant.

Open Spacing: Any distribution of parts in which the three upper members of a chord are not arranged in their closest possible relations.

Parallel Phrase Construction: Two or more successive phrases sharing the same rhythmic structure and similar contours.

Passing Tone: A decorative pitch that connects two different basic pitches, or a basic pitch and its secondary. In a harmonic context passing tones may be either consonant or dissonant.

Perfect Terminal Cadence: See *Terminal Cadence*.

Period: Two or more consecutive phrases which avoid an implication of finality at interior cadences.

Progressive Cadence: Represents a break in tonal flow but with the suggestion of continuation. Both the half and the deceptive cadence belong to the general classification *Progressive Cadence*.

Scale: A step arrangement within the span of an octave of the notes that serve as the pitch basis for a composition.

Secondary Pitches: Decorative pitches that elaborate by skipping to and from a basic pitch.

Sequence: Successive repetitions at different pitch levels.

Stable Intervals: See *Basic Consonance*.

Step-Progression: The ascending or descending motion by steps that outlines a melodic line over the whole or a large segment of a passage.

Structural Intervals: See *Basic Consonance*.

Suspension: A decorative figure in which (1) a basic pitch is prolonged by means of a tie or rearticulation, (2) extending it into a metric or rhythmic accent, (3) then moving by step to an unaccented basic or decorative pitch. In a harmonic context step *1* generally is consonant, step *2* generally is dissonant, and step *3* generally is consonant.

Syncopation: Syncopation occurs when the accents normal to the metric or rhythmic framework are contradicted. Such contradictions can be brought about by duration, dynamic stress, etc.

Terminal Cadence: Cessation of activity, represented by tonic as the cadence pitch (*perfect terminal cadence*) or by a pitch relation having tonic as its root (*imperfect terminal cadence*). In a harmonic context, authentic (V—I) and plagal cadences (IV—I) belong to the general class of *Terminal cadence,*

Tonality: The property of pitch focus in music.

Tonality Framework: A kind of "floor and ceiling" within which the melodic parts will all sound as related elements of the tonal design. In many melodies the tonality frame is bounded by some relationship of tonic-dominant, tonic-tonic, tonic-mediant, or some other distribution of these scale degrees.

Transient-Terminal Cadence: A cadence on any scale degree other than tonic in which the cadence pitch momentarily has the importance of a tonic.

Two-Voice Framework: The total pitches of any texture reduced to the basic outer parts.

Unstable Intervals: See *Dissonant Intervals.*

INDEX OF MUSICAL EXCERPTS

A

Anonymous: *En ma dame* (Trouvère Rondeau), 32; *L'homme armé*, 126; *Nun komm, der Heiden Heiland* (German chorale), 133; Spanish folksong, 172; *Vater unser im Himmelreich* (German chorale), 127

Ashley: *In memoriam . . . Esteban Gomez*, 460

B

Bach, J. S.:

Art of the Fugue: Contrapunctus I, 255, 260; Contrapunctus II, 248; Contrapunctus V, 256–57; Contrapunctus VI, 257; Contrapunctus IX, 273

Chorale Preludes: *Alle Menschen müssen sterben*, 137; *Christ ist erstanden*, 135; *Christ lag in Todesbanden*, 134–35; *Gotte, durch deine Güte*, 139; *In dulci jubilo*, 140; *Nun komm, der Heiden Heiland*, 132, 133; *Wo soll ich fliehen hin*, 130–31

English Suite in F Major, Prelude, 2–6; Fugue in G Minor, 259

Inventions: *(three-voice)* F Minor, 363; E-flat Major, 89; F Minor, 235, 241–42; *(two-voice)* C Major, 212, 218, 219, 226; C Minor, 214–15, 223; D Major, 211, 218, 222, 230; D Minor, 208–10, 212; E Major, 216–17, 220; E Minor, 211, 219, 225, 229; E-flat Major, 221; F Major, 213–14, 225, 229; F Minor, 212, 226–27; G Major, 212, 215; G Minor, 228; A Minor, 212, 213, 219, 228; B

Bach, J. S.: *(cont.)*

Minor, 211, 223–24, 227; B-flat Major, 211, 216, 224

Passacaglia in C Minor, 175–77; Solo Violin Sonata in E Major, Gavotte en Rondeau, 33

Well-Tempered Clavier (Book I)

Fugues: C Major, 244–45; C Minor, 247; C-sharp Minor, 261; D Minor, 241, 245, 251, 260–61, 271; D-sharp Minor, 258; E Major, 265; E Minor, 234, 249; E-flat Major, 257; F Major, 237–39, 255; F Minor, 264–65; F-sharp Minor, 252; G Minor, 246, 254, 271–72; A Major, 232–33; A-flat Major, 263; B-flat Minor, 252, 256

Preludes: C Major, 109; D Minor, 103; E-flat Major, 99; E-flat Minor, 147–48; F Minor, 89.

Well-Tempered Clavier (Book II)

Fugues: C Minor, 242; C-sharp Major, 256; D Minor, 250; E Major, 257; G Minor, 275

Bacharach: *What the World Needs Now*, 49

Barber: Piano Sonata, Op. 26, I,* 388; II, 43; IV, 246, 248–49, 250–51, 266; Symphony No. 1, 178–79; Variations on *Wondrous Love*, 138–39; Violin Concerto, I, 382–83

Bartók: Concerto for Orchestra, I, 369, 416–17; II, 435–36; IV, 255; V, 243; *Contrasts*, III, 386–87; *Little Pieces for Children*, Vol. I, No. 7, 76

Mikrokosmos: Vol. VI, No. 146, 367; No. 148, 370; No. 150, 428

---

*Roman numerals indicate movement quoted.

Music for Strings, Percussion, and Celesta, I, 268, 381; IV, 44; Piano Concerto No. 3, II, 81; Piano Sonata, I, 421; III, 391, 392

Quartets: No. 1, I, 262–63; III, 267; No. 3, I, 374; No. 4, I, 432, 439; No. 5, Finale, 269–70; No. 6, I, 440–41

Sonata for Two Pianos and Percussion, II, 376; Sonata No. 2 for Violin and Piano, I, 396; Suite, Op. 14, I, 401; II, 375

Beethoven: Bagatelle, Op. 119, No. 9, 142; Concerto for Violin, III, 41; "God Save the King," 108

Piano Sonatas: Op. 2, No. 1, I, 279; Op. 10, No. 1, I, 72; Op. 14, No. 1, III, 53; Op. 27, No. 2, III, 144; Op. 31, No. 2, I, 146; Op. 31, No. 3, I, 111; III, 95; Op. 49, No. 2, I, 296–97; Op. 53, II, 338; Op. 81a, I, 100; II, 338–39; Op. 106, II, 334; III, 362; Op. 110, I, 340–41

Quartets: Op. 18, No. 2, IV, 164–65; Op. 18, No. 3, I, 288; Op. 18, No. 4, IV, 156–57; Op. 18, No. 5, II, 191–92; III, 170; Op. 18, No. 6, IV, 58; Op. 59, No. 2, I, 151; Op. 131, I, 263–64; IV, 193–96; Op. 132, III, 356–57

Symphonies: No. 1, IV, 303; No. 3, I, 63, 327; No. 4, II, 52; No. 6, I, 104; No. 7, III, 42; No. 9, I, 92; III, 63

Berg: *Schlafend trägt man,* 408; Violin Concerto, I, 440; *Wozzeck,* Act I, Lullaby, 390

Bizet: *Carmen,* Act II, "La fleur que tu m'avais jetée," 75

Blacher: Epitaph, Op. 41, 368

Böhm: Fugue for Organ, 255

Boulez: *Le marteau sans maître,* III, 370

Brahms: Chorale Prelude, *O Welt, ich muss dich lassen,* 138

Intermezzi: Op. 116, No. 1, 90; Op. 116, No. 6, 91; Op. 119, No. 3, 361

Quartet, Op. 51, No. 1, I, 145, 292–95; Rhapsody, Op. 79, No. 1, 347–48; *A German Requiem,* II, 144; VI, 57

Symphonies: No. 1, I, 169, 304–5; II, 327; No. 2, I, 301; No. 3, I, 110; II, 316; IV, 354–55; No. 4, II, 148

Variations on a Theme of Haydn, 197–200, 274

Bruckner: Mass in F Minor, *Crucifixus,* 158; *Sanctus,* 162

Buxtehude: Fugue in D Minor for Organ, 258

C

Carter: Piano Sonata, I, 381; II, 367; Sonata for Flute, Oboe, 'Cello, and Harpsichord, II, 396–97

Chopin: Ballade in F Major, Op. 38, 85; Impromptu in A-flat Major, Op. 29, 336

Mazurkas: Op. 7, No. 1, 43; Op. 7, No. 2, 150; Op. 17, No. 2, 67; Op. 17, No. 4, 326

Nocturnes: C Minor, Op. 48, No. 1, 82; E Major, Op. 62, No. 2, 82; G Major, Op. 37, No. 2, 83; G Minor, Op. 37, No. 1, 71

Prelude, Op. 28, No. 6, 111; Prelude, Op. 28, No. 20, 146; Sonata in C Minor, IV, 158; Sonata in B-flat Minor, I, 162; Waltz, Op. 69, No. 1, 84

Copland: *Appalachian Spring,* 80, 87–88, 425; Fantasy for Piano, 390; *Music for the Theatre,* 419–20; Piano Sonata, 391, 404; Symphony No. 3, I, 427

Cowell: *Persian Set,* III, 373; String Quartet No. 5, II, 403

Creston: Symphony No. 2, I, 387

D

Dallapiccola: *Cinque Canti . . . ,* 380

Debussy: Prelude to *The Afternoon of a Faun,* 346, 364–65; Ballade, 87; *The Blessed Damozel,* 86, 123–24; *Clair de Lune,* 61; *Danse,* 119; *Pélléas et Mélisande,* Act IV, 123; Preludes, Book I, No. 4, 342–43

Dello Joio: Piano Sonata No. 3, I, 187, 193; Variations, Chaconne, and Finale, 182–83

Donovan: *Adventure,* 424–25

Dufay: *Missa L'homme armé, Kyrie* I, 126–27

Dupré: Chorale prelude, *Christ lag in Todesbanden,* 136

Dutilleux: Sonatine for Flute and Piano, 370

F

Fauré: *Poème d'un jour,* III, 66
Franck: Praeludium, Chorale, and Fugue,
      113; Prelude, Aria, and Finale, 330

G

Gershwin: Prelude No. 3 for Piano, 119
Gesualdo: "Io pur respiro," 166
Giannini: *A Canticle of Christmas,* 233
Godowsky: *Nocturnal Tangier,* 78
Gounod: *Faust,* Act I excerpt, 319
Grieg: *An der Bahre einer Jungen Frau,* 86

H

Handel: *Messiah:* "Rejoice Greatly," 147;
      "Surely He Hath Borne Our Griefs,"
      83
   Passacaille, 180–81; Suite No. 5, Air with
      Variations, 185–86; Suite No. 12,
      Gigue, 52
Harris: Symphony No. 3, 255
Haydn:
   Piano Sonatas: D Major, III, 40; E
      Minor, I, 116–17, 145; E-flat Major,
      I, 152–53; III, 362–63; G Major, I,
      201–2
   Quartets: Op. 74, No. 3, III, 155; Op. 76,
      No. 3, I, 167; Op. 76, No. 6, I, 159
   Symphonies: No. 88, IV, 34; No. 104, I,
      298–99; IV, 280
Heiden: Sonata for Piano Four-Hands, I,
      231–32
Helm: Concerto for Five Solo Instruments,
      Percussion, and Strings, 400
Hindemith: Chamber Music for Five
      Winds, 442
   Ludus Tonalis: Fuga Prima, 267; Fuga
      Secunda, 234, 247, 261; Fuga Tertia,
      243; Fuga Quarta, 240, 269, Fuga
      Sexta, 258; Interludia, 325, 450–51
   Mathis der Maler, 56, 259, 418, 426; *Nobilis-
      sima Visione,* III, 389; *Philharmonic
      Concerto,* 376
   Sonatas: Flute, I, 336–37, 433–34; Organ
      No. 1, II, 387; Piano No. 1, I, 402–3;
      Piano No. 2, I, 418–19; III, 383, 395;

Hindemith: *(cont.)*
      Piano No. 3, II, 44–45; Trumpet, III,
      137
   Theme and Four Variations, 190, 203–5
Honegger: Symphony for Strings, III, 421;
      Symphony No. 1, I, 388; Symphony
      No. 5, I, 394; II, 244

I

Ives: *Majority,* 393

K

Kabalevsky: "Novelette," 146
Kodaly: Cello Sonata, Op. 4, III, 320;
      Symphony No. 1, I, 26–30
Krenek: "The Moon Rises," 79; Toccata,
      424

L

Leoncavallo: *I Pagliacci,* Act I, "Recitar," 65
Ligeti: *Aventures,* 372
Liszt: *A Faust Symphony,* 375; Piano Concerto
      in E-flat Major, I, 114; Piano Sonata
      in B Minor, 163
Lutoslawski: Paroles Tissées, 377–78

M

Mahler: *Songs of a Wayfarer,* I, 98; Symphony
      No. 8, Finale, 169
Mendelssohn: Andante con Variazioni, Op.
      82, 75
   Elijah: "Behold, God the Lord Passed
      By," 56, 79; "Be Not Afraid," 73; "Yet
      Doth the Lord See It Not," 82
Messaien: *Couleurs de la Cité Céleste,* 411
Milhaud: Quartet No. 9, III, 437–38;
      Saudades do Brazil, 420; *Suite Française,*
      V, 45
Monteverdi: *Ariana,* "Lasciatemi morire,"
      53
Mozart: *Eine kleine Nachtmusik,* K. 525, I,
      295–96; Motet: *Ave verum corpus,* 64

Mozart: (*cont.*)
  Operas: *Idomeneo, Re di Creta,* Act I, sc.
    1, Recit.: "Quando avran fine,"
    7–15; *The Magic Flute,* Overture, 66;
    The Marriage of Figaro, Sextet from
    Act III, 63
  Piano Concerto, K. 466, III, 157
  Piano Sonatas: K. 309, III, 62; K. 330,
    III, 104, 105; K. 331, I, 187–89; K.
    332, I, 48, 115; K. 333, I, 287; K. 457,
    III, 74–75; K. 533, II, 113; III, 74;
    Sonatina in C Major, III, 34–35;
    Viennese Sonatina in C Major, III,
    35–37
  Quartet in B-flat Major, K. 458, III, 110;
    Sonata for Violin and Piano, K. 526,
    I, 289–91
  Symphonies: No. 38, I, 282–85; No. 40,
    I, 52; No. 41, IV, 299–300
Mussorgsky: *Boris Godunov:* Coronation
    Scene, 345; Act III, Polacca, 357–58
  Songs and Dances of Death, IV, 161

O

Offenbach: *Les Contes d'Hoffman,* Act III,
    "Elle à fui . . . ," 85

P

Palestrina: Motet, *Dies Santificatus,* 50; *Missa
    Dies Sanctificatus,* "Agnus Dei I," 274
Penderecki: *Anaklasis,* 412–13; *Threnody: To
    the Victims of Hiroshima,* 455–59
Persichetti: Piano Sonata No. 4, II, 417
Piston: Sonata for Violin and Piano, III,
    38–39
Prokofiev: Piano Concerto No. 3, I, 430;
    Piano Sonata No. 2, I, 385; Violin
    Concerto No. 2, III, 46
Puccini:
  La Boheme: Act I, "Si, mi chiamano
    Mimi," 51, 65; Act II, "Quando
    me'n vo," 78; Act IV, "Sono andati,"
    88
  Tosca: Act II, "Vissi d'arte," 83
Purcell: *Dido and Aeneas,* "Ah, Belinda,"
    174–75

R

Rachmaninoff: Prelude in E-flat Major,
    323–24
Rameau: *La Poule,* 112
Ravel: *Jeux d'eau,* 57; *Le Gibet,* 324; *Pavane,*
    90; Quartet, IV, 369; *Le Tombeau de
    Couperin,* 99, 311, 317
Reger: Quartet, Op. 109, I, 108
Rochberg: Bagatelle No. 5, 405–6

S

Scheidt: Variations on *Ei, du feiner Reiter,*
    184–85
Schoenberg: *Das Buch der hängenden Gärten,*
    400; *Moses and Aaron,* Act I, sc. 2, 346;
    Piano Piece, Op. 11, No. 1, 423, 432;
    Quartet No. 2, Op. 10, IV, 367;
    Quartet No. 4, Op. 37, I, 378, 407,
    431; Serenade, Op. 24, 382; Suite for
    String Orchestra, Fugue, 242
Schubert:
  Lieder: *Am Meer,* 165–66; *Frühlingstraum,*
    321; *Der greise Kopf,* 51; *Gute Nacht,*
    64; *Morgengrüss,* 119; *Der Müller und
    der Bach,* 143; *Rast,* 159; *Schwanenge-
    sang,* 341–42, 360; *Sei mir gegrüsst,*
    359–60; *Ständchen,* 321
  Mass in G Major, *Sanctus,* 147; Piano
    Sonata in D Major, III, 334–35; IV,
    43; Piano Sonata in B-flat Major, I,
    145; Quartet in C Minor, I, 149;
    Quartet in D Minor, 67; Quartet in
    A Minor, I, 116; Symphony No. 4,
    I, 94; Symphony No. 5, I, 61, 73; III,
    72–73, 112
Schuman, W.: *A Free Song,* 394; *American
    Festival* Overture, 266; Symphony
    No. 3, Fugue, 236; Symphony No. 4,
    II, 402
Schumann, R.: *Davidsbündler Tänze,* I,
    321–22; Fugue for Piano, Op. 72,
    254, 258, 270–71; *Kinderszenen,* Op.
    15, No. 1, 106; *Nachtstücke,* Op. 23,
    No. 2, 107; *Phantasiestücke,* Op. 12,
    318–19; Symphony No. 2, III, 95, 98,
    150–51, 168; Trio, Op. 80, II, 16–24

Shostakovitch:
   24 Preludes and Fugues: Fugue No. 2, 255;
      Fugue No. 4, 262; Fugue No. 5, 246;
      Fugue No. 9, 241
   Symphony No. 5, I, 427
Sibelius: Symphony No. 3, I, 346
Stockhausen: Electronic Study II, 414;
      Klavierstück X, 371
Strauss, R.: *Also sprach Zarathustra,* 346
Stravinsky: *The Firebird,* Finale, 389; *In
      Memoriam Dylan Thomas,* 380; Octet
      for Winds, 312, 368–69; *Petrouchka,*
      76; *The Rake's Progress,* 395; *The Rite
      of Spring,* 438; *The Soldier's Tale,* 437;
      Sonata for Two Pianos, I, 425; Sym-
      phony in Three Movements, I, 434–
      35; III, 325; *Symphony of Psalms,*
      444–46; Symphony of Wind Instru-
      ments, 422

T

Telemann:
   Chorale Preludes: *Christ lag in Todesban-
      den,* 132, 136; *Herzlich thut mich ver-
      langen,* 129; *Vater unser im Himmelreich,*
      128
Torelli: Violin Concerto, 40
Tschaikovsky: *Legende,* 64

V

Vaughan Williams: Symphony No. 5, III,
      373
Verdi: *Otello,* Act III, 166; *Requiem:* "Req-
      uiem e Kyrie," 87; "Ingemisco," 61;
      "Libera me," 62
Villa-Lobos: Quartet No. 3, IV, 392

W

Wagner: *Lohengrin:* Prelude, 149; Act II,
      Procession, 152; *Die Meistersinger:* Act
      I, 120; *Siegfried,* Act III, 121; *Tristan
      und Isolde:* Prelude, 100, 121–22, 315,
      344–45; Act I, 90, 328; Act II, 93,
      330–32, 349–53
Webern: Five Movements for String Quar-
      tet, Op. 5, 347, 377, 399, 443–44; Six
      Pieces for Orchestra, Op. 6, IV, 436;
      Symphony, Op. 21, II, 379, 422–23;
      Variations for Orchestra, Op. 30,
      409, 446–49
Wolf: *Italienisches Liederbuch,* 346; *Mörike
      Lieder,* 353–54; *Spanisches Liederbuch,*
      97, 312–14, 318, 364

INDEX

A

Aeolian, 353
Asymmetric, 27, *367ff,** 438
Atonal, atonality, 307, 376–81, 422–24
Augmentation, 226, *242*
Augmented sixth chords. *See* Chord,
    augmented sixth

B

Basic "blues" progression, *180*
Bichord, *393*–97
Binary form, 220, 277
Bi-thematic, 200–2
Bitonal, 27, 394, 420–22, 451
Bridge, 235, 240, 247*ff*, 279, 282, 299

C

Cadence, 56, 60*f*, 66, 72, 74, 78, 81*ff*, 99*f*,
    147, 153–55, 285, 329, 430–34
  deceptive, 329
  Phrygian, 147
  in twentieth-century music, 430–34
Cancrizans, 243 *fn*
Canon, canonic, 39, 139*f*, 213*ff*, 380, 429,
    437*f*
Cantus firmus (C.F.), *126ff*, 172*ff*, 429, 446
Chaconne, 173, *180*–83
Chance, 371, 429, 459
Chorale prelude, 126–40
  embellished, 134–40
  fugal, 127–34
  imitative, 127–34

Chord:

  added fourth, 389
  added second, 389
  added sixth, 60, 118
  augmented eleventh, 315–18
  augmented sixth, 141*f*, 153–71
    French six-four-three, *154*
    German six-five, *154*
      enharmonic resolution, 163*ff*
      as modulatory pivot, 163*ff*
    inverted, 160–63
    Italian Sixth, *154*
  diatonic seventh, 48–88
  diminished seventh, *49*, 69–76, 102–17
    enharmonic spelling, 105, 115
    irregular resolution of, 110–12
    as modulatory pivot, 112, 114–17
    regular resolution, 106
    and tonal instability, 112–14
  diminished third, 170
  dominant augmented eleventh, 315
  dominant eleventh, 310–15
  dominant ninth, 70, 91–97
  dominant thirteenth, 318–24
  eleventh, 310–18
  embellishing diminished seventh (°7/),
    102–25
    enharmonic spelling, 105
  embellishing diminished triad (°/),
    102–25
  embellishing half-diminished seventh
    (°7/), 117–24
  half-diminished seventh, *49*, 58*ff*, 69*ff*,
    117–24
    enharmonic spelling, 121–23
  leading tone seventh, 49*f*, 69–76

---

*Note: *Italic* type indicates pages on which the definition of a subject appears.

Chord: (cont.)

Major-Major seventh, *49, 76ff*

Major-minor seventh, *49,* 118, 164

mediant ninth, 97–99

mediant seventh, 85–88

minor-minor seventh, *49,* 58–68

Neapolitan, 141–53

ninth, 88–100

nondominant ninth, 97–100

nondominant seventh, 48–88

nondominant thirteenth, 324*f*

passing, 53

prime, 70, *102,* 117

quartal, *389f,* 398

quintal, *391*–93, 398, 402

secondary dominant, 3, 12, 84, 102*ff,*
   116

   of Neapolitan, 149*f*

secundal, 391, 398

seventh, 48–88

subdominant ninth, 97–99

subdominant seventh, 49*f,* 53–55, 79–84

submediant ninth, 97–99

submediant seventh, 84*f*

succession in twentieth century, 401–4

supertonic ninth, 97–99

supertonic seventh, 58–68

   as pivot chord, 67

thirteenth, 318–25

tone cluster, *392*

tonic ninth, 97–99

tonic seventh, 76–79

MM_7, *49,* 56, 76, 79, 84*f*

Mm_7, *49,* 102*f,* 118, 164

mm_7, *49,* 76, 79, 84*f*

mM_7, 49*fn*

MMM_9, 98*f*

mmM_9, 97*f*

$°7$, *49,* 69*ff,* 102–25

$\uparrow°7/V$, 109*f*

$\downarrow°7/V$, 109*f*

$ø7$, *49,* 58*ff,* 69*ff*

N, 146

N_6, 143–46

N six-four, 147

Chords:

containing tritones, 69*ff,* 102*ff,* 344–47,
   408

linear, 347–53

parallel, 387, 403

Coda, 39, 210, 279, 281*f,* 291, 299, 306

Contrapuntal association, 226–30, 247

Counterexposition, 239

Countermotive, 132

Counterpoint, 127–40

   double, 216*f,* 272–75

   invertible, 216*f,* 270–75, 300*f*

Countersubject, 210, 220, 226, 270–75

D

Development:

   section, 217–21, 280, 289–91, 292–95,
      296, 306*f*

   thematic, 207–31, 278*f,* 280*f*

Developmental procedures:

   augmentation, 226, *242*

   change of key, 210

   change of mode, 240

   contrary motion, 210, 217, 226

   diminution, 128, *242*

   fragmentation, 210*f,* 217, 219, 240, 247,
      280

   melodic inversion, 240*ff,* 379

   modal change, 217

   pitch alteration, 210, 217, 241

   retrogression, *242ff*

   sequential statements, 210, 217, 220,
      225, 229

   stretto, *223f,* 239, 241, 244–47, 252,
      256, 429

   textural inversion, 216, 220

Diminution, 128, *242*

Dissonance, treatment of, 50–55

Distantly-related keys, 16–25

Double canon, 139*f*

Double counterpoint, 216*f,* 272–75

Double fugue, 270 *fn*

E

Electronic composition, 366, 413–15

Embellished chorale prelude, 134–40

Enharmonic, 18*f,* 23, 105, 121–23, 151,
   163*ff*

Episode, 138, 248

Exposition, 212, 232–36, 279, 297–99, 306*f*

F

Familiar style, 134
Follower, 213, 218
Form, *32*
  binary, 220, 277
  and dynamics, 39
  and instrumentation, 40
  Rondo, 32–47
  Sonata-allegro, 277–309
  ternary, 278
  theme and variation, 183–206
  tonal, *1*
  in twentieth-century music, 429–62
Fortspinnung, 3 fn
Fragmentation, 210*f*, 217, 219, 240, 247,
    280
Fugal, *231*
  chorale prelude, 127–34
Fugato, *231,* 281, 299, 429
Fughetta, *231*
Fugue, *231*
  answer, 258–60
    real, *258*–60
    tonal, *258*–60, 265
  bridge, 235, 239, 247–49
  counterexposition, 239
  countersubject, 270–75
  developmental sections, 237–47
  episode, 248
  exposition, 232–36, 254–75
    order of voice entry, 260–65
    tonality contrasts of entries, 235*f*,
      265–70
  sectional linkage, 247–49
  subject, 232*ff*, 254–58, 265
  tonality relations in, 250–53

G

Gavotte, 33
Grand pause, 29
Ground, *173*–75

H

Harmonic parallelism, 387, 403
Harmonic reduction, 23*f*, 332*f*, 352
Harmonic sequence, 333–37

Harmonic succession, in twentieth-century
    music, 401–4
Harmony, serialized, 404–7, 409*f*
Hexachordal tone row, *405*

I

Imitative chorale prelude, 127–34
Impressionism, 315
Interval content analysis, 398–401
Introduction, 302–5
Invention, 127, *207, 221*
  beginning section, 212–17
  closing section, 222–26
  developmental section, 217–21
Inversion:
  melodic, 240*ff*, 379, 406
  of seventh chords, 49
  textural, 216, 220

K

Key:
  allusion to, 7, *28,* 30
  Neapolitan relation, 151–53, 342, 362
Key relationship:
  by seconds, 340
  by thirds, 340, 361
Keys:
  near-related, 6, 16, 18, 25, 31, *250*
  and tonal form, 6*f*
Key scheme, 6, 15, 25. *See also* Tonal
    form; Tonality scheme

L

Leader, 213, 218
Leading tone:
  lower, 109, 141
  secondary, 102, 106, 109, 120
  upper, 109, 141
Lydian, 355–58

M

Melodic contour, 381–83
Melodic variation, 133

Melody:
    serial, 376–81, 409*f*, 446–49
    twentieth-century, 366–84, 408
        pitch organization, 372–84
        rhythmic structure, 366–72
Meter:
    asymmetric, 366–70
    complex, 366–72
    uneven division of common meter, 370*f*
Mixolydian, 373
Modality, 353–58, 372–74
Modulation, 1, 3, 31, 67, 112–17, 148–51,
        163–67, 219, 265, 277, 282–86, 291,
        302, 341, 357, 358–65, 426–28
Motive, 132
Motivic repetition, 438–40
Mutation, 92, 104, 267

N

Neapolitan chord. *See* Chord, Neapolitan
Neapolitan relation, 151–153, 168, 342, 362

O

Ostinato, 27, 418, 425, 429, 445

P

Pandiatonicism, 424*f*
Passacaglia, 173, 175–80
Pedal, 3, 29, 73, 229*f*, 286
Pentatonic scale, 374
Phrygian cadence, 147
Phrygian mode, 142, 148, 354
Pitch class, *378*
Polychord, 393–97
Polytonal, 420–22
Prelude, 1
    analysis of, 1–7
Prime (form of row), *379*, 406. *See also*
        Chord, prime
Proportional rhythm, 371

Q

Quartal chord, 382, *389f*, 398
Quintal chord, 383, *391*–93, 398, 402

R

Real answer, *258*–60
Recapitulation, *281*, 306*f*
Recitative, 7
    analysis of, 7–15
Refrain, 32–33
Reprise, 222*ff*, 251
Resolution of sevenths, 53–55
    deceptive, 54–55
    irregular, 54
    regular, 53–54
Retrograde, *379*, 406
Retrograde inversion, *379*, 406
Rhythmic invariance, *3*, 135–37
Rondeau, 32–33
Rondo form, 32–47
Rondo theme, *33*

S

Scale:
    chromatic, 374
    Mixolydian, 373
    modal, 353–58, 372–74
    natural minor, 372*f*
    pentatonic, 374
Scherzo, *41*
Sectionalization, 1, 247–49, 292–96
Secundal chord, 391, 398
Sequence, 8, 12, 151, 220, 225, 229, 249,
        286, 333–37, 427, 439
Serialized harmony, 404–7, 409*f*
Serialized melody, 376–81, 446–49
Silence, as structural element, 455
Sonata-allegro form, 277–309
    coda, 281*f*, 306
    development, 280, 288–91, 292–95, 296,
        306*f*
    exposition, 279, 306*f*
        monothematic, 297–99
    introduction to, 302–5
    recapitulation, 281, 306*f*
    retransition, 286–91
    tonal design, 277, 282–86, 307*f*
    transition, 302
    twentieth-century, 306–8
    variables in, 296–302
Sonatina, *296*
Stacked chords, 393–97

Stasis, *205,* 454*ff*
Stretto, *223f,* 239, 241, 244–47, 252, 256, 429
Subject, 208, 211*ff,* 232*ff,* 254*ff*
Symmetric, 27, 39

T

Third relation, 41
Through-composed, 7
Tonal allusion, 7, *28,* 30
Tonal answer, *258,* 260, 265
Tonal form, *1,* 3–31. *See also* Key scheme; Tonality scheme
Tonality:
    ambiguous, 325–29, 340–42
    enrichment of, 334–40
    expanded, 30, 401
    suspended, 123
    in twentieth century, 416–22, 426–28, 450–54
    variability of, 325–65
Tonality frame, 374
Tonality scheme:
    of a contemporary movement, 25–31
    and distantly related keys, 16–25, 31
    and form, 1–31, 426–28
    and near-related keys, 6
    in twentieth-century music, 426–28

Tonal regions, 3, 7, 13, 19, 26*f,* 30, 66, *358*–65, 426
Tonal shift, 357, 427
Tone cluster, *392*
Tone row, *378*
Triads, 385*ff,* 401*ff*
Tri-thematic, 202–5
Tritones, 69*ff,* 102*ff,* 344–47, 408

V

Variation:
    cantus firmus, 173–83
        chaconne, 173, *180*–83
        ground, *173*–75
        passacaglia, 173, *175*–80
    forms, 172–206
    harmonic variations, *196*
    independent, 173, 183–206
        bi-thematic, 200–2
        tri-thematic, 202–5
    melodic, 133
    in rondo form, 39
Variation process, in twentieth-century music, 440–49
Vorimitation, 128f, 132, 135